D0535311

THE WINES OF
SPAIN
&
PORTUGAL

Charles Metcalfe & Kathryn McWhirter

Consultant Editor:
Joanna Simon

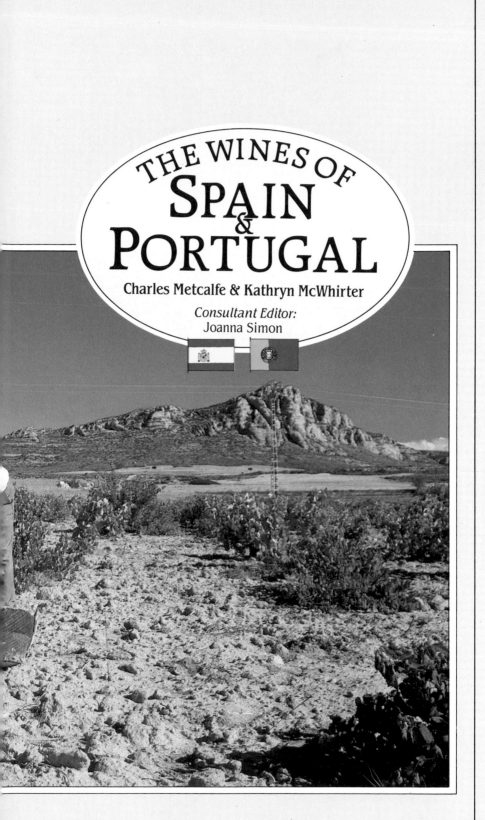

THE WINES OF
SPAIN
& PORTUGAL

Charles Metcalfe & Kathryn McWhirter

Consultant Editor:
Joanna Simon

a Salamander book

Published by Salamander Books Limited
LONDON • NEW YORK

A Salamander Book

Published by Salamander Books Ltd,
52 Bedford Row,
London WC1R 4LR,
United Kingdom

© Salamander Books Ltd 1988

ISBN 0 86101 359 X

Distributed in the UK by
Hodder & Stoughton Services,
P.O. Box 6,
Mill Road, Dunton Green, Sevenoaks,
Kent TN3 2XX

All rights reserved. No part of this book may be reproduced, stored in a retrieval system or transmitted in any form or by any means, electronic, mechanical, photocopying, recording or otherwise, without the prior permission of Salamander Books Ltd.

All correspondence concerning the content of this volume should be addressed to Salamander Books Ltd.

Credits

Editor:
Philip de Ste. Croix

Designer:
Roger Hyde

Colour artwork:
Ann Winterbotham and Sebastian Quigley
© Salamander Books Ltd

Maps:
Sebastian Quigley
© Salamander Books Ltd

Index:
Jill Ford

Filmset:
SX Composing Ltd, England

Colour and monochrome reproduction:
Melbourne Graphics Ltd, England

Printed in Belgium by Proost
International Book Production, Turnhout

*To Rachel Cecilia,
our unseen and uncomplaining research assistant*

AUTHORS

Charles Metcalfe is Associate Editor of *WINE* magazine (which he started with Robert Joseph in 1983) and wine correspondent of *TODAY* and *Homes & Gardens*. He first became interested in wine while studying English Literature at Oxford University, and twice successfully represented the Oxford team in the annual match against Cambridge. He repeated this competitive success on the Evening Standard/Grants of St James's wine-tasting team. In its four years of existence, the Standard team won matches against teams from France, Germany and the USA, and when Charles Metcalfe left the team in 1982, he was the captain and longest-serving member. He started to work as a freelance wine writer, side by side with his career as a classical singer, and has also written for the *Observer*, the *Which? Wine Guide* and numerous other magazines. As well as writing about wine, he has lectured on wine and wine-tasting on P&O Cruises and for Leith's School of Food and Wine.

Kathryn McWhirter was editor of the *Which? Wine Guide* for two years, and won the 1986 Glenfiddich Wine Book of the Year award for the 1986 edition. She also won the Glenfiddich Wine Trade Writer of the Year prize for her work on *Wine & Spirit* magazine, which she edited for four years. Her enthusiasm for the subject grew from visits to the Loire, and, after a short spell in the wine trade, she joined the staff of *Wine & Spirit,* rising to the position of editor within a year. The foreign languages she studied at university have assisted her to an understanding of the technical aspects of winemaking unrivalled in British wine-writing circles, and she still contributes a monthly column on technological innovations to *Wine & Spirit*. While working for the Consumers' Association, she wrote a monthly newsletter, *Which? Wine Monthly* and edited *The Good Wine Bar Guide*. She has also written on wine for the *Observer, Good Housekeeping, Time Out, WINE* and *The Good Food Guide*.

ACKNOWLEDGEMENTS

The authors would like to thank the many wine producers of Spain and Portugal who have been so generous with their time and their wines. We are most grateful also to Jeremy Watson, David Balls, Nicola Speakmann and Lynn Cockett of Wines from Spain, João Henriques and Lina Brandão of the Portuguese Government Trade Office, and Graham Hines and Bryan Buckingham of The Sherry Institute for all their help and support; to those employees of ICEX, INDO and ICEP who have helped and guided us; and to Domingos Soares Franco and Peter Bright for replying so assiduously to our telexes.

CONSULTANT EDITOR

Joanna Simon has edited two of the foremost wine journals in the English language: *Wine & Spirit* magazine, which she joined as assistant editor in 1981, becoming editor in 1984, and *WINE*, which she edited between October 1986 and December 1987. She has travelled extensively in Europe and Australia, has tasted for a number of wine magazines, as well as *The Financial Times*, and has written for a wide range of trade and consumer publications on wine-related subjects. She is currently wine correspondent for *The Sunday Times*, and Contributing Editor of *WINE* and *Wine & Spirit*.

CONTENTS

FOREWORD

ood wine costs less in Spain and Portugal. Both countries have their expensive rarities: Spaniards will pay a fortune for Vega Sicilia and a small fortune for the white Albariño wines of the northeast, while Americans are prepared to pay top prices for newcomer Viña Pesquera; Portugal has its Barca Velha, Palacio da Brejoeira and, of course, its vintage ports. But such wines, some of them selling at inflated prices thanks to reputation and demand, are great exceptions. Most of the Iberian peninsula's finest wines sell at very reasonable prices, and wines in the middle quality ranges are positively cheap.

It is among the red wines of both countries that almost all the really interesting discoveries are to be made. Good white winemaking is difficult in hot climates, though certainly possible, given expertise and the right sort of equipment. But to compound the problem, the white grape varieties grown in Spain and Portugal are on the whole rather dull, and could never be turned into great wines even with the most advanced techniques and equipment in the world. Reds are a different matter. Black grapes are more suited to hotter climates, and some of the Iberian native varieties are capable of producing really exciting flavours.

Modern methods have been slow to arrive in Spain and Portugal, except in a few advanced areas and some forward-looking individual companies. Until very recently, Portugal had no department of viticulture or oenology in any of its universities, nor even a specialised college. Aspiring young winemakers who were dissatisfied with the usual course of learning from their elders were obliged to study in France, at colleges in Montpellier, Bordeaux and Beaune, or even in California or Australia.

The effects of post-graduate winemaking have been evident in Spain for some years, but Portugal is only just beginning to benefit. Co-operatives, who make a large proportion of both countries' wines, have been even slower to change than private companies, though grants now available from the EEC as well as the national and regional governments could bring about a real revolution in the next few years.

A revolution is also on its way in the official systems of wine region demarcation of both countries. Portugal so far has very few officially demarcated regions, but rules and geographical boundaries for several more are currently being drawn up. There may be another 26 *Regiões Demarcadas* by the early 'nineties. Spain's equivalent, the *Denomina-*

Metric/Imperial Equivalents

The Spanish and Portuguese wine industries use metric measurements to express volumes, weights, dimensions, etc. This book, therefore, also uses metric units for such measurements. For those readers unfamiliar with the metric system, or who are more comfortable thinking in Imperial units, listed below are the necessary conversion factors.

$$1 \text{ metre (m)} = 3.281 \text{ ft}$$
$$1 \text{ kilometre (km)} = 0.6214 \text{ miles}$$
$$1 \text{ hectolitre (hl)} = 100 \text{ litres} = 22 \text{ UK gallons or } 26.4 \text{ US gallons}$$
$$1 \text{ hectare (ha)} = 10,000 \text{m}^2 = 2.471 \text{ acres}$$
$$1 \text{ kilogramme (kg)} = 2.205 \text{lb}$$
$$1 \text{ tonne} = 1,000 \text{kg} = 2,205 \text{lb}$$

ciónes de Origen, already number 30, with one more due by the end of 1988. But here, too, sweeping changes to existing DOs are under consideration for the 'nineties. Spain has already introduced another category of wines, *Vinos de la Tierra* (like French *vins de pays*, a super-category of basic table wines) and Portugal should come up with some *Vinhos Regionãos* by 1991.

This book covers all Spain's DOs and *Vinos de la Tierra*, all the existing *Regiões Demarcadas* of Portugal, and Portugal's other main (as yet undemarcated) winegrowing regions,

as well as a few estates or wineries such as Marqués de Griñon in Spain or the Buçaco Palace Hotel in Portugal that fall completely outside any of the official regions, but are nevertheless excellent in their own right. There can be immense variations in quality between neighbouring wineries in the same region, and, indeed, between different wines made under the same roof. For each region, we have highlighted our personal selection of the best wineries, and within those wineries the best wines, that Spain and Portugal have to offer.

Over 60 per cent of all the wine made in both Spain and Portugal passes through the growers' co-operatives. Spain has more than 1,000 wine co-operatives, Portugal 300. These communal wineries serving growers in single villages or sometimes whole regions have sprung up since the beginning of this century, but in much greater profusion since the 1950s. The initial building and any subsequent improvements are subsidised by loans from the national or local governments (now also grants from the EEC), and co-operatives benefit, too, from paying agricultural taxes rather than the much higher commercial taxes exacted from private wineries. Co-operatives are generally run by a committee of elected growers headed by a president, and unfortunately this can mean inflexibility and lack of progress, especially since the committee generally changes every five years or so, and co-operative policy with it.

Co-operatives have become so popular in Spain and Portugal because the tiny plots farmed by most growers make it unprofitable for them to make their own wine. Many farm their land only as a hobby, in the evenings and at weekends; others grow vines only on their poorest land, where the crops that form their major source of income will not grow.

As members of a co-operative, they can be rid of their grapes in the autumn, usually for a small payment on the spot, followed by further payments, costs deducted, as the wine is sold.

Of course, they can also sell their grapes to private wineries for more immediate payment in full (though often slightly less money overall). Private wineries fill their needs in a variety of ways. Some have their own vineyards supplying all or a part of their raw materials. Some buy grapes from growers, either on the open market or under regular contracts. They may buy juice ready-pressed in the co-operatives, or even ready-made wine from co-operatives or private growers, which they then blend and sometimes age before selling. It is quite common for a winery to buy its raw materials in a combination of all these ways. From the quality point of view, the earlier in the chain they can buy, the better, so that they can keep a technical eye on the whole process.

Until recently, the big commercial wineries had a near-monopoly on *bottling* wine. Small-scale growers and co-operatives sold their wine either by the tankerload to private wineries or foreign buyers, or by the large plastic tub or five-litre jar to locals and passers-by. In the co-operatives, things have

Annual Rainfall and Average Yield for the Main Wine Areas

Portugal

Region	Rainfall	Yield (hl/ha)
Alentejo	500mm	46
Ribatejo	650mm	70
Douro	700mm	31 (at the lowest)
Bairrada	950mm	32
Dão	1,250mm	25
Minho (Vinho verde)	1,750mm	48

Spain

Region	Rainfall	Yield (hl/ha)
Jumilla	300mm	6.87
Yecla	322mm	11.54
Cariñena	350mm	18.69
Toro	350mm	25
Almansa	375mm	7.77
Rioja	380mm	15.37
Campo de Borja	400mm	19.12
Terra Alta	400mm	n/a
Alicante	400mm	10.74
Utiel-Requena	400mm	5.54
Méntrida	400mm	11.37
Rueda	415mm	22.12
La Mancha	450mm	22.75
Málaga	475mm	38.4
Ribera del Duero	475mm	20.5
Valencia	480mm	15
Somontano	485mm	20
Valdepeñas	500mm	19.68
Penedés	514mm	52.76
Ampurdán-Costa Brava	545mm	16.2
Navarra	550mm	20.88
Condado de Huelva	550mm	22.91
Alella	559mm	17.79
Tarragona	564mm	36.27
Priorato	600mm	4.62
Jerez	600mm	59.97
Montilla-Moriles	600mm	29.73
Valdeorras (Galicia)	925mm	12.89
Ribeiro (Galicia)	950mm	34.12

Note: Other factors, such as the proximity of the sea and night dew, can affect humidity, and the consequent yield, and the need to protect vines against mould, e.g. in the Penedés in Spain and the Minho in Portugal.

been changing, however, though the majority of the wine is still sold in bulk as before. Many have installed their own bottling lines, or have plans to do so, and are bottling a proportion of their production. In some areas, co-operatives have joined together forming super-co-operatives to take charge of the bottling for the whole group, and some even employ proper management and sales staff, even export staff in a small minority of cases.

Few small estates or small producers bottle their own wine, but it is exciting to note that more and more are now beginning to do so. This movement is particularly strong in Portugal, and especially in the Vinho Verde district, but it is beginning in Spain, too. These are not the typical small-scale growers with their little cellars and archaic concrete vats, but dynamic people who are aware of advances in winemaking elsewhere, and have invested in sparkling new stainless steel equipment, and often new oak barrels to age their wine. Interest in these individual wines in countries brought up on large-scale blends has been so great that, significantly, the large wineries are now beginning to feel that they must join in to supply a market demand. They, too, are beginning to plant private estates, sell wines from their existing estates as individual wines, or form links with small estates so as to be able to offer such wines in their range.

Left: *Blackboards outside the Godelleta Co-operative in Valencia announce the picking programme: whites on Thursday, Moscatel only on Friday and Saturday.*

G ood winemaking starts in the vineyard, and the changes that have revolutionised the world's vineyards in the past two decades have only recently begun to be reflected in vineyard practice in Spain and Portugal.

Since the vine-root-gnawing louse phylloxera struck the vineyards of the Iberian peninsula at the end of the 19th and the beginning of the 20th century, the old indigenous varieties of vine have had to be grafted on to roots of phylloxera-resistant American species of vine, which come in all sorts of variations to suit different conditions of soil fertility and composition and climate. Because the soils of few vineyards have been properly analysed before planting, the wrong rootstocks are often chosen. This is not the only obstacle to optimising a vineyard's potential: another area in which both Spain and Portugal are behind the times is in cloning (long-term selection of the best, most disease-resistant, yet flavourful strains of particular varieties). Clones of some Spanish and Portuguese varieties are now available, but they have been "perfected" over a much shorter period than the vines of France, Germany or even Italy. True cloning takes decades of careful selection. The sherry country of Jerez has been in the forefront of cloning progress.

The number of vines in a given patch of vineyard is also important. Famous viticulturist Miguel Torres points out that Spanish winegrowers have largely ignored research done years ago which concluded that even in Spain's dry conditions, vines planted at a density of 4,000 to 5,000 plants per hectare produced better quantity *and* quality than vines grown in Spain's traditional wide spacing of 1,500 to 2,700 per hectare. Planted close, the roots delve more deeply in search of underground water (vine roots can force their way ten metres or often more down through earth or rock fissures) while the ground between the vines is better shaded by foliage. Most of the highly successful Torres vineyards are planted at this greater density (their most recent vineyards

Above: *Dancing a jig on top of one's trailer in the time-honoured way of this La Mancha grower might squeeze in a few extra bucketfuls of grapes, but it does little for the quality of the wine. Ideally, grapes are picked into small, stackable plastic containers, and delivered to the winery intact.*

En vaso with 3 branches   *En vaso with 2 branches*   *Bairrada*

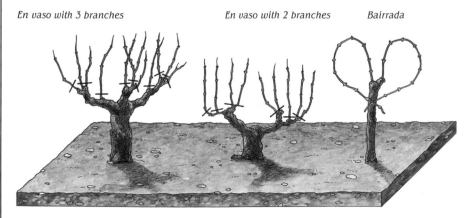

Above: *Pruning en vaso with either two or three main branches is common in almost all parts of Spain. These vines are shown with their summer growth, which often* trails down to the ground, shading the grapes. Bairrada (above right) has its own training method, shown here just after winter pruning.

even more so), and are worked by tractors that span the top of a row of vines. Traditional Spanish growers will swear that native Spanish vines such as the Tempranillo cannot be grown along wires, and that closely spaced, wired vines cannot cope in Spanish conditions, but some of Spain's best wines prove the contrary to be true.

Admittedly, the foreign Cabernet Sauvignon, always grown along wires, has to be irrigated in the hot, dry conditions of Toledo and Costers del Segre, but native Spanish varieties are better adapted to Spanish conditions. Irrigation is theoretically illegal throughout the EEC, but here as everywhere, producers seem to be able to get away with it by classing their vineyards as "experimental", despite the fact that the resulting wines are very much for sale. Indeed, even growing on wires is against the rules of some regions, including Rioja, but permitted for "experimental purposes". As can be seen from the table on the previous spread, Portugal is less in need of irrigation than Spain, since the influence of the Atlantic brings much heavier rainfall.

In most parts of Spain and sometimes in Portugal, vines are pruned into small bushes, a shape known as *en vaso* (or *en taça* in Por-

tuguese). This consists of a small trunk with a variable number of short branches, from which the fruiting canes sprout. The number of branches allowed to grow depends on the fertility and climate of each region: very dry areas, like Jumilla and Yecla, prune *en vaso* with fewer branches than the wetter Penedés or Montilla regions. In really dry areas, the branches may be left longer at pruning time so that the summer growth sprawls down to the ground, shading the grapes and the surrounding earth.

Bairrada in Portugal has its own method of training vines, which are cut into two fairly short branches, then bent and tied into a heart shape. Traditional sherry vineyards use the *vara y pulgar* (stick and thumb) system, consisting of a long branch with seven or eight buds for this year's growth, and a stump with a bud left to make next year's "stick". Both the Portuguese of the Minho (*vinho verde*) district of northern Portugal and the neighbouring Galicians of Spain, who share the coolest, wettest part of the peninsula, train their vines up high posts and along overhead trellises in an attempt to contain the vigour such a climate encourages, and to allow air to circulate around the grapes to discourage attacks of mould.

Rarely in Spain do you come across modern, trim rows of tightly-wired vines. Jerez, where half the vineyards are on wires, is one major exception to this. A few enlightened producers such as Torres in the Penedés, Domecq in Rioja, Raimat in Costers del Segre and Marqués de Griñon in Toledo on the great, dry central plains also train their vineyards on wires. In Portugal, on the other hand, wired vines abound: in this respect, Portugal is the more advanced of the two countries. Wiring greatly facilitates mechanisation.

Vines lie dormant from about November to the end of April, during which time they are pruned. Life begins to return to them in April, and they flower in April or May when the temperature reaches around 15 to 16°C. The grapes ripen some time between August and November.

Because of the low humidity, vineyard care is easier in much of Spain and the drier parts of Portugal than in many other winegrowing countries of Europe. In the driest parts, sprays are rarely needed against fungal diseases, which thrive on moisture, whereas in more humid climates like the Penedés it might be necessary to spray 15 to 20 times during the growing season. In dry conditions, weeds are also less of a problem. Occasional ploughing is fairly effective, and growers resort far less to herbicides than in the more northerly countries of Europe. Pruning is almost universally done by hand,

though half the Torres vineyards in the Penedés are now pruned mechanically.

Although most of Spain and Portugal is bakingly hot throughout the summer, there is a big difference in *night* temperatures depending on height above sea level. Up in the hills or mountains temperatures at night can drop enormously. If nights are hot, the vines burn up both aromatic constituents and colouring matter in the grapes. (An important exception to this is the Moscatel grape, in which the main flavour compounds, known as terpenes, consist of such tiny molecules that they do not get burnt up – hence the highly aromatic, super-sweet wines for which the Moscatel is famous.)

The best, most aromatic and flavourful grapes (given a good variety in the first place) often ripen late, in places of high altitude. It is important to choose precisely the right moment for picking. As grapes get riper, they become sweeter and sweeter, but their acidity diminishes, as do their aromatic and flavour-giving compounds. Traditionally, grapes have been picked extremely ripe in Spain and Portugal, and growers have been paid according to the amount of sugar in them (the more sugar the higher the alcohol of the wine). But the resulting wines lacked aroma as well as the acidity that makes both reds and whites taste fresh. The modern tendency is to pick earlier, but in many areas, the old traditions of high alcohol, low acid and aroma still persist.

Ramada or Latada

Barra

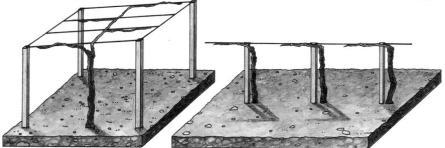

Above: Vinho verde *vines trained in the traditional* ramada *or* latada *system, along wires stretched between three-metre-high posts. Such trellises often surround fields of maize or kiwi fruits.*

Above: Barra, *the most modern method of training vines for* vinho verde, *along a single wire about 1.7 metres high. Whole vineyards are dedicated to vines planted on* barra, *not just the borders.*

Double Guyot

Single Guyot

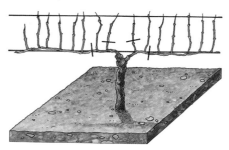

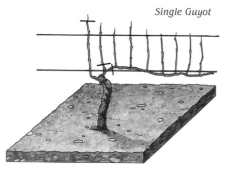

Above: *Vines grown in modern vineyards along wires are generally pruned in the* Double Guyot *system (left) or Single*

Guyot *(right). Canes of the previous year's growth tied flat along the wires send up this year's fruiting shoots.*

The story of the vineyard does not end until the grapes are in the *bodega*. Even if grapes are picked at the perfect stage of ripeness, all can be spoiled if they are squashed, damaged or delayed between picking and delivery. Some firms in Spain and Portugal provide their grape suppliers with stackable plastic crates to help keep the grapes from being squashed during transportation. Because bacteria and yeasts on the grapes soon begin to spoil them if they are left hanging around in hot climates, it is vital to get the grapes to the wineries as quickly as possible. This may present problems, since growers with small vineyards may have other jobs or trades during the week, and so prefer to leave picking to evenings and weekends, when other members of the family can help. Half-filled trucks of grapes may sit around from one evening to the next, the grapes oozing and spoiling in the autumn sun. Nowadays, however, private wineries and even co-operatives generally work out a picking plan before the harvest, so that growers appear on an appointed day with approximately the expected quantity of grapes, so reducing queueing and delay. Most private wineries would refuse grapes that had clearly been sitting around for longer than was good for them.

Picking machines are not yet very common; they can in any case only be used where vines are trained on wires, and they are too rough with thin-skinned grapes (like the Palomino Fino of Jerez). But with tougher grapes, modern machines are sufficiently gentle, and have the great advantage of speed. Machine-picked grapes can be guaranteed to reach the winery within a couple of hours, a great plus for quality.

Left: *Vines grown on the* cruzeta *system in the experimental vineyard at* vinho verde *estate Quinta da Aveleda. A great improvement on the* ramada, *this allows tractors to work between rows.*

Cruzeta

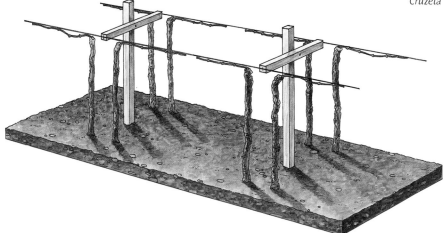

Above: *The* cruzeta *(meaning "cross") was the first step up for Portuguese growers from the traditional, untidy* ramada *or* latada *training. But the even simpler* barra *system is more popular in the newest vineyards.*

*T*hroughout the winemaking world, the production of white wines and the wines themselves have changed spectacularly over the past two decades. However, it was not until well into the 'eighties that such changes became at all widespread in Spain, while Portugal (apart from a few international grade *adegas*) is only now beginning to upgrade its white winemaking.

There have been two major elements in the revolution: cooling equipment and stainless steel. With stainless steel tanks, unlike concrete or wood, there is no danger of the receptacle tainting the taste of the wine, and since it is easy to clean, there is less likelihood of off-flavours developing because bacteria have escaped the scrubbing brush.

As steel is also a good conductor of heat, the liquid inside stainless steel tanks can easily be cooled, and keeping the temperature down means that important aromatic substances remain in the fermenting wine, rather than bubbling furiously away into the atmosphere. Steel tanks are usually cooled either by running cold water down the outside, or by enclosing the tank in a thermal jacket. Other fermentation vessels may be cooled by pumping the wine through a heat exchanger (coils of cold water interwoven with coils of wine). Wineries without cooling equipment sometimes control temperature by filling the fermentation vats little by little, progressively adding cold juice to quieten the fermentation.

On delivery to the winery, white grapes are weighed, sampled and tipped into a reception trough (ideally made of stainless steel) in the bottom of which is a screw to carry them through to the crusher. (Grapes of different qualities and degrees of ripeness are usually kept separate right through the process.) The best crushers consist of gentle rollers, which barely burst the grapes open, but, especially in co-operatives, the job is often done more roughly in a centrifuge.

A new technique is sometimes used at this point by some of the most enlightened winemakers when vinifying grapes with particularly aromatic skins. They remove the stalks before crushing and leave the crushed grapes to stand for between two and 12 hours. The maceration time must be carefully judged to extract the maximum of aroma but the minimum of astringent substances from the skins and pips: these would not only spoil the taste, they would hasten browning.

Normally, however, the grapes, complete with their stalks, pass on to the press. The best, most pure and fragrant juice is the "free-run" juice, which flows from the grapes simply by the action of gravity, but the first, light pressing also gives good results. Many large wineries and co-operatives use "continuous presses", huge, upward-tilted screws, which are quick and efficient, but detract from the quality of the juice, as they tend to mangle the grapes and release harsh and bitter-tasting substances. Better for quality are modern horizontal presses, cylindrical in shape, sometimes with metal plates at either end which gradually press in towards the centre, or else with an inflatable

Right: *Vacuum filters are becoming quite a common means nowadays of cleaning white juice before fermentation. The revolving drum, coated with an earth filter, dips into a bath of juice, and sucks it by vacuum into its centre.*

Below: *Delivering Parellada grapes into a stainless steel reception trough at the Torres winery in Pachs del Penedés.*

Why Sulphur Is Used

*I*n almost every case, sulphur dioxide is used throughout the winemaking process to kill and inhibit yeasts and bacteria and to prevent oxidation – the combination of components of the wine with air, which turns white wines yellow, then brown, and red wines orangey-brown, and makes both taste dull and fruitless, cardboardy or sherry-like. Most wineries add sulphur dioxide in the form of potassium or sodium metabisulphite as soon as the grapes arrive in the winery, and gradually top up the sulphur dioxide level right up to the time of bottling.

The EEC dictates strict maxima of sulphur dioxide that may be present in wine. Although it is not harmful (except to asthmatics), an excess of sulphur dioxide tastes dirty and makes you cough, and combined with other compounds in the wine, it can make all sorts of unpleasant smells and flavours, reminiscent of anything from cabbage and rotten eggs to blocked drains and sweaty socks. The cleaner the equipment, the cooler the fermentation and the less the wine and juice are exposed to air, the less sulphur dioxide is needed.

bag that squeezes the grapes outwards against the inside of the cylinder.

The next stage is the clarification of the juice before fermentation. Traditionally, it is simply sulphured to protect it from oxidation and to subdue wild yeasts and bacteria, and then left to stand for 12 to 48 hours, until most of the solid particles have drifted to the bottom. This is still the most common method (sometimes helped along by added enzymes or fining agents), but some wineries now use centrifuges, while the most affluent

have invested in vacuum filters – huge, slowly rotating cylinders that draw the wine through a clay-like substance into their centre, leaving the solid particles behind to peel off the outside in a sheet as the cylinder turns.

The clean juice is analysed, and if necessary a little tartaric acid is added to raise the acidity. (This acid is naturally present in grapes, but rapidly reduces under the hot Iberian sun in the latter stages of ripening.) The juice now passes to the containers in which it is to ferment. Traditionally, this

happened in huge clay Ali-Baba pots called *tinajas* in Spain, *amforas* in Portugal, sunk into the ground and rising up so that their mouths often just protrude through the ceiling into the room above. Such pots are still very common in Spain, though now usually made of concrete. But they are difficult to clean – a man must be lowered inside on a rope – and difficult to cool. Square concrete vats, sometimes lined with ceramic tiles or epoxy resin, are the next stage up, but best of all is stainless steel.

Most Iberian winemakers allow the grapes' natural yeasts to ferment the juice, having knocked out unwanted species of yeast with sulphur dioxide. But some "culture" selected natural yeasts in special tanks at the very beginning of the harvest, while a few purchase commercially selected yeasts. The yeasts absorb the grape sugar in order to divide and multiply, producing enzymes called diastases, which release alcohol and carbon dioxide from the sugar, as well as energy; a host of by-products and products of side reactions give the wine its distinctive fermented flavours, some of them highly aromatic, depending on the variety of grape used. This "tumultuous fermentation", which occurs while the yeasts are dividing rapidly, produces a lot of heat, and fermentations, left to their own devices, can shoot up to temperatures above 30°C, especially in the hotter, southern parts of Spain and Portugal. This is the point where cooling is vital in white winemaking (to somewhere between 16 and 18°C) if the wines are to taste fresh.

Once the tumultuous phase is over, the young wine continues to bubble gently until the sugar is used up, or the yeast dies of alcohol poisoning. White wine fermentations usually last between ten and 15 days, but can be over in only a week at excessive temperatures, or last seven weeks if kept really cool. If the wine is to be sweet or semi-sweet, the fermentation can be stopped by chilling followed by filtering or centrifuging to remove the yeasts, or, less satisfactorily, with a massive dose of sulphur dioxide; fortified wines are "stopped" by the addition of alcohol, since yeasts die at a high alcoholic degree.

In the cooler parts of Spain and Portugal, principally Galicia and the Minho, white wines contain a lot of malic acid (the acid found in apples and cool-climate fruits), and unless the winemaker takes steps to prevent it, this will be converted to lactic acid some time in the few months following the alcoholic fermentation by the action of naturally present malolactic bacteria. Lactic acid tastes less acid than malic, so wines that have undergone a malolactic fermentation taste less sharp. This second fermentation is difficult to control, however, and often leads to dirty flavours if equipment and winemaking knowledge is poor. Some wineries choose to prevent malolactic fermentation in order to preserve the wine's original flavours, or because the resulting wine would fall below the legal regional minimum for acidity. The best *vinhos verdes*, contrary to popular

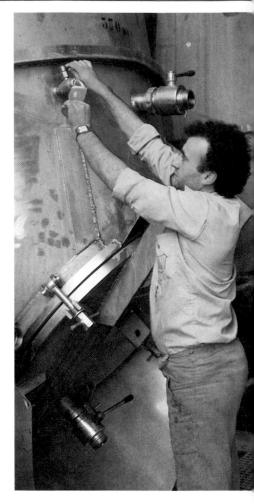

Above: *Taking samples from stainless steel fermentation tanks at Torres in Pachs del Penedés. These tanks are usually used for red wines, the spent skins sliding out through the openable base once the wine has been run off.*

Right: Tinajas *at Alvear in Montilla. Once made of clay, more recent* tinajas *such as these are cast in concrete.*

belief, do *not* undergo a malolactic fermentation. Filtration or a generous dose of sulphur dioxide will stop it happening.

The next step is "racking", transferring the young wine to a new container, leaving the solid products of fermentation, the lees, behind. This is done perhaps three times during the winter. Even then, however, some solids still make the wine cloudy, and it is necessary to "fine" or clarify the wine. The solid particles have a natural electrical charge, and the fining agent used has an opposite charge, so attracting the particles and dragging them with it to the bottom of the containers, where they can be left behind in a final racking. The most common fining agents are isinglass (from sturgeons' air bladders), gelatine, bentonite (a sort of powdered clay) and less and less these days, the traditional beaten egg whites. No trace of the fining agent is left in the wine.

Before bottling, the better wines are now nearly all chilled to prevent the formation of tiny, sugar-like crystals once the wines are bottled. These are insoluble tartrate salts, formed when tartaric acid, either added or naturally present, combines with calcium or potassium, also natural constituents of grapes. If the wine were left untreated, this would happen gradually, though the reaction is accelerated by any drops in temperature, and although the crystals are harmless, customers sometimes complain. The solution is to chill the wines before bottling and keep them at between 4 and 6°C for about a week in insulated tanks, so that most of the tartrates drop out, because they are less soluble at low temperatures. Loss of tartrates means a loss of acidity, however, and this must be taken into account at the beginning of the winemaking process when deciding whether and how much to acidify.

Almost all white wines are filtered before bottling. Large wineries usually use "diatomaceous earth", while smaller ones use pad filters. Most quality wines from good wineries are now passed finally through a fine membrane filter, which should exclude all yeasts and bacteria and leave the wine pure and stable. Cheaper wines are pasteurised, but this would spoil the flavours of better wines and reduce their keeping abilities.

Most white wines from Spain and Portugal are best drunk young, within a year or little more of their harvest, before they begin to yellow and taste dull or oxidised. But there are still many wineries that follow the traditional method of ageing their whites, in tank and/or wooden vat or barrel, before release. Usually, this destroys any quality they might once have possessed, but a few high-quality whites, particularly in Rioja, benefit from ageing and can become quite spectacular.

*R*ed wines get their colour from the skins of black grapes – their flesh is just as colourless as that of white grapes, with the one exception, in Spain and Portugal, of the red-fleshed Garnacha Tintorera, the "dyeing" or "staining" Garnacha. By modern, international standards, skill in red winemaking means extracting the desired amount of colour while at the same time minimising the extraction of bitter, harsh components from the skins, pips and stalks. This is all the more important in hot climates, where not only colouring matter but also the harsh tannins are formed in much greater profusion. But old-fashioned Spanish and Portuguese reds did not even attempt this balancing act (and some still do not), turning out dark *and* tough. However, some entire regions and some individual winemakers on the Iberian peninsula mastered the modern art many years ago, and many more are now adopting modern methods.

Ideally, red grapes should be de-stalked on arrival at the winery. Left in during the fermentation, stalks can make the wine unpleasantly bitter. Old wine-making practice in Spain and Portugal was to ferment the wine with the stalks, however, and the practice is still widespread among co-operatives and small-scale growers. Quality-minded wineries, if buying ready-made wine rather than grapes or juice, generally try to persuade their suppliers to dispense with stalks. If de-stalking machines *are* used, the French type, which tear the grapes off the stems, are vastly preferable to the fast, modern centrifugal destalkers, as these often bruise and crush the stalks during the process, releasing as many (if not more) bitter compounds into the juice as if de-stalking had not been done at all.

Above: *Winemaker Jaume Mussons i Estabanell inspecting red wine samples in the laboratories of the Cellers de Scala Dei in Priorato, Catalonia.*

Right: *The most traditional of winemaking in an underground cellar at Benavente in León: raking skins and stalks out of the* lagar *after fermentation.*

From the de-stalker, the grapes pass on to a crusher. The best, as for whites, consist of gentle rollers, but rougher, centrifugal crushers are more common, especially in co-operatives. The broken mass, the "must", is analysed, and more tartaric acid may be added if necessary before fermentation. A whole variety of fermentation vessels is used in Spain and Portugal. The traditional old

Above: *Samples are taken to check the specific gravity at the Cartaxo co-op*

in the Ribatejo. Many co-operatives still pay more for sweeter grapes.

lagares, shallow open troughs, are still in use, as are larger rectangular concrete vats, sometimes open at the top, sometimes enclosed, sometimes lined with ceramic tiles or epoxy resin. There are big wooden vats, lined steel tanks and, best of all, stainless steel, sometimes equipped with cone-shaped, openable bottoms through which the grape skins can be extracted, sparing the labour of men with pitchforks. As with white wines, some winemakers prepare cultured yeasts, while others let the natural yeasts take their course.

Reds have to ferment at a higher temperature than whites because heat is necessary to extract the colour. The ideal temperature for red wines is between 26 and 28°C, but many fermentations become much hotter, with the result, if temperatures shoot up much above 30°C, that the wine tastes jammy and bitter. In the most modern wineries, temperature is controlled for reds in similar ways as for whites. Heat and alcohol both accelerate the extraction of colour from skins, and over the first few days, as the growth of the yeasts makes the must hotter and hotter and more and more alcoholic, the juice gets darker and

darker. However, the harsh, bitter-tasting substances, the tannins, are slower to emerge. Richest of all in tannins are the pips. These are coated with a waxy layer, which must be dissolved by the alcohol during the first few days. As fermentation continues, colour extraction diminishes, while tannin extraction increases.

Winemakers who want to make light, soft, fruity reds exploit this cycle by removing the skins very early in the fermentation process, and allowing the juice to continue fermenting by itself. Red wines usually ferment on their skins for between one and two weeks. A few wineries heat the must to about 28°C to give the colour extraction a head start, and some even flash-heat their must to as much as 60 or 70° for a very short time. This latter method makes very colourful, agreeably soft wine but it must be drunk young, as it soon loses its freshness. Wines intended for longer ageing *need* the astringent tannin to preserve them throughout their maturation, and these wines will taste really tough by the time their skins are removed.

For maximum colour and tannin extraction, the skins must be kept constantly

steeped in juice, which is difficult because the carbon dioxide generated by the action of the yeasts gets trapped in the skins so that they float to the surface and form a solid layer or "cap", known in Spanish as the *sombrero* and in Portuguese as the *manta* or blanket. This must periodically be mixed in. It is normally done by pumping the must out through a pipe near the bottom of the fermentation vessel and spraying it back in at the top, once or more every day. In Portugal, especially for port production but also in other regions, "autovinificators", rather like coffee percolators, do the job (see page 31) and these are very occasionally seen in Spain. A few very modern wineries have temperature-controlled, rotating tanks not unlike washing machines. Simplest of all is to poke the skins under the surface with some sort of instrument – this is the usual method adopted in old-fashioned, open *lagares*.

Rioja has its own tradition of red winemaking, still observed by most small-scale growers and by a few of the large *bodegas* for some of their wines. Similar to the method used in Beaujolais, it makes light, extremely fruity wines. Far from being crushed, the grapes must be kept as intact and undamaged as possible. During transport and loading into the open vats, some grapes split, however, and their juice begins to ferment in the bottom of the vat, bathing the grapes above in carbon dioxide. This stimulates enzymes within the grapes, which bring about a fermentation *inside* the grape skins, killing the skin cells, producing alcohol to extract the colour and tannin, and softening the skins till they ooze juice.

From about the third day, part way into this process, Riojan growers generally intervene, actually leaping into their shallow vats

Above: *Sampling the wares at the Rosado Fernandes winery in the Alentejo, bought by José Maria da Fonseca Successores.*

and pressing the grapes by foot once a day. Eventually, any whole grapes that still remain swell and burst. The juice is run off and left to ferment to completion. This method is sometimes known as "semi-carbonic maceration", as opposed to full "carbonic maceration". The latter involves taking extraordinary care to keep almost all the grapes whole, bathing the tank in added carbon dioxide even before an ordinary fermentation is able to start, and allowing the carbonic fermentation to progress much further before pressing. The resulting wines are very fruity, with characteristic, almost bubble-gum-like aroma and flavour. This method is also used in a few Spanish and Portuguese wineries for a proportion of their wines.

Whatever the method, the skins left behind after the wine has been run off contain between 15 and 20 per cent of the total potential liquid, and this is retrieved by pressing. Initially this is done gently; then, after the juice of the first pressings has been collected, it is done really firmly to squeeze out the last drops. The final pressing is almost always sent for distillation, but the liquid from the first couple of pressings – dark, tannic wines – may eventually be blended back, in part or in total, into the main batch if this is considered to need more colour, body and firmness. Otherwise they will be blended into cheaper wines.

Meanwhile, the fermenting wine that was drained off the skins continues to ferment more slowly for perhaps another 20 days. After fermentation is over, it is "racked"

Above: *The winemaker checks temperatures of fermenting must at the Cellers de Scala Dei in Priorato, Catalonia.*

Above: *The new Esporão winery in the Alentejo, modelled partly on the Torres vinification centre in the Penedés.*

(transferred to another container, leaving its deposit behind) several times. Any solid bits left over from the fermentation are thus discarded, along with a certain amount of the colouring matter, which falls out of solution, so that the wine begins to lose the purplish colour of its very early youth.

Most red wines in Spain and Portugal undergo a malolactic fermentation (see pages 16 and 17) some time during this period, becoming softer and rounder. Some wineries warm the wine to about 20° after the *alcoholic* fermentation, since the bacteria that cause the malolactic fermentation are happiest at this temperature. An unskilled winemaker may not always manage to induce, or to complete, the malolactic fer-

mentation, with the result that the wines may remain rather tart.

The wine is then clarified or "fined" usually with isinglass, gelatine or occasionally beaten egg whites. Alternatively, any remaining unwanted solids can be spun out of it in a centrifuge. If it is to be sold immediately as young wine, it will then be coarsely filtered, and then if it has any pretence of quality, very finely "sterile filtered"; otherwise it will be pasteurised. Before bottling, reds for drinking young are generally chilled, like white and *rosé* wines, to precipitate tartrates which might otherwise form unsightly crystals in the bottle. Wines that are to undergo further ageing do not need this treatment, since they will have time to lose their tartrates naturally in the maturation barrels or tanks.

Rosés and claretes
Wines of various shades of pink are obtained by leaving the juice in contact with the skins for a shorter period. Portugal has only two categories, red and *rosé*, but Spain has an intermediate level, *clarete*. A *clarete* is generally made from a mixture of white and red grapes, which have by law to ferment for a period with the skins, usually three to four days, before the liquid is drawn off to finish fermenting alone. The result is a pale red or a dark *rosé*. For a true *rosé* wine, the juice is left in contact with the skins for no longer than a day. Like red wines, *rosés* lose a little of their colour during their first few months, and are therefore made a little darker than the desired end result.

Not all wines are suitable for maturation. Red wines selected for wood ageing are generally big and dark, with fairly aggressive, bitter tannins and good acidity – all aspects, along with the alcohol, that help to preserve wine, as does any additional tannin extracted from the oak. Ideally, lighter reds should spend a much shorter time in wood, if they spend any time at all.

Traditionally, white wines have also been wood-aged in Spain and Portugal, and many still are. Usually this results in no more than a slow process of oxidation; a gradual yellowing, a loss of fruitiness and the development of a dull, cardboardy or sherry-like flavour. The Iberian peninsula's white grape varieties rarely stand up successfully to much wood ageing, though a few months in young oak barrels can add a little complexity, and longer oak ageing can, on occasion, produce stunning results in Rioja, notably at Bodegas Marqués de Murrieta.

In France, Australia and the USA, red wines for ageing tend to be put into oak barrels in the spring after their harvest, and are then transferred into bottle for further ageing after a period of wood maturation; by contrast, the Spanish and Portuguese tend to mature their reds for a year or more in big tanks or vats before barrel-ageing, racking them every four months or so. The period of barrel-ageing also tends to be rather longer. The result may be wines with slightly less fruit and more woody flavour, but there are many variables.

The main variable is the wood itself. A new barrel has a lot of vanilla and sawdust-like aromas and flavours as well as hard-tasting tannins to pass on to a wine stored inside it. But after five years' use, very little if anything remains to be extracted. Most Portuguese and Spanish winemakers keep their barrels for many years. After five years, a barrel serves simply as a container, more or less permeable to damaging air, and such barrels contribute no flavour to a wine. Some wineries attempt to rejuvenate their casks by scraping a layer off the inside, but experiments have shown that this is of little use, and can even lead to the creation of undesirable bitter flavours.

Different types of wood have different effects. American oak, most common in Spain and Portugal, imparts a very strong flavour very quickly. Oak from France takes longer to contribute its more subtle flavours, and oak from different parts of France gives different nuances of flavour: oak from the forests of Tronçais and the Vosges is thought to be best.

Even the method of manufacture of the barrels affects the taste: sawn staves impart a different taste from split ones, and barrels shaped under the effects of steam give a different flavour from those shaped (and singed) over an open fire. The degree of charring inside the barrel makes a big difference to flavour in the latter case. Smaller barrels give more oak flavour, since proportionally more wine is in contact with the wood. The most usual size is 225 litres. Actually, there is no reason why a barrel should be barrel shaped: Torres is currently experimenting with much cheaper *square* "barrels", the sides of which can be cheaply replaced to provide fresh wood character.

Though the authorities in both Spain and Portugal stipulate how long various classes of matured wine should spend in oak barrels, there are no guidelines as to how old or of what type these barrels should be. So wines

Below: *João Pires age their Quinta da Bacalhôa in new wood in the cellars of J. M. da Fonseca Internacionales.*

Below: *An impressive array of new and nearly new oak casks in the ageing warehouse in Pesquera of the Ribera del Duero's new star Alejandro Fernandez.*

Above: *Old, cobwebbed bottle-ageing cellar at CVNE. This bodega always has a large stock of wines maturing in bottle, usually around three million.*

in the same official category may have a distinct vanilla-oak flavour or none at all.

As red wine ages, its fruitiness gradually mellows and eventually fades, while colour and tannin also decrease in intensity. If all the elements were in ideal proportions at the outset, the wine should at some stage in its life reach a point where all its various elements are in perfect balance.

Colour pigments start out as tiny, purple-red particles, which link up as the wine ages, forming chains of an increasingly red, then brown colour. Finally, some particles become so big that they drop out of solution as a solid deposit, and the colour gradually becomes less intense. At the same time, the taste becomes less harsh and astringent, since the larger particles react less with the inside of our mouths than the far more numerous tiny particles which are present at the wine's birth.

The last stage of maturation occurs in the bottle. Most countries sell their wines as soon as possible after wood ageing, leaving the bottle ageing, and the decision as to when the wine is ready to drink, to the consumer. But winemakers in Spain and Portugal rarely release a wine before it is mature. Bottles may be stacked in the cellars for any time between a few months and many years before sale. The changes detailed above continue slowly in the bottle (though the wine has often thrown all the deposit it is going to throw before bottling) and it also develops distinctive mushroomy, pruney, "bottle-aged" flavours that make it more complex.

Not so many years ago, sherry making was full of mysteries and unexplained quirks of nature. In the year after the vintage, the wines in some butts (barrels) grew a thin veil of squashy, flaky, oatmeal-white yeast called *flor* (flower), and as they aged these wines remained pale and took on tangy-fresh flavours; the wine in other butts remained *flor*-free, tasted heavier, and gradually began to take on a darker, brownish colour and rich, nutty flavours. The lightest, finest *flor*-covered wines would be classified as *finos*, meaning "fine"; *flor*-less wines were termed *olorosos* ("richly fragrant"). (A full description of the various styles of sherry appears in the box on pages 100-1.) How much of each type a *bodega* managed to produce was quite beyond its owners' powers of control.

Fortunately for present day sherry producers trying to make particular styles of wine in pre-determined quantities, *flor* no longer appears as if by magic. A *bodega* ought to be able to hit its annual target for *finos* and *olorosos* fairly accurately by controlling the source of the grapes, the winemaking and fortification.

The selection begins in the vineyards. The finer wines for *finos* are more likely to come from the chalky white *albariza* soil than from the region's heavier land. Older vines are more likely to produce *finos*, too – grapes from vines younger than ten years rarely produce wine that is elegant enough to make a good *fino*.

But one of the most decisive moments that helps determine the elegance and quality of the finished wine lies between the vineyard and the fermentation vat. Fifty years ago, all the pressing was done in presshouses in the vineyards. The grapes arrived by the cart-load to be pressed under leather boots in receptacles that were washed without wasting too much water, since water was at a premium at these isolated vineyard presses. Any dirt or pick-up of astringent compounds from the grape skins or stalks would increase the likelihood of the wines' tasting dull, heavy or spoiled. Then the juice was loaded into butts for the hot journey to the *bodegas* in Jerez, Sanlúcar or Puerto de Santa María, still the only centres where sherry may be matured. Each butt was equipped with an expansion pipe to control the juice and gas on the journey – because everyone knew that the hot sun would set the must fermenting before it reached town.

Today, the *bodegas* control most of their own pressing and fermentations in hygienic conditions (though there is still a thriving market in grape juice and young wine). The grapes (principally Palomino) arrive as ripe as possible, whole and unbattered from the vineyards in 14-kilo plastic crates, which stack on top of one another without putting any pressure on their contents. The stalks are gently removed by machine. According to the regulations, only 70 per cent of the potential juice may be squeezed from the grapes to make sherry, 70 litres from 100 kilos. In practice, however, this alone does not guarantee top quality juice from good grapes – the type of press is also vitally important. Some *bodegas*, particularly the co-operatives, use continuous presses incorporating long, sloping steel screws. The juice from these contains more tannic and astringent substances, as well as unwanted solids from the grapes, which can lead to off-flavours. Best for quality and by far the most common in Jerez are horizontal presses, which press batches of grapes at a time, extremely gently. The best juice for *finos* is the "free-run" juice, extracted with little or no pressure, while a little more pressure can be applied to extract slightly coarser juice for *olorosos*. Some firms, however, choose to use their finest juice to make their best *olorosos*, too.

Traditionally, gypsum or plaster (*yeso*) was added to sherry juice in certain years to "correct" the acidity. Its effect was to convert the naturally present potassium bitartrate, which would later cause a sediment, into an instantly removable sediment, calcium tartrate, while adding to the natural tartaric acid of the juice. Some firms still do this, but a more modern and more accurately controllable alternative is to add a little tartaric acid before fermentation, and then to super-chill the finished sherry before bottling, since the potassium tartrate crystalises and precipitates out at low temperatures.

Above: *Cleanliness and gentle handling of grapes in the vineyards are the vital first steps in good sherry making. These attractive but unhygienic baskets are gradually giving way to plastic crates.*

Below: *The finest sherry grapes grow on chalky white* albariza *soil. It absorbs winter rainfall like a sponge, providing an underground supply for the vines long after the surface has dried to a crust.*

Most firms simply leave the juice to settle for about 24 hours before fermentation to get rid of the majority of the solid particles, although some clean it with centrifuges. Traditional fermentation vessels are huge Ali-Baba-style concrete vats (still used by the co-operatives) or wooden butts. Most *bodegas* have done away with both in favour of vats of stainless steel or other modern materials, but a few continue to ferment all or part of their wine in butts. More often than not, this is not because they prefer the quality of barrel-fermented sherry: what they are after are the wine-impregnated butts. They may need them to replace or supplement their barrels used for maturation; there is also quite a trade selling sherry fermentation butts to the Scotch whisky industry, since sherry butts impart a richer, rounder flavour to whisky than the bourbon casks they would otherwise use. Sherry fermented in wood is used for *oloroso* style wines, since the wine extracts oaky and astringent flavours that would spoil *fino*.

With an outdoor temperature at vintage time of between 24 and 29°C, it is absolutely essential to cool the fermentation if the wine is to turn out fine and elegant, with its maximum aroma and fresh flavour. By no means all *bodegas* have cooling equipment, but the best keep their *fino* fermentations down to 25°C or under (ideally lower) and *oloroso* vats to 30°C or below.

So much for the factors deciding the elegance of the wine. Whether or not *flor* will grow on a given cask of wine depends very largely on the degree to which it is fortified after fermentation. (*Flor* also develops best on wine of a certain acidity, and a suitable humidity and temperature – between 15 and 22°C – but the wines and *bodegas* of the sherry region almost always fall within the correct limits in these respects.) *Flor* will not live on wine containing over about 16.2° of alcohol. Not so long ago, the cellar master would taste each butt in the spring and add a fairly rough measure of grape alcohol to fortify the wine for maturation. Not surprisingly (though it was all a mystery to him) the more lightly fortified wines grew a film of *flor*, while the stronger wines remained clear. Nowadays, wines intended for *finos* are carefully fortified to just 15 or 15.5°; heavier wines for *olorosos* are more highly fortified up to 18°.

The air of the sherry region's *bodegas* is alive with *flor*. It consists of three strains of yeast, which are present in different proportions in different *bodegas*, giving the *flor* of each one a slightly different character. Down by the sea in Sanlúcar de Barrameda, the *flor* contains notably more of one of the strains, *Saccharomyces beticus*, and this contributes to the different flavour of the Manzanilla made there in the *fino* style.

Sanlúcar is cooler and more humid than inland Jerez, and the *flor* grows in a thicker layer. In Jerez, and even in the hotter seaside town of Puerto de Santa María, it is necessary in summer to keep the *bodegas* closed against the dry heat and to hose the floors with water every couple of days to maintain a cool enough temperature and high enough humidity to sustain the *flor*. There is no such problem in Sanlúcar.

Quite a large area of *flor* is in contact with the wine, since the 600-litre butts are filled only five-sixths full. As it grows, the *flor* protects the wine from the damaging effects of oxygen in the air, but it also alters the wine in various ways. It reduces the alcoholic degree, so that a *fino* starting life at 15.5° is likely to be down to around 14.7° by the time it is ready for bottling perhaps four years later. (Some *bodegas* would like to change the regulations and sell it in this more delicate state, but at present it must be refortified up to at least 15.5°, and 16.2° is more typical.) *Flor* also feeds on vinegar (acetic acid), ethyl acetate (the chemical that gives pear-drop flavours) and acidity (*fino* is one of the least acid wines in the world). The sharp, aromatic, tangy flavour of a *fino* sherry comes not, as one might imagine, from its acidity, but from a high concentration of a compound called acetaldehyde formed by the *flor*.

It takes a legal minimum of three years, but in practice more like four or more years for a *fino* sherry to take on the expected intensity of aromas and flavours. Untouched in a single butt, however, the *flor* covering would thin out and die for lack of nutrients within perhaps a year or eighteen months.

Above: *The* fino sherry in the right hand glass has been drawn from under the layer of flor with a venencia, *a metal cup on a long, flexible handle. To the left is a scoop of the* flor *itself.*

This is where Jerez's famous *solera* system comes to the rescue.

A *solera* is usually pictured as three or four tiers of butts lying on wooden supports one on top of the other. When wine is needed for bottling, a quarter or a third of the wine is drawn off the bottom butt (the actual

Above: *Contrary to popular belief, the different scales of a* solera *are rarely stacked one above the other. They may be kept in quite separate places. This bodega, Las Copas at Gonzalez Byass, contains 80,000 butts of sherry.*

solera), which is topped up from the butt above (first *criadera*), which is topped up from the one above that (second *criadera*) and so on for however many levels or scales (*escalas*) a producer requires, with young wine topping up the whole system. The result is that younger wine refreshes each barrel on the way down, and just enough nutrients pass down to the older wines to keep their *flor* alive. *Flor* can be kept going in this way for five and a half to six years. In practice, the different scales of a *solera* may be kept in quite different *bodegas*, and the wine from a large number of butts in one scale may be syphoned out, mixed together and poured into an equal number of butts of the next scale. Each scale might consist of just one, or a thousand or more, butts.

Though the *solera* system is vital for *finos* and *manzanitlas*, it is also the traditional way of blending all types of sherry to a con-

sistent style. After fortification, *oloroso* sherries, like *finos*, are filled into 600-litre butts up to the 500-litre mark so that they are in contact with a large volume of air. Slow oxidation produces the *olorosos'* rich, nutty, aromatic flavours and dark brown colour. Wines from the different casks are gradually blended together through the *solera*; *olorosos* also must be a minimum of three years old when drawn off for bottling – though really good *olorosos* would be matured for much longer. Their alcoholic degree *increases* as the wine very slowly evaporates, so that they are sold at between 18 and 20°.

The other major style of sherry goes through a mixture of the production processes of both *fino* and *oloroso*. *Amontillado* starts life as a *fino*, then gradually loses its *flor* and continues to develop, turning to a dark amber, through slow contact with air. It may lose its *flor* because it has been re-fortified in order to speed it on its way into the *amontillado* style, or it may have been left for six years or more under *flor* until the *flor* thinned out and died naturally. Really good *amontillados* are then aged for several years more through *amontillado soleras*. They are sold at between 16 and 18° of alcohol.

*A*ll the sherries described so far, whether *fino, amontillado* or *oloroso,* are *dry.* Sweet sherries are made by adding specially-made sweet wines either during the maturation process or before bottling. For dark cream sherries this is usually "PX", the super-sweet, dark, concentrated, fortified juice of the Pedro Ximénez grape. Jerez is not really hot enough to ripen PX to the required sweetness, and so it tends to be imported from Montilla, though this trade is officially frowned upon. The grapes are dried to raisins either on traditional mats in the sun or under plastic tunnels, and have to be milled to extract the thick, sweet juice. Ideally unfermented, the juice is fortified up to about 12° of alcohol and generally put through *solera* for a year or two. Fortified raisin juice (*mistela*) from local Palomino grapes is also sometimes used for sweetening. This paler liquid nowhere near approaches the sweetness of PX, and it can be used only for medium sherries. Pale creams are sweetened simply by the addition of vacuum-concentrated grape juice; liquid sugar was once extensively used, and no doubt still finds its way unofficially into some pale cream sherries. A very few *bodegas* use fortified Moscatel juice, but this gives a very scented, grapy flavour untypical of sherry.

The darkest of sherries are made by the addition of *vino de color,* a treacly liquid in colour, texture and taste, made, for the cheapest dark sherries, simply by boiling up grape juice to a third or a fifth of its original volume. This boiled juice is cooled and added to fermenting natural grape juice for use in more expensive sherries.

Fino's Fleeting Freshness

*F*INO SHERRY needs a sell-by date almost as much as a pot of yoghurt. *Oloroso,* having spent its whole maturation period in contact with air, still tastes good after months and months in an open bottle. But *fino* and *manzanilla* sherries, matured under a film of *flor,* have been protected from oxygen up to the moment of being drawn off the *solera* for bottling. After that they behave rather like schoolboys just released from a single-sex school. They have never seen oxygen before – and grab every bit they can get.

Most wines can be protected from oxidation by the preservative sulphur dioxide, but this is little help in the case of *fino* sherry, since it binds together with products of the *flor.* A bottle that has hung around for too long in a warehouse or on a shop shelf might already taste dull by the time it is opened.

Many of the recent improvements in sherry making have helped reduce this problem by making the wine cleaner and less prone to oxidation from the start. A few *bodegas* top up their *fino* bottles with the inert gas nitrogen before corking, as a protection against air. Domecq go a stage further, chill their *fino* and bubble nitrogen through it before bottling, bringing the level of the air dissolved in the wine since it left the *flor* to just 15 per cent of its original volume.

Sadly, when faced with an array of *fino* sherries on the shop shelf, there is usually no way of telling how long ago they were bottled. It is safest to choose a shop or supermarket that seems to have a fast turnover, and to buy in small quantities for drinking fairly soon.

Once opened, a bottle of *fino* or *manzanilla* sherry certainly needs drinking up as quickly as you would any white wine, before it loses its freshness. It helps to keep it chilled (it tastes better that way, too), to decant half for future drinking into a corked half-bottle, or to suck out the air remaining in the full-sized bottle with special gadgets sold for the purpose by wine merchants.

Above left: *Grapes drying in the sun under the plastic tunnels that have now largely replaced the traditional* esparto *mats. Both Pedro Ximénez and Palomino grapes are dried in this way.*

Above: *You need steady nerves to pour 100-year-old* manzanilla pasada *with a* venencia, *a traditional cask-sampling tool of Jerez. This* venenciador *is at work in the* bodegas *of Barbadillo.*

The Douro must be one of the world's few wine regions where they still tread grapes by foot – including some of the region's finest. The sight of an enormous stone *lagar*, or fermenting trough, with a line of bare-legged men in shorts or swimming trunks rhythmically wading through a red-purple sea of juice and skins, raising their knees above the surface at each step, is one never to be forgotten. At the end of the line, the leader shouts out the beat, and by the evening the *adega* (winery) has become host to a large and noisy party: the treading continues until the fermentation is well under way, with music, dancing and drink to revive the treaders' flagging energies.

When the treading stops, the work of keeping the colour- and tannin-loaded skins on the churn and giving their all to the juice is done by men standing on planks balanced over the *lagares*. Prodding and stirring the bubbling cauldron of skins and juice with long wooden sticks, they work intermittently until the new wine has reached an alcoholic strength of between six and seven degrees. The wine, still with more than half its original natural grape sugar remaining unfermented, is then run off through channels opened in the bottom of the *lagares*, to be mixed with grape brandy up to a strength of about 19 per cent alcohol. This fortification stops the fermentation by killing off the yeasts, and the infant port is left to settle and recover from the shock of birth.

This is the *traditional* way of making port, dating from the days when there was little or no electricity in the Upper Douro. Most port was made on small *quintas* (or farms), under the supervision of the port shipping companies, and it was wine, rather than grapes, that the shippers bought to blend and mature.

Now, though some of the top vintage ports still come from isolated little farms with traditional *lagar* vinification, the major companies have all installed electricity and large modern vinification plants. Mechanical grape crushers have almost completely replaced the human foot, and most winemaking is carried out in "autovinificators". These were originally devised to overcome the lack of electricity, and are still popular as an effective means of cutting electricity bills.

The process is called "autovinification" because the naturally expanding volume of gas given off during fermentation acts as a pump to spray the must over the floating mass of skins and pips, breaking it up and extracting colour and flavour. Wineries that do not use autovinificators have electric pumps instead.

The diagram illustrates how an autovinificator works. As the must begins to ferment, carbon dioxide is released. The increasing volume of gas drives the fermenting juice up through the escape tube and into the open trough on top of the vat. At the same time, water is forced out of the water-valve into the holding tank. When all the water has been

Above: Picking at Taylor's Quinta de Vargellas in the Upper Douro.

driven out, the built-up carbon dioxide rushes out of the vat, creating a vacuum that sucks the must in the upper trough back down the central pipe of the autovinificator. The fermenting must showers up through the outer tube of the autovinificator and down on to the floating cap of grape skins and pips, breaking it up and extracting colour and flavour as it seeps down through the skins. At the moment the must gushes back into the vat, water is drawn back into the water-reservoir through its return valve, and the whole process begins again. When the fermentation is in full swing, this cycle is repeated every 10 to 15 minutes, and the required alcoholic degree is reached in about 36 hours. The vat illustrated has an opening through which the remaining skins and solid matter can be emptied when the wine has been drawn off.

Some wineries are *really* modern, equipped with temperature-controlled stainless steel vats, or revolving paddles to agitate the must and break up the cap, but most shippers maintain that autovinificators are adequate for the greater part of port making. There is a general move towards the installation of temperature control equipment throughout the industry. Average temperature during fermentation is 28°C, but unusually hot (or cool) weather at harvest time can mean that fermentations overheat or

stop. As one shipper put it: "With temperature control equipment, we can make more
good wine, more predictably."

Legislation in force at present obliges producers to ferment wine destined for white
port (made from white grapes) similarly to
red, with some or all of the skins. This may
change, as the high fermentation temperatures and inclusion of the skins result in
rather coarse wines, often charcoal-filtered
to remove excess golden colour.

Above: *Music revives flagging treaders at
Quinta do Noval. Most port grapes are
crushed mechanically nowadays, but
some* quintas *still rely on the human foot.*

Below: *Autovinificators were invented in
Algeria and proved invaluable in the
Douro region before electricity was
available, as carbon dioxide given off
during fermentation acts as a natural
pump to spray juice over the skins.*

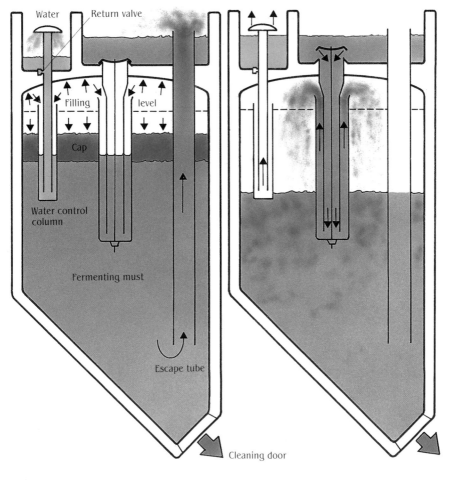

Although port is *made* in the Douro, most of it is matured in Vila Nova de Gaia, a small town just across the Tagus river from Oporto, and this is where the young wine is taken early in the year following the vintage, after analysis and a first classification have been made, and more brandy added to bring the wine up to 19° alcohol if necessary.

In Gaia, the wines are classified once again, this time to decide their final destiny. Potential vintage wines are kept firmly separate, to await developments in the next two years. Others of similar character are married together into *lotas* (parcels), given an identity number, and left to rest in wooden barrels and casks of varying sizes until they are considered ready for blending and subsequent bottling.

Every so often they are racked off their lees into a clean vat or barrel, at least once a year when they are young, and less frequently as they grow older. The red colouring matter is gradually precipitated out over the years, which is why old tawny ports are paler in colour than young ruby.

Right: *A blender at work in the tasting room of Graham & Co at Gaia.*

Below: *The double decker bridge, designed by Eiffel, which spans the river between Oporto and Vila Nova de Gaia.*

Port Types

Ruby The youngest of the red port styles. It should be fresh and fruity, with a good, red-purple colour. Ruby can be bottled and sold after three years of cask ageing (the statutory minimum).

Vintage Character Superior ruby port with longer in wood (between four and six years on average) before bottling. Wines intended for these blends are said to come from the better quality vineyards, but sometimes this superior quality is hard to perceive, let alone any similarity to real vintage port.

Tawny With cheap tawny, this is purely a description of colour, the result of blending basic ruby with white port, to give a tawny, or deep gold wine. These wines are most widely drunk as aperitifs in France and Belgium. There are some definitely superior tawnies (about eight years old) sold under various brand names, but no certain way of distinguishing the good from the basic on a shop shelf. See also **Old Tawny**.

White Usually medium-sweet, and quite light in colour.

Dry White White port made drier than the version above, and sometimes aged for as long as six years, until it takes on a nutty flavour.

Old Tawny Known officially as "Indication of Age" ports, these are blends of tawny wine matured for a long time in barrel, then bottled and sold as 10, 20 or 30-year-old wines. These figures represent a rough average of the blend's age, since some of the components may be older than the age stated, but the mixture will always contain some younger wine to give freshness to the blend.

Dated (Colheita) port Not much seen in the export markets, but popular in Portugal. Dated port is wine from a single vintage that has been matured in wood for at least seven years before bottling. So, essentially, it is single-vintage tawny, *not* to be confused with vintage port. The year of bottling must also be stated on the label.

Port Types

Late-bottled vintage (LBV) Port from a single year, matured for between four and six years in wood before being bottled. Most LBV has no inherent superiority to decent ruby, and was invented to satisfy the demand of the hotel and restaurant trade for port with "vintage" on the label that did not need decanting. However, a few shippers make LBV that develops in bottle and may throw a deposit and need decanting. The latter wines usually have the year of bottling mentioned on the label as well as that of production.

Crusted (or Crusting) Usually a blend of good ports from two or three years, matured in wood for three or four years, then bottled. Further ageing in bottle will cause the port to throw a deposit, or crust, hence the name. Crusted port had almost disappeared until a few years ago, and was not even defined in the 1974 regulations governing aged ports. However, recently there has been a revival of interest in crusted ports, representing as they do a traditional type of port that has been subjected to less pre-bottling treatment than the various types of exhaustively filtered rubies.

Single quinta port Each shipper has some *quintas* (farms) whose grapes make up the backbone of their top wines. In years not thought good enough for vintage declaration, some companies bottle the production of one of these top quintas as a sort of "off-vintage" vintage. In recent years, restrictions obliging would-be exporters of port to mature their wines in Vila Nova de Gaia have been lifted, enabling Douro farms to sell their wines direct to the public. At present, only three estates do this.

Vintage The top wines – port from an outstanding year, bottled two years after it was made, and needing up to 20 years' further maturation in bottle before it is ready to drink. On average, only two per cent of the industry's entire production becomes vintage port. Since 1975, it has been obligatory to bottle vintage port in Vila Nova de Gaia.

*W*hile most of the wine-making world strives to keep winemaking and maturation temperatures *down*, winemaking in Madeira is based on deliberate *heating* of the wines during their maturation period. The practice developed in the 19th century as a means of reproducing the effects of long sea journeys across the equator in the previous century, which had proved beneficial to the quality of the exported wine. (In addition to wine bound for India, wine shipped to other destinations also did the round trip, as a means of quick maturation.) Customers grew to like the "cooked" flavour, and the Madeira producers thought up less laborious ways of producing it on the spot. The modern substitutes for sailing ships are *estufas*, literally "hot houses", in practice either huge "kettle-tanks" (*cubas de calor*) or hot rooms (*armazemes de calor*).

In other respects, the production of Madeira differs very little from that of other fortified wines, such as port. There are two main bands of quality (see pages 148 and 149 for further details): cheaper wines (including cooking wines), made from the officially "noble" but actually not particularly exciting Tinta Negra Mole grape, and more expensive wines, labelled "reserve" "special reserve", or occasionally "vintage" or "solera", made from the more flavourful "noble" grapes, Sercial, Verdelho, Bual and Malmsey. Confusingly, the cheaper wines also bear these four names, even though they consist simply of Tinta Negra Mole made in the (respectively) dry, medium dry, medium sweet and sweet style of the four top wines.

The actual process of winemaking begins when the grapes for Madeira are transported to the wineries for pressing in more or less modern equipment, grapes of different varieties and from different altitudes of the precipitous island being kept separate. Growers are generally paid according to the sugar content and therefore the potential alcohol of their grapes – since Madeira is a fortified wine, more natural alcohol means less expensive fortification.

For Sercial, Verdelho and Tinta Negra Mole, the juice ferments alone, but with Bual and Malmsey, the skins are usually also added for a couple of days in order to extract more colour, and more tannin and aromas. The wine ferments at anything between 18 and 35°C (ideally towards the lower end), either in tanks or traditional wooden casks.

All the British firms on the island (Britain has a long-standing connection with Madeira) stop their fermentations at the desired point of sweetness by adding grape alcohol up to about 17°. Some Portuguese companies ferment all their wines right out to dryness, sweetening them up later with *vinho surdo*, grape juice prevented from fermenting by the addition of alcohol, either before or after the *estufagem* (heating) process. After fermentation, the young wine is racked off its deposit.

If the wine was not fortified during fermentation, it may either be fortified now or

Above: *Coopers sorting barrels at The Madeira Wine Company's San Francisco Lodge. Reserve wines must mature for five years, Special Reserves for ten.*

left (often the case with cheaper wines) until the heating process is complete. About two degrees of alcohol are driven off in the *estufa*, and some companies feel this would not be cost-effective for their cheaper wines, although adding the alcohol before *estufagem* makes for better quality.

The *estufas* for the simpler, cheaper wines are large tanks or wooden vats equipped inside with hot water-filled pipes or coils, and sometimes with propellers or pumps to keep the wine circulating; these heat the wines to between 45 and 50°C for a minimum of 90 days. Better wines, intended for reserves and special reserves, are filled into pipes (large casks holding approximately 600 litres). These are then stacked in store rooms above the hot tanks used for the cheaper wines, or in lodges heated by hot water pipes to much gentler temperatures, usually between 35 and 40°C.

After the heating period, the wine is left to cool for three to four weeks. This is a dangerous stage, and many Madeiras develop excessive volatile acidity (vinegary flavours)

Left: *Real Sercial grapes. The EEC is to put an end to the confusing practice of labelling dry wines made from Tinta Negra Mole grapes as "Sercial".*

filtered. All wines are left to rest in casks or tanks for a minimum of eighteen months. The cheapest wines are sold after eighteen months to three years, but reserve wines must by law be five years old, and special reserves must be ten years.

Generally, the wines sold are blends of several batches of wine, or *lotes*, most likely of different years. However, Madeira does also produce a very few vintage wines, which must age in cask for a minimum of 20 years, followed by two in bottle before sale. Some of these are undoubtedly genuine, but there are also some very dubious "ancient" bottles on sale on the island.

There have always been a very few *solera* wines, too (see pages 26 and 27 for an explanation of the *solera* system). Wines entering the *solera* must be special reserves, though they may be blended with ten per cent of the wine of the year. However, because Portuguese politicians failed to include Madeira's *soleras* in their negotiations leading up to Portugal joining the EEC, until this is put right *solera* Madeiras are officially illegal.

on top of the desired caramelly, tangy and slightly bitter flavours produced by the heating. The wine is then fined, possibly filtered and those wines not fortified before are fortified now to about 17° of alcohol. The more expensive wines are re-fortified (they will be fortified again up to somewhere between 18 and 21° sometime before bottling), fined and

ost famous of all the ways of making
wine sparkle is the Champagne
method, generally known in Spain as
cava or, occasionally, método champenoise,
and in Portugal as *método champanhês*
(until, that is, the latter term becomes illegal
in 1994 as a result of an EEC directive). In this
type of winemaking, still wine is mixed with a
carefully measured quantity of sugar and a
new supply of yeast. It is then bottled, firmly
sealed with metal caps, and the bottles are
stacked away on their sides in a cool cellar for
a second fermentation to take place. Most of
the second fermentation is over within a
couple of weeks, but the process slows down
as the pressure in the bottle increases, and
only peters out gradually.

In theory, the bottles could be prepared
for sale at this stage, but EEC and local
regulations require a minimum ageing
period of nine months from second fermentation to final corking. Unfortunately, most
of the Iberian peninsula's white grapes are
not really suitable for such long ageing, and
the wines emerge from the cellars with rather
less fruitiness than they had at the outset
(though the sparkling wine does age more
slowly than the equivalent still wine would
owing to the pressure and low temperature,
and the absense of air since the wine is sat-
urated with carbon dioxide). The French
stress that their Champagne method wines
pick up a special yeasty flavour from pro-
longed contact with the dead yeast cells
during this ageing process, but Spanish and
Portuguese Champagne method wines very,
very rarely have any yeasty character, and
their producers generally deny that such flavours are the object of the exercise.

This deposit of dead yeast cells trapped

Above: *The traditional way of teasing the
sediment down on to the cork is now
largely giving way to quicker methods.
Even where the racks persist, they are
now generally made of concrete.*

inside the bottle poses problems, however; it
is not a simple matter of slapping on a label
once the producer has decided the wine is
ready to sell. If this were the case, the murky,
yeasty sludge would come churning up with
the bubbles when the bottle was opened. The
solution is to trap the sediment in the neck of
the bottle, where it can be frozen in a plug of
wine by immersing the bottle neck in a bath
of freezing brine, after which the plug is
ejected by the pressure of the fizz on removal
of the bottle cap.

Simply tipping the bottle up on to its cap
is no use, however, because the sticky sludge
adheres to the bottle side and the finer particles cloud up into the wine. Instead, the traditional Champagne method involves placing
the bottles "head first" into heavy, hinged
rectangular wooden boards bored with holes
in such a way that the bottle can be held hori-
zontally, vertically or at any angle in between.
Skilled cellar workers "riddle" the bottles
gradually twisting and tipping each bottle
daily for several weeks until they are virtually
upside down and the sediment has sunk into
the bottle neck.

Some Spanish and Portuguese sparkling
wine producers still use this old method
(though generally replacing the wood with
racks moulded out of concrete), but firms in
the Penedés region of Catalonia pioneered a
new, less labour-intensive device that has
now become almost standard equipment.

Above: *The* girasol, *a Catalan invention, is now used worldwide, even in Champagne itself. It enables 504 bottles to be turned in one go, doing away with the twisting and turning of single bottles.*

Above: *Latest in* cava *technology are "agglomerating yeasts" for the second fermentation, which form easily moveable clumps instead of the fine, sticky sediments left by the ordinary yeast.*

The *girasol* (Spanish for sunflower) consists of a metal crate big enough to hold 504 bottles neck-down, standing on an octagonal base. Every eight hours or more, the *girasol* is turned by two workers on to the next facet of the base, and the sediment gradually spirals down. Variations on the *girasol* have a "rocking chair" base, and sometimes even motors to replace manual labour altogether.

Once the iced sediment has been success-fully ejected, the bottles are topped up with more wine, sometimes some brandy, and generally a little sugar to bring the wine up to the required sweetness, then the cork is inserted and secured with wire.

The next most common way of making sparkling wine is the tank method, the equivalent of the French *cuve close* or Charmat method, called *granvas* in Spanish, *método continuo* in Portuguese. The base wine is blended as for the Champagne method with a measured quantity of sugar and yeast, but instead of being bottled, it is left to ferment in a sealed pressure tank. By Portuguese and Spanish law, the wine has to spend 21 days in the tank, after which it is fil-tered to remove the sediment, and bottled, all under pressure. The resulting bubbles tend to be larger, and do not last quite so long in the glass, but these wines can be good if the base wine is decent in the first place.

Simplest and cheapest of all is to inject the base wine with carbon dioxide up to the required pressure just before bottling. Such wines are termed *vino gazificado* or *vinho espumoso*. This results in big, coarse bubbles that fade quickly in the glass, and since the method is usually applied only to very basic wines, these are best avoided. Por-tuguese *vinhos verdes* almost always have their prickle of fizz injected.

Portugal can also boast an oddity, sparkl-ing wine made by the Russian continuous method. It is used in Europe by only one firm, J.M. da Fonseca Internacional, to make their sparkling Lancers (see pages 154-5 for further details).

Awine label *should* be the key to understanding what is in the bottle. Too often, however, you need a key to the puzzles the label itself presents. It is not just a language problem. There are good and bad labels, although the more obscurely phrased examples are disappearing from Spanish and Portuguese bottles since their entry into the EEC.

One vital yet basic piece of information that may be missing is the vintage. This can be particularly frustrating for a wine made to be drunk young, like a Portuguese *vinho verde*. A few *vinhos verdes* from single estates have their vintage on the label (often in small print on a back label), but there is no way of knowing how old most of the commercial brands are – and hence how long a bottle may have been sitting neglected on a shop shelf.

There is a further problem in Spain (although you will rarely meet it nowadays on bottles with export labels, and it is seen less and less even within Spain). The traditional method of age-indication does not tell the whole story. *1° año, 2° año, 3° año* (and so on) mean that the wines were bottled respectively during the first, second and third calendar years after they were made.

If a wine labelled like this *also* tells you the date of the vintage (as happens with the Valbuena wines from Bodegas Vega Sicilia), you have a fairly complete picture. You know when the wine was made and how long it spent in vats or barrels before it was bottled. Usually, however, there is no vintage indication, and a *1° año* wine that happened to be made in 1985 (ie bottled during 1986) intended for early consumption *may* have been lurking in ambush on a sunny shop shelf for a couple of years before being bought by an unsuspecting customer in 1988.

Apart from these difficulties, though, Spanish and Portuguese labels are simple enough to understand: it is just a matter of knowing what the key words mean. As with wine labels from any country, the words to look for are those that tell you the wine *type*, region, quality level and, above all, the name of the producer.

Contents in centilitres — Name of the *bodega* that made the wine — Registered trade mark — Registration number of the *bodega* — Alcoholic degree — Name of viticultural region — Seal of the *Consejo Regulador* — Town where *bodega* is situated — Brand name

Spanish label Vintage

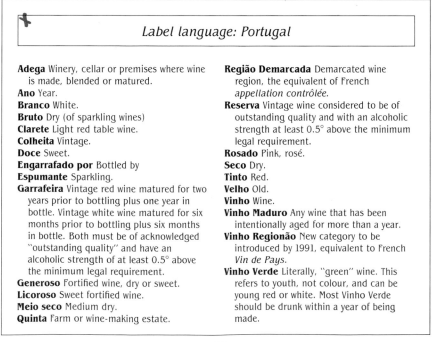

Label language: Portugal

Adega Winery, cellar or premises where wine is made, blended or matured.
Ano Year.
Branco White.
Bruto Dry (of sparkling wines)
Clarete Light red table wine.
Colheita Vintage.
Doce Sweet.
Engarrafado por Bottled by
Espumante Sparkling.
Garrafeira Vintage red wine matured for two years prior to bottling plus one year in bottle. Vintage white wine matured for six months prior to bottling plus six months in bottle. Both must be of acknowledged "outstanding quality" and have an alcoholic strength of at least 0.5° above the minimum legal requirement.
Generoso Fortified wine, dry or sweet.
Licoroso Sweet fortified wine.
Meio seco Medium dry.
Quinta Farm or wine-making estate.

Região Demarcada Demarcated wine region, the equivalent of French *appellation contrôlée.*
Reserva Vintage wine considered to be of outstanding quality and with an alcoholic strength at least 0.5° above the minimum legal requirement.
Rosado Pink, rosé.
Seco Dry.
Tinto Red.
Velho Old.
Vinho Wine.
Vinho Maduro Any wine that has been intentionally aged for more than a year.
Vinho Regionão New category to be introduced by 1991, equivalent to French *Vin de Pays.*
Vinho Verde Literally, "green" wine. This refers to youth, not colour, and can be young red or white. Most Vinho Verde should be drunk within a year of being made.

Label Language: Spain

Abocado Medium sweet table wine.
Aguja Very young wine with a strong prickle of gas remaining from the fermentation.
Almacenista Private stockholder of fine individual sherries.
Amontillado Re-fortified *fino* (qv) left to mature till it becomes dark amber in colour and nuttily pungent.
Año Year.
Blanco White.
Bodega Winery, wine cellar, wine warehouse or wine-producing company.
Brut Dry (of sparkling wine).
Brut Natur(e) Very dry (of sparkling wine).
Cava Catalan for "cellar", but used to describe Spanish sparkling wines made by the Champagne method in certain specified regions, and the companies that make them. Now a *Denominación de Origen* defining various regions of origin, and the production method.
Clarete Light red table wine.
Comarca Vinícola Viticultural region.
Con crianza Wine that has been aged (*crianza* means ageing) for the minimum time in oak and bottle specified by the local *Consejo Regulador* (regulatory body) of each region, or for a minimum of two years if the local *Consejo* does not specify otherwise.
Cosecha Vintage.
CVC Stands for "Cupage de Varias Cosechas", or blend of different vintages. Sometimes written as "Sin Cosecha" (non-vintage).
Denominación de Origen (DO) Guarantee of wine's authenticity issued by local *Consejo Regulador*. Equivalent of French *appellation contrôlée*.
Denominación Específica Now obsolete quality level, which used to fall between DO and basic Comarca (qv). Still seen on vintages before 1987.
Dulce Sweet.
Elaborado por Made, matured or blended by.
Embotellado por Bottled by.
Espumoso Sparkling.

Fermentación en botella Sparkling wine made by the transfer method. Secondary fermentation takes place in bottle, but the wine is filtered in tanks before bottles are refilled for sale.
Fino Pale, delicate, pungent fortified wine matured under a layer of *flor* yeast in Jerez and elsewhere.
Gasificado Artificially carbonated.
Generoso Fortified wine, sweet or dry, drunk as aperitif or dessert.
Gran Reserva Top-quality wine, aged for a minimum of two years in oak casks and three in bottle for reds, and a minimum of four years for whites and rosés, of which six months must be in oak barrels.
Granvas Sparkling wine made by the tank (*cuve close* or Charmat) method of secondary fermentation in sealed tanks.
Joven Young.
Mistela Blend of grape juice with wine alcohol, drunk as aperitif.
Nuevo New, young.
Rancio Deliberately maderised (oxidised) wine (usually baked in the sun in glass jars or wooden barrels), drunk as aperitif or after a meal.
Reserva Good quality wine, reds aged for a minimum of three years (of which one must be in oak barrels), and whites and rosés for two years (of which six months must be in oak barrels).
Rosado Pink, rosé.
Sangría Blend of wine (usually red) and fruit juice.
Seco Dry.
Semi-seco Medium dry.
Tinto Red.
Vendimia Harvest.
Vino Wine.
Vino de la Tierra New super-category of table wines, equivalent of French *Vins de Pays*.
Vino espumoso natural same as *fermentación en botella*.
Vino gasificado Sparkling wine made by adding carbon dioxide (carbonation).

Portuguese label

1981 ———— Vintage

Alcoholic degree —— 12% VOL.   75 CL —— Contents in centilitres

Dão
—— Name of viticultural region
REGIÃO DEMARCADA —— Demarcated region
VINHO TINTO —— Red wine
ENGARRAFADO NA REGIÃO —— Bottled in the region

São Pedro de **Grão Vasco** —— Brand name

Producing company —— VINÍCOLA DO VALE DO DÃO, LDA.
VISEU-PORTUGAL   PRODUCE OF PORTUGAL

Town where *adega* is situated

*I*t is simply not true that vintages do not matter in Spain and Portugal. Years *do* vary – there may be rain at picking time, droughts, hail, damaging rain or winds at flowering time, and spring frosts. Yes, while the tourists are sweating down in the disco after a hard day on the beach, growers up in the Ribera del Duero are out lighting fires amongst their vines to protect the new growth from frost. Some areas have a much more constant climate than others, however, and the chart opposite deals only with the red wine regions where vintages really matter. (A guide to vintage port vintages will be found on pages 124-5.)

There is no need to look at a vintage chart to work out which vintage of *white* and *rosé* wines you should be drinking. From the spring after the vintage, seek out the previous year's wine and enjoy its fruitiness and freshness while you still can. Vintages vary, but the most recent one will almost invariably be the best choice.

Vintage charts can be misleading for red wines, too. Skill in winemaking can often compensate for inadequate raw materials,

and a talented winemaker is likely to make a better wine in a "poor" year than a bad or careless producer in a good one.

Until recently, the Spanish and Portuguese preferred to buy their wines, white, red or rosé, well aged. Even if no old wine was available, it was possible to satisfy customers with an elderly-looking label outside the bottle and a relatively youthful wine within. This still goes on, but far less so today than a few years ago. Tastes amongst the younger members of the populations of Spain and Portugal are changing in favour of younger, fresher wines, and controls in some regions have become a little stricter.

Be cautious if offered wines without a vintage. This could well be a means of masking tired old wines with fresher, younger vintages, and the result is never a success. The exceptions are sherry, Malaga, Montilla, non-

Below: *Vintages in reserve at the João Pires winery on the Setúbal Peninsula. Winemaking skill often has a far greater bearing on quality than vintage.*

Spanish Reds

Jumilla Excellent **1980, 1981**. Very good **1978**.

Penedés Some Penedés reds are made for drinking very young, and few remain at their best after five years (with the exception of some Torres wines and Jean León). All the vintages of the '80s have been quite good and **1981, 1982** and **1987** were especially good.

Priorato 1975 and **1976** were excellent, and **1982** was a great vintage. Very good: **1978, 1979, 1980, 1981**.

Ribera del Duero Excellent **1970, 1981**. Very good **1973, 1975, 1976, 1977, 1979, 1982, 1983, 1985**. Styles of wine vary enormously, and it is even more impossible than elsewhere to generalise about keeping potential.

Rioja Wines labelled "Crianza" are for drinking between five or six years after the vintage, though some will not last this long. Most Reservas are at their peak between six and eight years old and Gran Reservas at about ten, though a few will keep for many years longer. The good recent vintages are **1985, 1983, 1982, 1981** and **1980** (especially **1982**). **1978** Gran Reservas are extremely good now or to keep for a few years, and some **1976, 1973** or especially **1970** Gran Reservas are very good, but many are now past it.

Utiel Requena Very good **1981, 1982, 1983**.

Valdepeñas From most *bodegas*, the young reds, made to drink in their first few years, are best. Top *bodegas* make Reservas and Gran Reservas that develop well for six to 12 years. Excellent **1981**. Very good **1980, 1983, 1984, 1985**. The best Gran Reservas of **1975** are still good, but beginning to go into decline.

Yecla Very good **1983, 1985**.

Portuguese Reds

Alentejo Best vintages of the best Alentejo wines on the market now are the excellent **1978** and **1980** and very good **1982**. **1983**s will be excellent when ready, and **1984** and **1985** very good.

Bairrada Made in the traditional style, Bairrada needs about five years to soften to drinkability, and the best may be in their prime after 12 years. **1975** and **1980** were excellent, and **1982** and **1983** very good. **1985**s will be excellent when mature.

Dão Best recent vintages were the excellent **1985** and very good **1983**. **1980** Reservas are mostly fading fast. Styles vary enormously, and some Dão wines have lost their fruit even before bottling.

Douro Good vintages for the table wines correspond to those for port (see pages 124-5).

Ribatejo Styles vary enormously. Good recent years were **1980, 1982, 1984**.

Setúbal Peninsula Best recent vintages were the excellent **1980**, very good **1982**, excellent **1984** and very good **1985**.

vintage ports and other fortified wines, as well as many sparkling wines, where the best wines, as well as the worst, are blended from a variety of vintages.

For some years, the trend in Spain has been towards less ageing in old wooden barrels. The Portuguese are only just beginning to adjust to the tastes of the outside world, however: the flavour of wine long aged in barrel has been popular there for years, whereas most of the rest of Europe prefers wine that has been bottled sooner after it was made. This lengthy barrel-ageing had tended to even out the considerable differences between vintages. All wines would reach the public in a state of near-exhaustion – good vintages were the ones that were still just drinkable. Now this is changing, but some regions still insist on the long, tiring stay in barrels, and top Garrafeiras and Reservas, like the Reservas and Gran Reservas of Spain, have to spend minimum periods in wood before they can be bottled.

Almost all Spanish and Portuguese reds are sold, in theory, ready to drink. Some will keep a few years, while some may have gone over the hill since (or even before) release from the winery. In regions other than those mentioned below, young reds, no more than a few years old, are usually the best bet.

SPAIN

Spain has more land under vine than any other country in Europe – indeed, with its 1,600,000 hectares, it can boast almost half the vineyards of the EEC (European Economic Community). That does not mean that Spain is producing half Europe's wine, however. Much of the country is dry and infertile, vines are widely spaced to cope with drought conditions, and irrigation is illegal. Results: yields average just over 23 hectolitres of wine per hectare of vines, compared with averages in France of 60 and in Germany of nearly 100 hectolitres per hectare. The income from grape growing in many parts of the country is pitiful.

Of the 36 to 40 million hectolitres of wine Spain makes each year, only 28 million hectolitres is eligible for sale as *wine* under the EEC's alcohol regime. Most of the remainder is distilled, for either brandy or industrial alcohol. The Spanish government is as eager as the EEC to reduce the excess vineyards. Grants are available for uprooting vines and planting other crops. The fine wine areas are unlikely to reduce in area – indeed, Rioja has recently been granted leave to *extend* its vineyards by 1,000 hectares – but a great many vines are likely to disappear over the next few years in Extremadura, La Mancha, Alicante, and other impoverished areas.

Things had already been changing in Spain in recent years without the spur of the EEC, however. The back street bars of Madrid, Seville and Barcelona still serve their litre bottles of alcoholic, brownish whites and rough, astringent reds, but they have other wines on offer, too, in a fresher, lighter style, and Spain's young wine drinkers are *asking* for modern wines, even if their fathers stick to the old stuff. Tastes – and winemaking know-how – have progressed much further in Spain than across the border in Portugal.

Only a few years ago, every co-operative in Spain (and 65 per cent of Spain's wine is made in co-operatives) paid its members according to the sugar content of their grapes, the more sugar, and hence potential alcohol, the better. Now many pay according to quality, and advise their members to pick sometimes three weeks early, before the grapes become over-ripe and lose their aroma and acidity. More and more co-operatives and wineries (*bodegas*) have installed or are installing cooling equipment, especially for their white wines, to make them as fresh and aromatic as possible.

Since Spain's entry into the EEC, grants have been available for upgrading cellars, usually matched by local grants and cheap loans, and though the backwoods areas are only just beginning to catch on to the possibility, the more forward-looking areas are already taking advantage of such financial assistance. Government or local government-financed research stations and wine-making schools have also been set up.

Key to map

1. Rias Baixas.
2. Ribeiro.
3. Valle de Monterrey.
4. Valdeorras.
5. El Bierzo.
6. Rioja.
7. Navarra.
8. Campo de Borja.
9. Somontano.
10. Ampurdán-Costa Brava.
11. Toro.
12. Rueda.
13. Cigales.
14. Ribera del Duero.
15. Calatayud.
16. Cariñena.
17. Terra Alta.
18. Tarragona.
19. Priorato.
20. Conca de Barberá.
21. Costers del Segre.
22. Penedés.
23. Alella.
24. Cebreros.
25. Méntrida.
26. Madrid.
27. La Mancha.
28. Valdepeñas.
29. Utiel-Requena.
30. Valencia.
31. Binisalem.
32. Almansa.
33. Jumilla.
34. Yecla.
35. Alicante.
36. Bullas.
37. Tierra de Barros.
38. Condado de Huelva.
39. Jerez-Xérès-Sherry.
40. Montilla-Moriles.
41. Málaga.
42. Tacoronte-Acentejo.

Among Spain's finer wines, the world's drinkers have long been aware of the quality of Rioja and sherry and some wines of the Penedés, especially those of the remarkable firm of Torres. But there are exceptional or highly recommendable wines to be found now in practically every major winemaking region of Spain. And what other country does the wine drinker the service of ageing wine to drinkable maturity before releasing it for sale, as Spain does? (The great wines of France are shipped to the customer for ageing, still far too young to drink.) Spain's *crianzas*, *reservas* and *gran reservas* may possibly continue to improve after you buy them, but the *bodega* will not have released them until they are ready to drink.

Just over half of Spain's total wine production gets the official stamp of *Denominación de Origen* (DO), the equivalent of the *Appellation Contrôlée* of France. As in France, this in theory guarantees the wine's origin, that it is made from certain specified grape varieties, that yields were kept to official limits, and that quality in the area has reached a level to satisfy the local, national and now finally the Brussels bureaucrats. Spain now has 30 DOs, many of them granted in the last decade, Toro being the most recent in the summer of 1987. Costers del Segre should become the 31st in 1988.

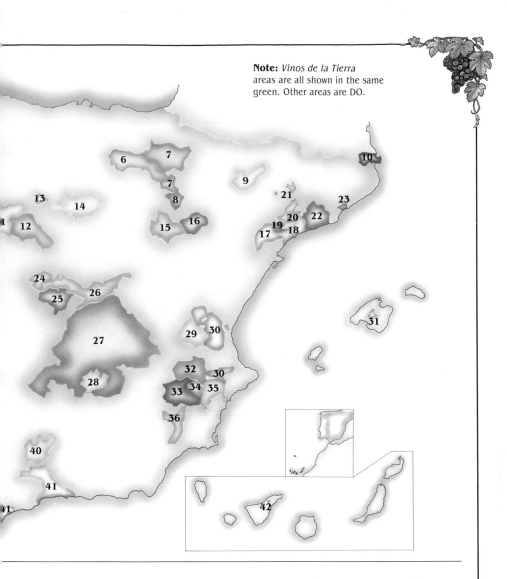

Note: *Vinos de la Tierra*
areas are all shown in the same
green. Other areas are DO.

Areas successfully on their way through the slow bureaucratic process of achieving DO status went until recently by the title of *Denominación de Origen Provisional*, with *Denominación Especifica*, preceded by *Denominación Especifica Provisional*, occupying the rung below; the remainder were simply *Comarcas Vinicolas*.

In December 1986, however, in preparation for entry into the EEC, Spain introduced a new category, *Vinos de la Tierra* (to match the French *Vins de Pays*). These must be made at least 60 per cent from the grapes authorised for each region, contain alcohol over certain minima, and stick within prescribed limits for the use of the preservative sulphur dioxide and for volatile acidity (vinegariness – a sign of poor winemaking or storage). They have to be labelled "*Vino de la Tierra*", along with the name of the *Comarca* or a *municipio* within the *Comarca*. Twelve *Comarcas* have qualified for this new status. No more DOs (except Costers del Segre) are to be declared for the next few years, and a massive revision of the whole DO system is expected to take place over the next decade.

Vinos de la Tierra

Comarca	Region	Previous status
Rias Baixas	Galicia	DOP
Valle de Monterrey	Galicia	CV
El Bierzo	Castilla-León	DEP
Cigales	Castilla-León	DE
Cebreros	Castilla-León	DEP
Calatayud	Aragón	DEP
Madrid	Madrid	DE
Bullas	Murcia	DOP
Tacoronte-Acentejo	Canaries	DEP
Conca de Barberá	Catalonia	DOP
Binisalem	Balearics	DEP
Tierra de Barros	Extremadura	DOP

Spain is said to have over 600 different vine varieties, but the 20 most extensively planted vines account for 80 per cent of the vineyards, and very many of the more obscure varieties are to be found in Galicia in the north-west. We tend to think of Spain as red wine country, but in fact vines producing white grapes are more numerous and planted over a greater area.

Assessing the importance of different grapes by the area they cover is misleading, however. The white Airén, for instance, though the first grape of Spain (and, indeed, of the *world*) in terms of vineyard expanse, covering almost three times as much land as any other Spanish grape, produces nowhere near three times as much wine as the number two, Garnacha Tinta. The tradition of widely spaced planting, and near drought conditions in the Airén's main habitat, the central plateau, result in tiny yields per hectare.

Things have been changing in the Spanish vineyards in recent years. Several difficult vines, prone to disease or poor in yield, have been replaced by more productive vines; the Graciano in Rioja, and the Malvasía in many parts of Spain have all but died out. There has been a move in several areas to replace lower-quality vines with better varieties: Garnacha and Airén are giving way to Tempranillo, for instance. But elsewhere, good vine varieties are still being abandoned in favour of more productive ones; the Airén (Lairén), for example, which is capable of high yields under favourable growing conditions, has gradually been swamping the traditional Pedro Ximén of Málaga.

Foreign varieties have also arrived. Vega Sicilia in Ribera del Duero has had Cabernet, Merlot and Malbec vines from Bordeaux established in its vineyards throughout this century. But several other estates now have established substantial plantations of foreign vines, especially Cabernet Sauvignon and Chardonnay.

Surprisingly, few of the vines grown in Spain are to be found across the border in Portugal. The Tempranillo appears in Portugal as the Tinta Roriz or Tinta Aragonez, but otherwise great similarities exist only between the grapes of Galicia in northern Spain and the Vinho Verde region, the Minho.

Above: *Cariñena grapes, grown in the region of Cariñena, where the variety is third in line after Garnacha and Bobal. Cariñena's main habitat is Catalonia.*

────── **Indigenous White Grapes** ──────

Airén Spain's most planted grape variety, covering 30 per cent of the vineyards, found all over the central plateau including La Mancha and Valdepeñas, and in Andalucia, where it is known as Lairén (and finds its way illegally into the *generosos* of Málaga). With old fashioned methods, it makes heavy, alcoholic white table wines; with modern methods and drunk very young, it is bland but fresh and fruity, often with a barely perceptible liquorice-like aroma.

Albariño Very sweet, low-yielding Galician grape potentially making complex high quality wines with higher acidity and alcohol than any other white Galician grape.

Cayetana Bland, high-yielding grape (for Spain), widely grown in Extremadura.

Garnacha Blanca Makes fat, flabby, alcoholic wines, short of acidity. Popular with growers for its high yields. Found mostly in the north-east, especially in Catalonia, but also in Rioja and Cariñeña.

Godello Aromatic Galician variety.

Lairén see Airén

Listan see Palomino

Loureira High quality Galician grape with a grapy aroma not unlike that of Moscatel. (Also, as Loureiro, a constituent of some of the best Portuguese *vinhos verdes*.)

Macabeo Most common white grape of northern Spain, known as Viura in Rioja, Navarra and Rueda, Macabeo in Somontano, Campo de Borja, Cariñena and Catalonia. Makes wines with good acidity, some fruit, slightly floral but generally rather bland flavour. With the help of a little added acidity, it responds well to oak ageing in Rioja, making, at best, rich, lemony, pine-flavoured wines.

Malvar Bland grape, found very widely in central Spain.

Malvasía Aromatic, musky-apricotty grape, quick to oxidise, grown in Valencia, Salamanca, Zamora, Albacete, and the Canaries. The Malvasía de Rioja may be a different variety.

Merseguera White grape grown widely in Valencia and, to a lesser extent, Alicante and Tarragona. It can be delicately perfumed but is usually very bland.

Moscatel de Málaga Makes grapy or raisin-flavoured, highly aromatic wines, usually very sweet. Málaga and Valencia are its major homes in Spain. Other former strongholds, such as the Canaries and Penedés, have dwindled. The best generally come from Málaga.

Moscatel de Grano Menudo This finer, grapier Moscatel (the finest of the Muscats of Alsace) is grown by Torres in the upper reaches of the Penedés to blend with Gewürztraminer in Viña Esmeralda.

Palomino de Jerez/Palomino Basto Once the main variety of Jerez. Coarser than Palomino Fino which has now practically replaced it entirely.

Palomino Fino Once the variety of Palomino growing only in the Sanlúcar area of the sherry region, this high-yielding grape now makes almost all sherry. Though it can produce base wines for turning into fine, delicate sherries, it tastes bland and quickly oxidises as a young white wine made in the modern style. In Condado de Huelva it is gradually replacing the local Zalema for *fino* production. It is to be found all over Spain as a dull constituent of white blends, often called the Listán or Jerez.

Pardillo Dull white making up 80 per cent of the vines in Badajoz by the Portuguese border, and also common in the provinces of Albacete and Cuenca.

Parellada The best of Catalonia's three major white grape varieties, used for both still and sparkling wines. It makes light, fresh, fruity whites, with a light, floral aroma; the alcohol content is usually low, between 9 and 11°, and the acidity good. They need drinking in their youth.

Pedro Ximénez Very sweet grape grown particularly for sherry-style wines in Montilla or dry to syrupy-sweet, dark, fortified wines in Málaga. It is in fact found all over southern Spain – Andalucia, Valencia and Extremadura – now sometimes made into a light, fresh but rather dull white wine, but more often yellowing, coarse and alcoholic.

Torrontés One of the indigenous white

Below: *Pedro Ximénez grapes of rather uneven quality on their way to the joint winery of a number of the major Málaga companies, in Mollina. PX is found all over southern Spain.*

grapes of the Ribeiro DO in Galicia; it gives a bitter, almondy tang to blends.

Treixadura Aromatic Galician grape especially important in the Ribeiro district. (Also a constituent of Portuguese *vinho verde*.)

Verdejo One of Spain's more characterful white grapes, grown in and around Rueda. Fresh and crisp, not too high in alcohol but full of body, with a nutty flavour.

Viura *see* Macabeo

Xarel-lo Native grape of Catalonia contributing body to the blends of both still and sparkling wines, though it is rather bland and often over-alcoholic. It is very common in the Penedés, Tarragona and, alias Pansa Blanca, in Alella.

Zalema Major but now declining variety of Condado de Huelva and the undemarcated area of Seville. It tastes bland, and easily oxidises.

──────── **White Foreign Imports** ────────

Chardonnay Makes fine, buttery-flowery wine that can be light or very full bodied. Grown in commercial quantities in various parts of Catalonia, and elsewhere on a very experimental scale. The finest is Torres' Milmanda from Conca de Barberá, but good ones also come from Jean León in the Penedés, and, still and sparkling, from Raimat in the *Denominación de Origen Provisional* Costers del Segre. Torres also use it for blending with local white grapes.

Gewürztraminer Spicy grape with a strong aroma reminiscent of the Chinese fruit lychee, grown by Torres in the coolest parts of the Penedés for their Viña Esmeralda.

Riesling German grape with a fresh, lemony flavour and good acidity, making wine much more alcoholic and full bodied than German Rieslings, much less freshly acidic, and much less fine. Grown on a commercial scale by Torres in the Penedés for their Viña Waltraud, and elsewhere experimentally.

Sauvignon Blanc An authorised grape in Rueda since 1985 and grown experimentally elsewhere. In Rueda, it makes soft, fruity, slightly grassy-flavoured wines.

------ **Black Indigenous Grapes** ------

Alicante *see* Garnacha Tintorera

Bobal One of Spain's most planted red varieties, making wines that are very darkly coloured but remarkably low in alcohol (around 11.5°) considering the hot climate. It is the main grape of Utiel-Requena, and it is also found in Alicante and Aragón, especially in Cariñena.

Caíno Characterful, aromatic variety found especially in Galicia.

Cariñena Produces deep-coloured wines, fairly high in alcohol, tannin and body, generally rather astringent. Its main habitat is Catalonia, where it is used as part of a blend with softer grapes. Alias the Mazuelo (or Mazuela) in Rioja, it now represents only a tiny proportion of the vineyards. In the region of Cariñena, where it is thought to have originated, the Cariñena grape is only third in line to the Garnacha and Bobal.

Cencibel *see* Tempranillo

Garnacha Tinta Vigorous, productive vine that does well in hot, dry places. It is the most extensively cultivated black grape in Spain, especially common in Navarra, Rioja, Penedés, Priorato, Tarragona, Terra Alta, Ampurdán-Costa Brava, Campo de Borja, Somontano, Cariñena, La Mancha, Méntrida and the area around Madrid, and Utiel-Requena, but also found to a certain extent almost everywhere except Andalucía, the Levante and Galicia. It tends to be alcoholic, and with the low yields it produces in Spain, red wines turn out quite dark (unlike in France, where high yields mean a low ratio between colour-giving skins and juice, hence pale wines). However, the colour falls out of Garnacha wines very quickly, and they are very prone to oxidation. Only rare examples, such as the richest and best of the Garnachas of Priorato, can stand up to much ageing. Elsewhere, the red is often drunk, fat and fruity, within the year as house wine in bars and restaurants, or everyday wine bought in bulk to drink at home. Much of Spain's Garnacha is made into *rosado*, which can also be excellent young.

Garnacha Tintorera Also known as Alicante, this is the only Spanish grape with red flesh. It is particularly common in Almansa, but also found in Alicante and parts of La Mancha.

Graciano High quality grape from Rioja and Navarra, quite rare nowadays because its low yields have made it unpopular. It makes subtle, well-balanced wine with a powerful, savoury aroma. The wine has good colour and ages well.

Jaen High-yielding, low quality grape covering a considerable area in central Spain.

Manto Negro Makes fruity red wines in the Balearic Islands.

Mazuela/Mazuelo *see* Cariñena

Mencía Grown in Galicia (especially Valdeorras), El Bierzo and León. Locals swear it is the Cabernet Franc, but from the taste this seems unlikely. Examples we have tasted have been herbaceous, like the Cabernet Franc, but bitter, though other authorities

Principal Black and White Grapes	
Grape	Hectares cultivated
○ Airén	476,300
● Garnacha Tinta	170,836
● Monastrell	108,138
● Bobal	106,114
○ Pardillo	37,234
○ Macabeo	35,852
● Tempranillo	33,633
○ Palomino	32,611
○ Pedro Ximénez	26,875
○ Cayetana	22,551
○ Zalema	19,627
○ Merseguera	19,463
● Jaen	17,297
○ Xarel-lo	17,065
● Garnacha Tintorera	16,459
○ Garnacha Blanca	16,329
○ Moscatel	15,100
○ Malvasía	14,460
● Cariñena	11,753
○ Malvar	8,689
● Mencía	8,850
● Moravia	8,218
○ Verdejo	7,041
○ Parellada	6,775
● Prieto Picudo	6,747
● Negra de Madrid	6,035
○ Albillo	3,500

○ White grape ● Black grape

Right: *A trailer-load of inky-black, succulent Bobal grapes in Utiel-Requena, where Bobal, the principal variety, is turned into very successful* rosado. *The Bobal is third most common red grape in Spain, very common also in Cariñena.*

have found it "delicate, sweet and aromatic".

Monastrell Spain's second most widely planted red grape variety gives high yields (by Spanish standards) of sweet grapes, making well-coloured, meaty, alcoholic wines that are capable of ageing if well made. It is particularly important in Alicante, and also abundant in Almansa, Jumilla, Valencia, Yecla and the Penedés. Much used to make *rosados*.

Moristel Principal variety of Somontano that can make fresh, fruity, raspberry-flavoured young red wine.

Mouratom Second most widely planted indigenous red grape of Galicia.

Ojo de Liebre *see* Tempranillo

Prieto Picudo Spain's 20th most planted variety, making wines similar to, though not as fine as, Tempranillo. It grows in León and the province of Zamora in the north-west.

Sumoll High-yielding, early-maturing Catalan grape, with an even greater tendency to oxidise than the Garnacha Tinta. Only in Conca de Barberá is it still much planted.

Tempranillo Makes elegant, well-coloured, herby, spicy wines, sometimes reminiscent of tobacco, sometimes of wild strawberries or sour cherries. Best grown in Spain's cooler regions, where it can achieve balancing acidity. The grapes are low in the enzymes that help to bring about oxidation, and therefore

easy to process successfully at grape and juice stage. It can make young, fruity, aromatic wines (often made by semi-carbonic maceration in Rioja), or firmer, more tannic wines that hold their colour well during oak-ageing. Although it is already grown very widely in Spain, it is being introduced to new areas, and its plantations are being extended in some others, in order to improve quality by using more Tempranillo in red blends. Cariñena and the Rioja Baja are two such areas, and experiments in Somontano have been very successful. The Tempranillo, sometimes slightly mutated over the years, goes by many other names in Spain: Cencibel in La Mancha and Valdepeñas, Tinto Fino in Ribera del Duero, Ull de Llebre or Ojo de Liebre in Catalonia, Tinto de Toro in Toro, and Tempranilla, Tinto del Pais and Tinto (de) Madrid elsewhere.

Tinto (de) Madrid, Tinto de Toro, Tinto del Pais, Tinto Fino and **Ull de Llebre** *see* Tempranillo

---

Black Foreign Imports

Cabernet Sauvignon Makes rich, dark, tannic, strongly blackcurrant wines that age well. There can hardly be a region of Spain where someone is not experimenting with Cabernet. It has already proved in many areas to make wonderfully complementary blends mixed about 15 per cent with Tempranillo. Of the new varieties, this was one of the first to be imported nearly a century ago by the Vega Sicilia estate in Ribera del Duero, which is increasing the current 25 per cent Cabernet in its blends. In the Penedés, where it is now an officially accepted variety, it is used in blends by Torres and several other *bodegas*, and as principal variety in the rich Jean León red. The Raimat estate in Costers del Segre (DO-to-be in Catalonia) uses it both to blend with Tempranillo and in a single varietal wine. A more recent arrival, Marqués de Griñon from near Madrid, is a wonderful example of a soft, rich, blackcurranty-oaky style.

Malbec Bordeaux vine, soft and early maturing, low in acidity and slightly reminiscent of blackberries. Part of the Vega Sicilia blend.

Merlot Bordeaux vine making tannic but soft, fleshy, plummy-fruity wines. It forms part of the Vega Sicilia blend, and several regions of Spain are experimenting with it.

Pinot Noir Native of Burgundy, a difficult vine to grow, giving fruity wines of moderate colour and a farmyardy and raspberry-like flavour. Torres grow it in the cooler vineyards of the Penedés and use it in blends. In Spain it totally lacks the delicacy and complexity of Burgundian examples.

Rioja

For a long time, Rioja *was* Spanish wine for serious drinkers. The reds were splendidly oaky, full of silky, penetrating fruitiness, and it did not take too much searching to pick up a cobwebby bottle proclaiming an unbelieveably ancient vintage for an unbelieveably tiny price. The whites were unctuously oaky as well, with a rich, mouth-filling character that made them some of the world's best alternatives to white Burgundy.

Things have changed in Rioja, but not all for the worse. For a variety of reasons, the reds are less oaky, but they reveal the flavours of the fruit itself more clearly than ever before. The ancient bottles have all but gone, but nowadays at least you can have more faith in the vintage date. There are fewer of the wonderful old-style, oaky whites, but many of those that have disappeared were badly made and oxidised anyway. Their replacements, modern and cool-fermented, may have less individual character, but, in theory at least, they are reliable, fresh, enjoyable wines.

If Rioja's oaky image is fading in all but the most traditionally-minded *bodegas*, such a change is long overdue. There had not been a major shift in Rioja winemaking since the Bordeaux winemakers arrived from across the Pyrenees in the 1860s and 1870s, fleeing from the destruction of their vineyards first by oidium (a type of mould), and then by phylloxera. They brought with them their habit of maturing red wine for long periods in 225-litre oak barrels, and long after the fashion for lengthy barrel-ageing had passed in Bordeaux, the Rioja producers hung on to it determinedly.

Oak barrels give wine an oaky (vanilla and sawdust) flavour only for the first few years of use. By the time a barrel is five years old, it has little or no flavour left to give, simply acting as a container in which wine will mature much faster than in tank or bottle. The tradition in Rioja was, and still is in many cases, to use the casks for 15 to 20 years, or until they fell apart, renewing a proportion each year when some wore out or stocks of wine increased. Old vintages would therefore rarely have had the intensely oaky flavour we have come to associate with Rioja.

The really oaky Riojas appeared in the 1970s, when sales soared and many new *bodegas* were founded, complete with warehouses full of new oak barrels, while many of the old ones expanded and increased their barrel holdings. The resulting oaky flavour became enshrined as red Rioja's main attribute, and the drinkers who had learned to love the sweet vanilla hallmark were dismayed when this taste seemed to wane.

Above: *Harvest at Briñas near Haro in the Rioja Alta. Note the bunches of white grapes – many of the older vineyards are still a mix of varieties.*

Since barrels cost a fortune and really needed to be replaced every five years or so once their flavour had been extracted, some *bodegas* found other ways of imparting the desired flavour. Oak chips suspended in a tank of wine, or little phials of gooey, brown, concentrated oak essence did the job well – albeit illegally. But much tighter control on the number and age of each *bodega*'s barrels by the Rioja authorities meant an end to such practices, and it is now much rarer to come across super-oaky wines from ancient barrels that clearly gave up their oaky ghost years ago. In any case, world taste in red wine has been moving towards fruitier styles, away from the oaky-mature.

Enforcing the Rules

*O*nly a few years ago, the vintage on a bottle of Rioja was not be be trusted. Customers wanted old wines – and that is what they *thought* they were getting. From the 1981 vintage on, things changed, however. The *Consejo Regulador*, the Riojan authorities, installed a computer on which quantities of grapes harvested and bought could be traced right through from vineyard to bottle. Each year, growers are issued with documents authorising them to pick so many grapes of such and such varieties, depending on the size of their vineyards and the yields expected that year. The document passes on to the *bodega* who buys the grapes or wine, and at the end of whatever treatment or ageing the wine is to undergo, the *bodega* receives from the *Consejo Regulador* a quantity of numbered back labels corresponding to the documents presented. Every bottle of Rioja sold by the *bodegas* since 1982 has by law had to bear this official back label. The *Consejo Regulador* also keeps detailed records of the number and age of each *bodega*'s oak barrels in order to check that they were in a position to fulfil the established ageing requirements.

The system *can* fail, however, if the growers' yields are lower than expected. This leaves unscrupulous *bodegas* the scope to buy in wine from elsewhere to make up the difference – the Penedes producers, for instance, tell of substantial sales to Rioja of their white wines.

Such are the variations in grape mixes and winemaking methods, climate and terrain throughout the Rioja region, that it is hard to predict the style of a particular *bodega*'s wines unless you are in the know. Most Rioja producers blend their finished wines from different grape varieties and from two or more of the three Rioja subregions, the Rioja Alta (High Rioja), Rioja Alavesa and Rioja Baja (Low Rioja), though a few do stick to grapes gathered only from surrounding vineyards.

The Rioja region slopes gradually downwards from the hilly or gently rolling Rioja Alta in the west to the flatter Rioja Baja in the east, with the Alavesa (and a small chunk of Alta) lying across the River Ebro to the north. The climate in the Alta and Alavesa is moderated by the influence of the Atlantic, with long, warm summers, cold, even frosty winters and sufficient rainfall (in normal times at least – in the mid-eighties they suffered drought like the rest of Spain). The Rioja Baja enjoys a Mediterranean climate, baking dry in its long, hot summers. In the Baja, vineyards compete for space with asparagus beds and cereals on fertile alluvial soil, making big, fat, alcoholic reds mostly from the Garnacha grape. Indeed, the Rioja Baja makes wines much more in the style of nearby Navarra – some of it lies, in fact, within the province of Navarra, and was included in the Rioja *denominación* in the thirties only out of habit, since it had always called its wines Rioja.

The style of the Rioja Baja wines may be distinctive enough, but it is impossible to lay down rules for the wines of the Rioja Alta and

Above: *Vineyards around the village of Paganos near the beautiful walled hill town of Laguardia in the Rioja Alavesa. The Sierra de Cantabria rises in the*

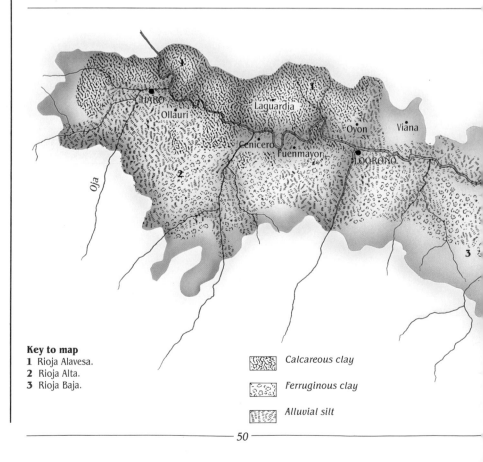

Key to map
1 Rioja Alavesa.
2 Rioja Alta.
3 Rioja Baja.

Calcareous clay

Ferruginous clay

Alluvial silt

background. Rioja's finest, reddest, most flavoursome wines come from the pale yellow calcareous clay found all over the Rioja Alavesa.

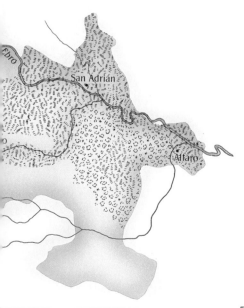

Alavesa. For a start, the border of the Alavesa region was not drawn to reflect wine styles or soil types at all: it simply follows the dividing line between the *province* of La Rioja (quite distinct in its boundaries from the wine region) and the Basque province of Alava. Had it not been for the bureaucrats, it would have made much more sense to divide the region up according to soil types, because that is what has the greatest influence on flavour variations within this western part of Rioja.

Rioja's finest, reddest, most flavoursome wines come from the pale yellow calcareous clay found all over the Rioja Alavesa, but also extending over adjoining parts of the Alta. As the map shows, the Alta itself is a hotch-potch of different soils. Much of it is alluvial silt like the greater part of the Rioja Baja, more fertile than is really good for vines. Both the Alta and the Baja also have large enclaves on higher ground of dark reddish-orange ferruginous clay. Even in the Rioja Alta, famous as it is for Tempranillo grapes, this sort of land is most suited to Garnacha, making rather pale wines which are best used for *rosados*.

But the best, calcium-rich land of the Alta is higher and cooler than that of the Alavesa and does uphold the sub-region's reputation for making elegant, long-lived reds with better balancing acidity than the softer, fruity wines of the warm, south-facing Ala-vesa slopes. These two sub-regions are the stronghold of what is undoubtedly Rioja's finest grape, the Tempranillo.

*F*ourteen thousand growers produce the grapes for 85 per cent of all the wines of Rioja. Many of them tend tiny plots, the result of the division of larger holdings through inheritance. Indeed, over half farm plots so small that vineyard work is relegated to weekends and evenings, after work in the factory or *bodega*. Many of the vines are old, yielding as little as 15 hectolitres per hectare against a permitted yield of 42 hectolitres for red wines, 63 for whites, but replanting would involve too much expense and trouble to be entertained. Pottering around the vineyard may satisfy the older growers, but the latest generation to inherit the tiny vineyards, dissatisfied with the low profit, is uprooting the vines in favour of asparagus, vegetables or fruit to sell to the thriving local canning industry.

Less than half of these small-scale growers make their own wine, often under rather primitive conditions; the greater proportion either sell their grapes directly to the *bodegas* or deliver them to the local co-operative. Those who do make wine sell practically all of it to the *bodegas* at a few months old.

While some growers are abandoning viticulture, and average yields are gradually decreasing as many of the vines reach old age, sales of Rioja are steadily increasing. And as grape prices have also risen dramatically in the past few years, it has become more and more attractive for *bodegas* to extend their own vineyard holdings, or at least to lease additional vineyards. Besides securing a regular supply for predictable costs, owning the vineyards enables them to control quality, and to decide for themselves upon the vital moment of picking.

Above: *At harvest-time, tractors and trailers queue up to have their loads of freshly-picked grapes weighed at the Labastida co-operative.*

Another reason for the incidence of low yields in recent years has been drought. Newly planted Tempranillo vines in the Rioja Baja have suffered especially, since the Tempranillo needs more water than the Garnacha (traditionally the Baja's almost exclusive grape). The Riojan authorities now advise that there should be 25 per cent Tempranillo (a much finer grape) in any replanting in the

Below: *Although many growers sell most of their grapes to co-operatives, tiny private* bodegas, *like this one in Cenicero, are to be found everywhere.*

well as wild strawberry-like flavours, it makes up at least half of the better red Riojas, and the totality of some. It is an adaptable grape – good for soft, fruity red wines, but capable, made in a more robust style, of long ageing. Forty-eight per cent of all vines in Rioja are now Tempranillo.

Garnacha used to be the Rioja's main grape, but it now accounts for a declining 27 per cent of the vineyards. However, it is still by far the major grape in the Rioja Baja, where it thrives in the dry heat. The Garnacha is a difficult grape. Its sugar level easily shoots up as the harvest approaches, and the resulting wines are heavy with alcohol. And though it can make fresh, fruity young reds and *rosados*, Garnacha wines need drinking young as they are prone to browning.

The other two permitted red Rioja grapes, Mazuelo and Graciano, are problematic to grow and have been in steady decline. The Mazuelo (local name for the Cariñena) is a sickly vine, planted in only 1.5 per cent of the vineyards. But the *bodegas* value it as a blending wine for its lasting colour, high acidity and substantial tannin content. The Graciano is now even scarcer, unpopular with the growers for its low yields, and found only in the oldest vineyards, although Bodegas Faustino Martínez have planted 15 per cent of their own extensive vineyard with the variety. The *bodegas* prize it, when they can get it, for its savoury aroma.

Rioja Baja, and this is actually a condition of membership of one of the Rioja Baja co-operatives. It is better suited to the cooler, higher land in the Baja, only recently planted with vineyards, than to baking lowlands.

The proportion of Tempranillo grapes is also increasing in the vineyards of the cooler Rioja Alta and Rioja Alavesa. The most elegant of the Rioja varieties, with savoury as

White varieties account for less than a quarter of the vineyards of Rioja. Most planted by far is the Viura with its good acidity but rarely exciting flavour, then Garnacha Blanca, making heavy, alcoholic wines, and the Malvasía with its musky, apricot-like perfume. Sadly, the Malvasía has dropped to 0.5 per cent of the vineyards owing to its low yields and tendency to oxidise. Bodegas Martínez Bujanda, however, have planted enough Malvasía in their vineyards to use 30 to 50 per cent in their whites.

Only these seven of the original 40 grape varieties are now "authorised" in the region. The old varieties still exist in some old vineyards, where different vines were traditionally mixed together in a haphazard way. The authorities now insist that new vineyards must be planted with the varieties clearly demarcated, so that they can be harvested and vinified separately, each variety at its correct stage of ripeness.

In recent years, "foreign" grapes have been arriving in Rioja. Though as yet unauthorised, some *bodegas*, notably Martínez Bujanda, Faustino Martínez, Marqués de Murrieta, Campo Viejo and Domecq, have planted varieties such as Cabernet Sauvignon, Pinot Noir, Gamay, Merlot, Riesling, Chenin Blanc and Sémillon. The authorities give a dispensation for these varieties to be trained "experimentally" on wires in the modern way, whereas the Rioja vines must be bush-pruned. Winemakers report excellent results from blending a small proportion of Cabernet with the Rioja varieties, especially Tempranillo, but this is as yet illegal.

Below: New American oak barrels are prepared for use in the large, recently-built extension for barrel-ageing at Bodegas La Rioja Alta in Haro.

Rioja is very much a *blended* wine. Traditionally, grapes were picked in a jumble of varieties and vinified together. Nowadays, varieties are generally fermented separately and blended before maturation, though some *bodegas* mix the grapes or juice in the desired proportions before fermentation. The wines are generally blended also from the different Riojan subregions, and the majority of Riojas are a blend of the production of many, many different growers.

Although we generally see the names only of the big Rioja *bodegas* even in the bars and restaurants of Spain, about half the wine is actually made by small-scale growers. The *bodegas* make just a quarter of the total themselves, half from their own vineyards, half from grapes bought in from the growers. The remaining quarter is vinified in the region's 30 co-operatives, who sell nearly their whole production to the *bodegas* in the form either of juice or of young wine. They sell only two per cent of their production direct to the public, and much of that goes to their own members. Ninety-five per cent of all Rioja goes out under the *bodega*'s labels.

The traditional method of making red Rioja by fermenting whole grapes, akin to that used to make the light, exceptionally fruity wines of Beaujolais, is still practised by very many of the growers. A few *bodegas* even use it for part of their production, notably Faustino Martínez, Riojanas, Palacio and Alavesas. This style of wine is not really suitable for ageing. It may be sold unblended as *vino de cosechero* (grower's wine), direct from growers for drinking within the year, *vino joven* (young wine) or *vino sin crianza* (wine

without ageing). It is more common nowadays for red grapes to be crushed in the standard way before fermentation. The resulting wines, usually fuller and firmer and less burstingly fruity, can also be sold *sin crianza* but, if made with sufficient body, they will certainly improve with varying lengths of ageing.

It is the *bodega*'s job to age and treat the wine before bottling it for sale. Indeed, the commercial *bodegas* have a monopoly of the job of oak-ageing wine, since the Consejo Regulador, the wine authority, insists that ageing *bodegas* should stock a minimum of 2,250 hectolitres of wine, at least half of it in wooden barrels of 225 litres.

Just over 40 per cent of Rioja's wines undergo wood ageing. From *bodega* to *bodega*, views differ on how long the barrels serve a useful purpose. The average age of Rioja's barrels is thought to be about 15 to 18 years. Some *bodegas* sell their barrels well before that, others keep them much longer, but only the wine in the youngest barrels (up to five years old) will extract from them flavour and tannin. Ageing in older barrels will simply make the wine taste older. Wines from casks of different ages are eventually blended together to achieve the desired flavour.

The effect of wood ageing varies between *bodegas* also because of the varying lengths

Below: *One of two huge bottle-ageing galleries at Bodegas Montecillo, which between them hold one and a half million bottles, stacked one at a time, by hand. Another million bottles are stored elsewhere for ageing before sale.*

Above: *New barrel-ageing cellar at CVNE. CVNE have about 19,000 barrels, a third of them made of French oak, the rest of American. They use them for between 15 and 20 years.*

of time they choose to leave the wines in wood. Under the regulations, a red *crianza* must spend a *minimum* of one year in barrel and one year in either bottle or in bulk (tank); a *reserva* must have three years' maturation, at least one in wood; and a *gran reserva* must spend at least two years in wood, three in bottle, or vice versa. Bodegas Marqués de Cáceres, at one extreme, works on Bordeaux principles and never leaves its wines in oak for longer than two years; Marqués de Murrieta always far exceeds the prescribed minima, sometimes by many years. Some *bodegas' reserva* might have spent even longer in wood than is required for *gran reservas*, yet still be labelled *reserva*. A number of forward-looking *bodegas* argue that the minimum oaking periods should be reduced: the regulations should take account of the age of the cask and the structure of the wine (light vintages might end up better balanced with less than the stipulated oak ageing).

There was at one time just as much variation in the maturation of white and *rosado* wines, but the modern trend to make them young and fresh has made them almost uniform in style. Modern white Rioja is almost always made entirely from the Viura grape, picked early before it loses its aroma and acidity and becomes too alcoholic. It is fermented at low temperatures in order to retain as much aroma as possible, and should be drunk within little more than a year to be at its best. However, the Viura generally has a rather dull flavour, and these wines are rarely more than adequate. *Rosados* made by these modern methods, whether made from the Tempranillo or the Garnacha, can turn out well-flavoured, light, fresh and fruity, however.

Among the whites, far more exciting are the few oak-aged wines. For aged whites, whether *crianza*, *reserva*, or *gran reserva*, the minimum wood-ageing period is now just six months, with a total of one year, two years and four years' total ageing periods respectively. Bodegas Marqués de Murrieta are notable for sticking to tradition and keeping their whites for much longer than this in oak. Added acidity (tartaric acid, a natural constituent of grapes) helps such wines to withstand long ageing.

Pick of Rioja

Campo Viejo This Logroño *bodega* is Rioja's biggest producer and market leader in Spain, owned by Savin, one of Spain's biggest wine companies. Quality at the bottom end of their range is sound, but the Reservas and Gran Reservas are excellent. A fifth of the wine comes from their own vineyards, half the rest being bought as grapes, half as young wine. Campo Viejo Reservas are generally powerful, full, ripe-tasting wines, made 80 per cent from Tempranillo. The Gran Reservas, Campo Viejo and the theoretically finer Marqués de Villamagna, are elegant and spicily oaky.

Co-operativa de Cenicero This co-op has recently been making big investments in cellar equipment, and is bottling its own well-made, cherry-fruity young red and good white, Santa Daria, both for drinking young.

Sociedad Vinícola Laserna (Contino) Small *bodega* owned half by CVNE (qv), half by local growers and other individuals. Their wine, most unusually for Rioja, comes from a single 45 hectare vineyard, the Viñedos del Contino, half way between Logroño and Laguardia. No grapes or wine are bought in. The vineyard, planted 80 per cent with Tempranillo, is dry and very sunny, and produces low yields of grapes that sometimes shoot up rapidly in sugar level, making big wines. Fermentation is in stainless steel, and the oak casks are half American, half French. Only Reservas and Gran Reservas are made here – the lesser wines go to CVNE – and they are rich, intensely fruity, and beautifully balanced. Best vintages of Contino Reserva are big, spicy, deep and complex and may benefit from a little more age after purchase.

Cosecheros Alaveses Tiny, high-quality co-operative of six growers on the outskirts of Logroño, who make their wines, largely Tempranillo, in their individual cellars by the traditional Rioja method, and age them jointly. Good, lemony-fresh, new-style white Artadi Blanco; rich, super-fruity, cherry-perfumed Artadi Tinto, and good, soft, cherry-oaky Valdepomares Tinto Crianza.

El Coto This immaculately clean, modern *bodega* was built in Oyón in 1970, releasing its first wines in 1975. Only Tempranillo goes into the red wines, nearly 60 per cent of it grown in their own vineyards, and only home-grown Viura in their whites. They make most of their own wine, and none of it is produced by carbonic maceration. The whites are no more than adequate, but the reds are very good in a light style: light, fruity El Coto, with six months' oak; pale, light, oakily mellow Coto Vintage Crianza with one year in cask and, at the top of the range, fruity, elegant strawberry-and-vanilla flavoured Coto de Imaz Reserva and Gran Reserva.

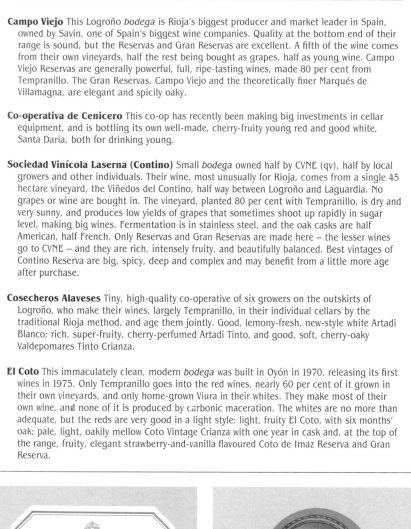

CVNE Though the initials stand for "Companía Vinicola del Norte de España", this top-quality Haro *bodega* is generally known as Cune (pronounced "coonay"). Medium-sized and fairly traditional, with a mixture of modern and old equipment, they get 65 per cent of their grapes from their own vineyards. None of their wine is made by carbonic maceration. They keep their casks for 15 to 20 years. In their white Monopole (20 per cent Malvasía, 80 per cent Viura), CVNE produce a successful cross between old and new style Riojas, with freshness and fruit as well as a little oak flavour; their new-style 100 per cent Viura Rioja Blanco Viura is also pleasantly soft, full and fruity. Youngest of the reds is CVNE Tinto (sold as CVNE Rioja Clarete in Spain), 80 per cent Tempranillo and one year in oak, a lovely, light, plummy, savoury wine; firm, plummy, rounded Viña Reál Crianza has the same grape blend but 18 months' oak, and there are Viña Reál Reservas and Gran Reservas in a similar style. Best wines of best vintages are sold as CVNE Imperial Reservas and Gran Reservas, with at least three years in oak, three in bottle: elegant, concentrated wines with savoury and wild strawberry-like flavours.

Faustino Martínez Large but high quality, family-owned *bodega*, the third biggest exporter of Rioja. Technically well-equipped and spotlessly clean. Half the grapes come from their own vineyards, which have an unusually high proportion of Graciano. Specialists in Reservas and Gran Reservas, with the accent on bottle-ageing rather than over-long wood-ageing. Best wines are red: fresh, fruity, concentrated but light Vino Joven or Viña Faustino made by carbonic maceration; light, fine, wild strawberry-scented Faustino V Reserva; deep, rich, spicy Faustino I Gran Reserva.

López de Heredia Extremely high quality, old fashioned family *bodega* in Haro. They grow half their own grapes and buy in the rest as grapes, not wine, all from the Rioja Alta. The equipment and techniques are old fashioned, extending to a working windmill, wooden fermentation vats, barrels repaired to their last stave by their own coopers, egg whites for fining and a total absence of filters. Most of the wine is red, but the whites are pleasant, especially the white Viña Tondonia, which is rich and spicily oaky after five years in barrel. The reds are all made from 50 per cent Tempranillo, 30 per cent Garnacha, 10 Mazuelo and 10 Graciano: soft, fine, lightly oaky Viña Cubillo with over two years in cask, three in bottle; and elegantly fruity, oaky Viña Tondonia, with five years' oak.

Marqués de Cáceres *Bodega* established with French technology in the mid-'seventies, obtaining its white grapes and red wines from a band of share-owning local growers with vineyards around Cenicero, and a local co-op. The whites, always made without wood ageing, were the first, and are still usually the most impressive of their style in Rioja, with a fresh, gooseberry-elderflower flavour more reminiscent of the Sauvignon than the Viura grape. The reds are aged, Bordeaux fashion, in new or nearly new oak for two years or less, making them atypical but fine and elegant with plenty of fruit to balance the oak, and usually firm tannin. Sometimes sold as Rivarey or Costanilla.

Below: *Looking south from the lower slopes of the Sierra de Cantabria over a recently planted Tempranillo vineyard in the Rioja Alavesa.*

Pick of Rioja

Marqués de Murrieta One of the most traditional *bodegas*, making some of Rioja's most imposing wines, remarkable for their long wood ageing. Even whites here are in the old, heavily oaked style. No wine spends less than two years in oak barrels, and Gran Reservas may be aged for 30 to 40 years in oak. Murrieta have a higher ratio of barrels to wine than any other Rioja *bodega*, mostly of American oak, but some bought from Châteaux Pavie, Lafite-Rothschild and Yquem in Bordeaux. Winemaking equipment is part modern, part old fashioned. The Ygay estate on which the *bodega* stands currently satisfies about 60 per cent of their grape needs, but with replantings they will grow all their own grapes in years to come. Murrieta's new owner, Vincente Cebrian, is tastefully restoring the buildings and estate, adding a museum and facilities for visitors. Wines: Etiqueta Blanca Crianzas are youngest of the range, but even they, white and red, have one year in tank, two in wood and up to a year in bottle before sale. The white is honeyed, oaky and lemony, the red elegant, soft and lightly fruity. White Reservas (which would actually qualify as Gran Reservas) are rich, buttery, slightly piney with lots of lemony acidity; they may spend ten years in wood, and some will keep for decades. Red Reservas are elegant, complex wines, with deep, plummy, soft fruit and flavours reminiscent of cedar, vanilla, figs and wild strawberries. Best wines of the very top years are labelled Castillo Ygay, the *current* vintage of which in the UK is 1942.

Martínez Bujanda This old family business recently expanded into a large, new, super-modern *bodega* making wines with delicious concentration of fruit and pronounced oaky character, only from grapes from their own vineyards. They are the only Rioja *bodega* to do a classic carbonic maceration (for a quarter of their red wines) in small, enclosed stainless steel tanks. Excellent technical equipment and control, to the extent of changing and filtering the air every night in the wood-ageing cellar, and purifying the water used to wash their equipment. Wines: soft, full young white Valdemar Blanco, usually half Viura, half Malvasía; good, soft and fruity, well-balanced Valdemar Rosado; lovely, light, super-fruity Tinto Valdemar made by carbonic maceration of Tempranillo; strongly oaky Reserva Conde de Valdemar with penetrating strawberry-like fruit, unusually 80 per cent Tempranillo, 20 per cent Mazuelo; rich, oaky-figgy Gran Reserva Conde de Valdemar. They will shortly start selling a Crianza.

Montecillo When the sherry company Osborne bought Montecillo in 1973, they immediately built a modern *bodega* in Fuenmayor. The *bodega* ferments at very low temperatures in self-emptying stainless steel tanks, and believes in long bottle ageing, rather than excessive wood ageing. The wood here is about a third Limousin, some of it bought from Bordeaux châteaux, two-thirds American. Montecillo have no vineyards, and buy only grapes, no ready-made wines. Viña Cumbrero Blanco is lovely, fresh, oaky-lemony; Viña Cumbrero Tinto Crianza is rich, zingy with raspberry-like fruit and a touch of oak and tannin; excellent savoury, rich, wild strawberry-like Gran Reserva.

Muga Medium-sized, very conservative *bodega* in which the family has a majority share. 40 per cent of the grapes are from their own vineyards, the rest bought in mainly as grapes, all from the Rioja Alta. Fermentation is in wooden vats, initial filtration through bunches of vine prunings, fining with egg white. They keep their casks for around 12 years. Most of the wines are red (the whites are traditional in the worst sense): fragrant, delicate Muga Crianza is 40 per cent Tempranillo with two years in oak; Prado Enea, sometimes Reserva, sometimes Gran Reserva, is more complex, but still honeyed and wild strawberry-like in its flavour, with 60 per cent Tempranillo, four years in cask and two or more in bottle.

La Granja Remelluri This immaculate farmhouse and estate (*granja* means farm) was renovated in the sixties by the Rodríguez family. The 20-year-old winery has recently been modernised, with the arrival of stainless steel tanks to replace wooden fermentation vats. All the grapes come from the estate, which is planted with 80 per cent Tempranillo, the rest with Viura, Mazuelo and Graciano, plus a few ancient Riojan varieties that are disappearing elsewhere. The only wine made is a Reserva, which has two to three years' cask ageing.

La Rioja Alta Century-old *bodega* making top-quality wines by traditional methods, including long oak-ageing. Over half the wines produced are Reservas and Gran Reservas. The wines still ferment in wooden vats, and there is a very high ratio of casks to wine. Casks are rotated about every 20 years. The reds are the *bodega*'s impressive wines: fruity, fresh, light Viña Alberdi has 18 months oak ageing; Viña Arana Reserva, an elegant wine with 70 per cent Tempranillo plus a mix of the other Rioja grapes, aged for three years in cask and two in bottle, contrasts with the fatter, richer, oaky Viña Ardanza, 60 per cent Tempranillo and 25 per cent Garnacha, which spends three-and-a-half years in oak, two in bottle. Gran Reservas 904 and 890 (made very rarely) are released from the finest vintages after six to eight years in cask, a further three to six in bottle.

Rioja Santiago Haro *bodega* now owned by Pepsico, who concentrate on the *sangría* side, leaving the Rioja *bodega* very much to its own devices. It is little known in Britain and the USA, since until recently exports were predominantly to Central and South America. No wine is made at the *bodega* – it is all bought in as wine for ageing. The whites and younger wines are unremarkable, but Gran Condal Reserva is excellent, rich, classic Rioja, woodily mature and darkly spicy. It has about 80 per cent Tempranillo, the rest Garnacha, and is aged one year in tank, two in oak, two in bottle. The same wine is sometimes sold as Vizconde de Ayala.

Riojanas Family-owned *bodega* in Cenicero with a mixture of modern and old-fashioned equipment. Unusually for a large commercial *bodega*, some reds are made by the traditional Riojan semi-carbonic maceration method as well as the classic method. When their barrels are ten years old they sell them to other *bodegas*. A third of the grapes come from their own vineyards. Monte Reál Blanco Crianza is one of Rioja's best whites, attractively soft, peachy, honeyed and oaky from one year in cask. Best of the reds are the Reservas: Viña Albina Reserva in a lighter, more elegant style, with soft, plummy, slightly farmyardy flavours; and Monte Reál Reserva, richer and more concentrated. Monte Reál Gran Reserva is also excellent, with a complex wild strawberry and cedar fragrance.

Below: *Moving barrels back into place after racking, in the underground cellars of Bodegas Riojanas, Cenicero.*

Navarra

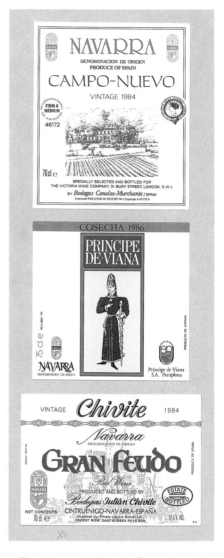

With Spain's most extensive vine and vinification research underway, Navarra deserves to succeed. The local government has been pouring money into new laboratories, experimental vineyards and research since 1980, and has even taken a financial share in one new and two established *bodegas*.

They have planted test vineyards all over the region with the local varieties as well as a selection of foreign vines (36 types in all), including Cabernet Sauvignon, Sémillon, Merlot, Riesling and Chardonnay. It is a little early to draw many definite conclusions, but the Cabernet Sauvignon, fairly tough and blackcurranty in Navarra, has already been listed amongst the "recommended" varieties, while Chardonnay, slightly more cautiously, is now among the "authorised" vines. Good results are reported for Riesling.

Before the phylloxera vine louse destroyed Navarra's vines at the end of the last century, the vineyards stretched up north into the foothills of the mountains beyond Pamplona. Now vines are practically limited to the hotter, drier land south from Pamplona down to the River Ebro, which they share with the fields of asparagus, artichokes, peppers, garlic and lettuces for which Navarra is famous. But it is the cooler northern hills that may better suit Riesling and Chardonnay.

Although red Garnacha still accounts for nearly 90 per cent of Navarra's production, growers are no longer allowed to replant it, whereas they get subsidies both for vines and, if they choose, trellising, for planting Tempranillo and Cabernet, which in any case fetch far higher grape prices once they come into production. Also recommended in the new regulations are the Graciano and Mazuelo (Cariñena) and among the whites Viura and Moscatel de Grano Menudo, with Garnacha Blanca, Malvasía Riojana, Chardonnay and Merlot only "authorised".

Rosados, made largely from Garnacha, were the rising stars of Navarra until 1984, when demand for reds began to increase. Reds now account for more than half of production, *rosados* for about 40 per cent, and whites for the rest. The most marked quality improvement in recent years, however, has been in the whites and *rosados*. The simple reason is the improvement in equipment in

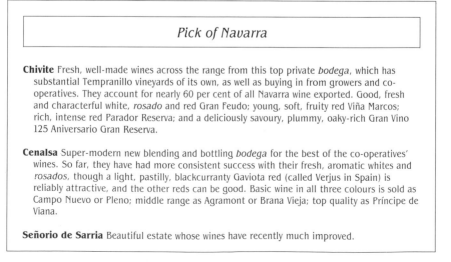

Pick of Navarra

Chivite Fresh, well-made wines across the range from this top private *bodega*, which has substantial Tempranillo vineyards of its own, as well as buying in from growers and cooperatives. They account for nearly 60 per cent of all Navarra wine exported. Good, fresh and characterful white, *rosado* and red Gran Feudo; young, soft, fruity red Viña Marcos; rich, intense red Parador Reserva; and a deliciously savoury, plummy, oaky-rich Gran Vino 125 Aniversario Gran Reserva.

Cenalsa Super-modern new blending and bottling *bodega* for the best of the co-operatives' wines. So far, they have had more consistent success with their fresh, aromatic whites and *rosados*, though a light, pastilly, blackcurrant Gaviota red (called Verjus in Spain) is reliably attractive, and the other reds can be good. Basic wine in all three colours is sold as Campo Nuevo or Pleno; middle range as Agramont or Brana Vieja; top quality as Príncipe de Viana.

Señorio de Sarria Beautiful estate whose wines have recently much improved.

the co-operatives. Over 90 per cent of Navarra's wine is made by co-operatives (as opposed to 40 per cent in Rioja), so this was where improvement had to begin. Back in 1984, not a single co-operative had the cooling equipment necessary to make fresh, aromatic whites and *rosados*. By 1985 there were two, nine by 1986, and 14 by 1987.

Foremost in creating a market for these new, fresher wines has been the impressive new blending and bottling *bodega* Cenalsa, funded jointly by the Navarra government, two local banks and the Union of Co-operatives. From a standing start, they are already providing nearly a quarter of Navarra's export wines and a fifth of Navarra wines for sale at home in Spain, and have really pushed up the proportion of Navarra wines sold in bottle.

Until recently, the co-operatives have taken little more interest in ageing than in bottling their reds, preferring to sell young wines to a small number of private *bodegas*

to do with them as they pleased. However proud the *bodegas* may be of their Reserva and Gran Reserva reds, they are rarely anything special. Until the proportion of Tempranillo is raised by the new plantings (with a bit of Cabernet for extra kick), these Garnacha-based wines age and fade quickly, and the old wooden barrels used in most *bodegas* add nothing to them and merely hasten the demise of the fruity flavours. So far, only Chivite among the private *bodegas* makes consistently good aged reds (as well as young reds, whites and *rosados*). For the rest, more pleasure is generally to be had from the plummily fruity *young* reds for which the Garnacha grape is better suited.

Below: *Vines share the beautiful Navarra estate of Señorio de Sarria with fruit trees, vegetables and cereal crops. Sarria's young wines are pleasant, but do not rank amongst the region's best.*

Aragón is bisected from west to east by the river basin of the Ebro. However, this fertile land near the river is used for growing vegetables, and the vines are relegated to the poorer soils, towards the Pyrenees in the north and the Iberian Cordillera in the south. All the wine regions of Aragón lie south of the Ebro valley except for Somontano. At present, only three out of nine have attained DO status.

 Cariñena

Cariñena, the largest and best-known of the Aragón DOs, is hot and dry. During the relentless summer days, the effect of the heat is compounded by a wind from the north, the *cierzo*, which, though cold, also has the effect of lowering atmospheric humidity. Much of the wine is basic and over-alcoholic and ends up anonymously in the bars of Madrid, but there are also pleasant reds under the Cariñena label.

The DO includes whites, *rosados*, *claretes*, reds (the last two both dry *and* sweet) and *rancios*, but it is for the reds that Cariñena is famous. Garnacha is the principal grape variety, although there is now about 30 per cent of Tempranillo and the aim is to raise it to 60 per cent. Other grapes for reds include the Cariñena (Rioja's Mazuela), Bobal, Monastrell and Juan Ibáñez, while the whites are almost all made from the Macabeo, sometimes with a little Garnacha Blanca.

About half the total production of Cariñena is still sold in bulk. Ninety per cent of the production is in the hands of co-operatives, and it is they who are leading the struggle to improve quality and bottle a higher proportion of wine.

 Campo de Borja

Only *rosados* and reds may be made within the Campo de Borja DO. Vinegrowing is less of a struggle here, since the region has more rain than Cariñena, and the proximity of the river Ebro and its mists means a consequent higher humidity.

As in Cariñena, the most widely grown grape is Garnacha, accounting for about 90 per cent of production. Traditionally, up to ten per cent of white Macabeo may be added to this, but more useful experiments are being carried out with Tempranillo and Mazuela. The locals hope for great things from both.

The struggle in Campo de Borja is to make wines with adequate acidity levels and not

overwhelmed by alcohol. Signs are encouraging, but beware – even a *rosado* can pack a 15° punch.

 Somontano

Somontano is the smallest of the three DOs in Aragón, the most recently demarcated (1985), and, frankly, the one with the most natural wine-making potential. "Somontano" means "under the mountain", and that is exactly where this region of 3,285 hectares is, in the foothills of the Pyrenees in the province of Huesca. It is an enchanting place, with little Pyrenean rivers working miracles of irrigation. Even in summer the fields and trees are green, except for the groves of ghostly poplars and stumpy grey olives. Although the average altitude is the same as the higher parts of Campo de Borja, the rainfall is much higher, and the problem is not one of over-ripeness, but one of under-ripeness.

Ninety per cent of Somontano's production is handled by the excellent local co-operative, and there are only five other producers. Three-quarters of the wine is red, and most of the rest *rosado*, although about five per cent is white.

The main grape variety is a purely local one, the Moristel, and second most common

Above: *Somontano, in the foothills of the Pyrenees, is the most promising of Aragón's three DOs. Even in summer, mountain streams and higher rainfall keep it fresh and green.*

is Garnacha. About a third of the grape production is of Macabeo, and there are experimental plantings of Tempranillo, Chardonnay, Cabernet Sauvignon, Riesling, Sylvaner, Pinot Noir, Merlot, Gamay and Chenin Blanc. The results with Tempranillo and Cabernet Sauvignon are very exciting already, although the Moristel is not to be underestimated.

Top-quality wine could be made in Somontano, and probably will before long. At the moment, the red wines made at the co-operative are fermented in auto-vinificators, cooled solely by opening the winery doors at night to let in the cold October air. The other *bodegas* are even more old-fashioned, although there is a new company (COVISA) just starting up with plantations of several foreign grape varieties, whose first harvest will be in 1989. Somontano is most certainly a region to watch.

Calatayud
Situated in the westernmost corner of Aragón, Calatayud is one of nine recently demarcated *vinos de la tierra*. The principal grape is the Garnacha, made into reds and *rosados* that can be pleasant but rarely as good as wines from the DO regions of Aragón.

Pick of Cariñena, Campo de Borja and Somontano

Bodegas San Valero (Cariñena) Huge modern co-operative handling a quarter of the DO's production, with temperature control for all wines. Young, spicy, unwooded Don Mendo red, and soft, almondy Don Mendo *rosado* are good, as are Gran Reserva Monte Ducay reds.

Sociedad Co-operativa Agricola de Borja (Campo de Borja) Co-operative producing oil, maize and animal foodstuffs as well as almost one third of the DO's wine. Best is the Pedernal Tinto Crianza, with good buttery-plummy fruit.

Co-operativa del Campo San Juan Bautista (Campo de Borja) Best of the DO's *rosados* comes from this co-operative: Crucillon Rosado, really fresh, with flavours of butter and almonds.

Bodegas Bordejé (Campo de Borja) Old family *bodega* in commercial production only for last 25 years. Wonderful underground cellars tunnelled into hill, with hardly any space to walk between rock and barrels. An unusual Beaujolais-style, carbonic maceration Tinto Joven and good Cava.

Co-operativa Somontano de Sobrarbe (Somontano) Main producer of DO, with good, young Selección Montsierras Rosado and Tinto, and excellent Señorio de Lazan Reserva (with some ageing in new oak barrels), mainly Tempranillo plus some Moristel, with deep, rich, concentrated raspberry fruit.

So enterprising and hard working are the Catalans that, with just 16 per cent of Spain's population, they contribute 25 per cent of her total industrial production and exports. It is hardly surprising, therefore, that Catalan *bodegas* have been among the leaders in modernising their winemaking, nor that the Catalans have been more eager and successful than their compatriots in applying for improvement grants in the early months of Spain's EEC membership.

Foremost of Catalonia's DOs for quality, technical expertise and wine exports is the Penedés, though the grapes for the sparkling wines may come from outside the Penedés region, and *cava* has had a separate DO since 1986. The other DOs are Ampurdán-Costa Brava, Alella, Tarragona, Terra Alta and Priorato, and another, Costers del Segre, should become a DO by the end of 1988. Promotion seems unlikely, however, for Conca de Barberá, which was also a Provisional DO until the category was abolished in 1986, and it became one of the few *vinos de la tierra*, Spain's equivalent of the French *vins de pays*.

Before the phylloxera wine louse devastated the vineyards at the end of the 19th century, 80 per cent of the wine made here was red, but more recently whites have taken over by far the majority of the production because of the demands of the ever more successful *cava* producers. Still whites are next most important, followed by reds, then the traditional fortified *rancios* and *generosos*, still popular with the older Catalans.

 *Penedés*

Of all the Catalan regions, the Penedés has always been in the forefront of wine trade and technology. The region bristles with efficient, modern companies, not least the headquarters of nearly all the *cava* producers. The base wines for their *cavas* may come from any DO in Catalonia, but most of the *cava* companies have a sideline in producing still wines of the Penedés, which sometimes

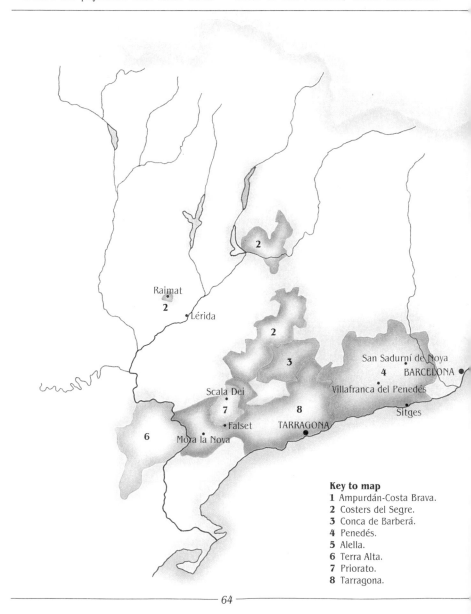

Key to map
1 Ampurdán-Costa Brava.
2 Costers del Segre.
3 Conca de Barberá.
4 Penedés.
5 Alella.
6 Terra Alta.
7 Priorato.
8 Tarragona.

Above: *The Penedés is dominated by the pinnacles and steep cliffs of the Montserrat, which translates from Catalan as "jagged mountain".*

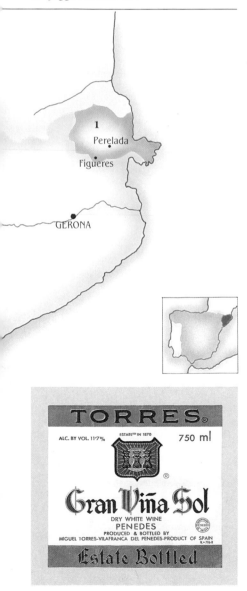

account for half their production, and many of the technological advances introduced for the benefit of the booming *cavas* have raised the quality of the still Penedés DO wines, too. The Penedés also houses a number of producers of still wines only who are well ahead of the Spanish times. Co-operatives are strong here, as elsewhere in Catalonia, but far more growers supply directly to the wine companies, advised by them on quality control, and about a fifth of the vineyard land belongs to the companies themselves.

Though the Penedés is predominantly a white wine region, it turns out a wide range of wine styles from a variety of grape types, both native and "international" in origin, in the very different growing conditions of different parts of the region. Lower Penedés along the coast is very hot, comparable to Central Spain or Andalucía. Right by the coast, the vineyards are suitable only for dessert Muscat grapes, but the native red varieties, Garnacha, Cariñena, Monastrell and Ull de Llebre will grow just a little way inland, away from the most intense of the coastal heat.

A range of hills divides the coastal section from Middle Penedés, a partly sloping, partly flat depression at between 250 and 500 metres above sea level. It is cooler here, sheltered from the hot Mediterranean winds, and traditionally planted with the native white varieties, Xarel-lo, Macabeo and Parellada, but now also with imported varieties (especially in the vineyards of innovators Torres): Cabernet Sauvignon, Pinot Noir, Chardonnay and Chenin Blanc.

Upper Penedés, up in the hills 40 or more kilometres inland in the north-west, is the really promising part for fine, aromatic wines. Few vineyards grow higher than 700 metres above sea level, though Torres have some up to 800 metres. This is a much cooler climate, since every hundred metres brings a drop of nearly one degree Celsius in average daily temperature, and, even more significantly for the grapes' aromas, temperatures fall markedly on summer nights. Traditionally, this has been the top spot for Parellada, but Torres have chosen it as their site for Gewürztraminer, Moscatel de Grano Pequeño (the Muscat à Petits Grains of Alsace), Riesling, Chenin Blanc and Pinot Noir.

However, the three native whites mentioned above, usually blended together, make up 90 per cent of Penedés' white production. Most of these wines are light, fresh, appley-lemony and simple, with little aroma but sometimes an attractive, creamy softness. Only a few companies make "native" whites of anything approaching real characater, because Parellada, and especially Xarel-lo and Macabeo, are grapes from which winemakers can extract little interest and aroma, however technically equipped they may be. Best of the native whites tends to be Torres' Viña Sol, made exclusively from Parellada grapes, the only one of the three native whites winemaker Miguel Torres considers worth using. He manages to extract a little more aroma by leaving the Parellada skins to macerate in the juice for four to six hours or so after crushing. Another interesting single variety Parellada is made by a young winemaker called Ramon Baladá at Celler Hisenda Miret from grapes from the family vineyards, one of an unusually good range of all three native whites. A few others make above average blends of all three.

But it is the imported varieties that demonstrate the real potential for whites in the Penedés, although some varieties are not yet officially allowed to carry the "Penedés" label. The local authorities accepted the Chardonnay only in September 1986, and they still consider grapes such as Gewürztraminer, Riesling and Chenin Blanc as "experimental". Torres make delicious, fresh, fragrant blends, for instance, of Gewürztraminer and Muscat (Viña Esmeralda), and Chardonnay with Parellada (Gran Viña Sol). Jean León makes a lovely, rich, California-style Chardonnay, and Chardonnay is just beginning to pop up as a small element in other companies' blends, too.

About the reds of the Penedés it is less easy to generalise. Good, rich reds such as the Cabernet Sauvignon of Jean León, or Torres' reds from local or French varieties show that the potential is there, as do lighter, fruity, sometimes oaky reds from good producers such as Cavas Hill or Josep Ferret. Other winemakers dismiss the reds as light and thin. It is no secret that a certain amount of illegal trading goes on between Rioja and the Penedés, reds moving coastward to beef up some Penedés reds by as much as a third, whites migrating inland to make up for the shortfall of white Rioja.

Conca de Barberá

It is sad that this attractive, rolling hill country just south-west of the Penedés, thick with almonds and hazels as well as vines, has never made a reputation of its own. Growing conditions are much the same as in the cooler parts of the Penedés, and there is great potential for white winemaking. So far,

however, the region lacks the technology to prove it. Co-operatives make almost all the wine, selling up to 80 per cent of their production in the form of grapes, juice or wine to the *cava* houses, or, less overtly, to other parts of Spain or France for blending.

So great has been the demand for *cava* base wines over the past decade that more and more vineyards are being turned over from red to white grapes. Almost three quarters of the production is now white, made from Macabeo and Parellada, with a little Sumoll, Trepat, Ull de Llebre (Tempranillo) and Garnacha making up the balance in *rosados* and reds. Even served via a hose straight from a concrete tank several months after the harvest, the whites can taste pleasantly fresh, lemony and fruity, the reds astringent but pleasant, though some co-operatives make very basic quality. For local sale, there are some delicious, raisiny *mistelas* and *rancios*, at unbelievably low prices.

Miguel Torres has demonstrated his belief in the region's potential by planting a 100ha estate around the 11th century castle-farmhouse of Milmanda near the famous monastery of Poblet. His Cabernet and Pinot vines are still too young, but the first Chardonnay vintage, 1985, is a glorious, rich, honeyed and oaky wine that could easily pass for a serious, complex Meursault. It will sell simply as Milmanda — the label says neither Chardonnay nor Conca de Barberá — for around

---

Pick of Conca de Barberá
———————**Torres**———————
Torres' wonderful, rich, oaky (and expensive) Chardonnay, Milmanda, comes from grapes grown in Conca de Barberá, but is fermented at the Torres headquarters in the Penedés.

the same price as the Torres Gran Coronas Black Label, at the top of their range.

Conca de Barberá was granted its DO by the regional government of Catalonia in 1985, but the Spanish Ministry for Agriculture refused to ratify it in 1986, when it became one of the newly denominated *vinos de la tierra*.

Above: *Torres' impressive red wine-making plant at Pachs del Penedés automatically pumps the fermenting juice over the cap, and controls the temperature to around 30℃. Once the wine has been run off, the sloping bases of the tanks allow the spent skins to slip out into trucks waiting below.*

Pick of the Penedés

Torres Super-modern, innovative winery, excellent for reds and whites from local and "foreign" grape varieties. Whites for drinking young: fresh, lemony Viña Sol, made from pure Parellada but fuller and more aromatic than others in the region; lively, spicy Viña Esmeralda, two-thirds Muscat d'Alsace, one-third Gewürztraminer; and floral, fragrant Waltraud from Riesling grapes. Whites with a little ageing: lively, pineappley, slightly oaky Gran Viña Sol, about half-and-half Parellada and Chardonnay; and rich, grassy, oaky Gran Viña Sol Green Label/Fransola, from Parellada grapes with a third Sauvignon Blanc. Full-bodied reds: big, rich, spicy-peppery Gran Sangre de Toro, two-thirds Garnacha, a third Cariñena; attractively soft, oaky, herbaceous-blackcurranty Gran Coronas, 70 per cent Cabernet with 30 per cent Tempranillo; and lovely, rich, blackcurrant-fruity Gran Coronas Black Label, 100 per cent Cabernet Sauvignon.

Cavas Hill Very good whites and reds as well as *cavas*. Fresh young whites: Blanc Cru and Oro Penedés Blanco Suave; and Rioja-like reds: Gran Civet and Gran Toc.

Jean León California-style vineyards and winery making oaky, pineappley, honeyed Chardonnays that benefit from a year or two's age, and firm, blackcurrant-scented Cabernet Sauvignon red, made lighter now than in the past, though still quite tannic when young.

Celler Hisenda Miret (Baladá) Small family company with excellent, fresh, fruity, single variety Parellada, Macabeo and Xarel-lo under the name Viña Toña.

Ferret i Mateu Small cellar making very good, light but richly fruity reds, super-fresh *rosados* and interesting whites, under various brand names including Vall de Foix and Viña Laranda.

Marqués de Monistrol Good, simple, fruity whites, Blanc de Blancs and Blanc de Noirs, better than reds.

Mont Marçal Fair to good whites, and good reds at the top of the range, especially Tinto Reserva. Good value.

Mas Rabassa Good, grassy-lemony white Gran Blanc from a small, well equipped private *bodega* belonging to a cousin of the famous Torres family.

Cellers Robert Family firm making very good dessert wines from Malvasía grapes in Sitges.

Cavas

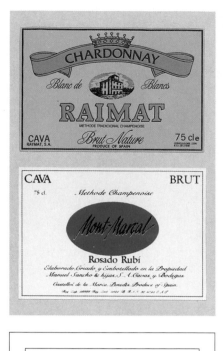

Buy a bottle of Spanish fizz and the odds are that it will have been made by the Champagne method (see pages 36-37), known in Spain as *cava*, in the ugly, sprawling Catalan town of San Sadurní de Noya, just off the motorway about 45 kilometres south-west of Barcelona. All but the tiniest proportion of Spain's *cavas* are made in Catalonia, and 76 per cent of the total is made in San Sadurní de Noya, home of 85 different *cava* companies.

The town lies in the heart of the Penedés, and many people think of its *cava* wines as Penedés wines. But in fact the *cava* DO is a *denominación* in its own right, and grapes for any *cava* producer anywhere in Spain may come from any of Spain's *cava* DO regions, blended together if the producer so wishes. However, a large proportion of the grapes used for the sparkling wines come from this area, some from the *cava* companies' own vineyards, but the vast majority bought from small-scale growers or co-operatives. A quarter of all the grapes grown in the Penedés end up as fizz. Some *bodegas* also buy in juice or wine, from the co-operatives of Tarragona and Conca de Barberá.

Conca de Barberá's speciality is the Macabeo grape (Rioja's Viura), one of a trio of grapes blended in various proportions in the *cavas* of Catalonia. Sharply fresh and fruity when well made and drunk young, though rather bland in flavour, it is usually blended with the slightly more flowery-aromatic Parellada and the Xarel-lo, which is a bigger, more alcoholic wine since Xarel-lo grapes ripen to a higher degree of sweetness, and thus contain more sugar which turns to alcohol during fermentation. Sadly, what all three have in common, apart from a fairly

---

Pick of the Non-Catalan Sparklers

Castilla la Vieja Not officially a *cava*, for reasons more concerned with politics than taste or method, the Brut, made from characterful Verdejo grapes in Rueda, is a lovely, soft, musky-grapy fizz.

---

bland flavour, is a tendency to age rapidly and lose their fruitiness.

"Drink them within the year", is the advice most Penedés *bodegas* would give for their *still* wines made from these same grapes. It is rather ironic, therefore, that the *cavas*, often made in the same *bodegas*, must legally be kept a *minimum* of a year before being sold to the public, while the "best", most expensive *cavas* are often cellar-aged pre-sale for as long as five years or even more. No wonder they often taste dull.

Pick of the Catalan Cavas

Raimat Our favourite Spanish sparkling wine comes from the fine, modern estate in Lérida, under the same ownership as the huge Penedés firm of Codorníu. The first *cava* to be made exclusively of Chardonnay.

Parxet Excellent, fresh, fruity, characterful Parxet Brut Nature and Parxet Brut Reserva from Alella. Under the same ownership as Marqués de Alella who make still wines.

Cavas Hill Penedés. Delicate, lemony Reserva Oro Brut Natur.

Mont-Marçal Penedés. Soft, creamy, appley Cava Nature is better than the Gran Reserva. They have been selling a pure Chardonnay *cava* since Christmas 1987.

Juve y Camps Traditional Penedés company. Brut Natural Reserva de la Familia is very good.

Segura Viudas Penedés. Pleasant, fresh Brut Reserva.

Codorníu Family-owned Penedés giant. Première Cuvée is clean, soft and lemony, Codorníu Chardonnay (sold only in USA at present) is toasty, honeyed and buttery, best of their range.

But attitudes are slowly changing in the Penedés as some *bodegas* realise that their customers want fruitier wines, and that to be fruity, these wines need to be young. Younger wines of course have the advantage of being cheaper to produce, so the best value and most enjoyable flavours are almost invariably to be found at the lower end of a company's price range, rather than up among the vintage and prestige brands.

At their best, from companies such as Cavas Hill or Mont-Marçal, the young *cavas* of the Penedés taste simple, clean, fresh and fruity. Still too often, however, *cava* has a flat, earthy taste from excessive ageing, sometimes accentuated by the use of specially super-aged wine for the final topping up after the removal of the sediment. Since the *cavas'* acidity is much softer than, say, that of Champagne, Penedés producers are quick to point out that you can drink more of their fizz without dire effects on your digestive system.

Here in the Penedés is where all the famous names are to be found: the gigantic Codorníu, largest single producer of Champagne method sparkling wine in the world, who process a million kilos of grapes a day during the seven weeks of the harvest; Freixenet, now owner or part-owner of a huge group including other local *cava* producers; and a host of other companies down to small family concerns.

There are a few *cava* producers in most of Catalonia's other wine regions, too, in Tarragona, Alella, Costers del Segre and Ampurdán-Costa Brava. Of these, most suffer from the poor quality of the base wines, and the only ones really worth seeking out are Parxet, from Alella, just up the coast from Barcelona, a simple, fresh, honeyed, appley wine made from the same trio of grapes grown in the nearby Penedés; and Raimat sparkling Chardonnay from Costers del Segre, light, flowery-fruity fizz with good, fresh acidity.

Above: *Macabeo grapes, one of the three types that make up the Catalan blends. Sadly, none of these native grapes makes characterful wine, and none of them is really suitable for long ageing.*

Below: *A giant bottle fittingly signals the way to Codorníu, largest Champagne method sparkling wine company in the world. Codorníu occupies a spectacular estate in San Sadurní de Noya, 60 kilometres south-west of Barcelona.*

*B*ecause Catalonia almost monopolises Spain's *cava* production, the Catalan authorities were given overall control over the whole country's *cavas* when *Cava* became a *Denominación de Origen* in 1986, though the rules about where the wines could be made and from which grapes were drawn up by officials in Madrid. Rather than basing their decisions on the suitability of each set of local conditions, they granted *cava*-dom to regions and in some cases just towns or villages that had already established a tradition for making *cava* – provided they applied for the honour by a certain date, and provided the wines were made from certain "suitable" grapes.

The resultant *cava* map is a rather illogical patchwork up in the north-eastern corner of the country. A scattering of little villages in Rioja, for instance, have the right to call their sparkling wines *cava*, while neighbouring villages, growing grapes just as suitable for making *cava*, are banned. (Rioja *cavas* are never exciting anyway.) Some mediocre *cavas* have been authorised in Campo de Borja. Worse, a strong contender for Spain's most delicious Champagne method sparkling wine, from Castilla la Vieja in Rueda, has been denied the name *cava* since it was considered a wine of no established tradition, and made from a grape unauthorised for *cava*, the Verdejo – which just happens to be one of Spain's most interestingly flavoured native white grapes.

Apart from the three Catalan grapes, the *cava* DO accepts the Rioja white grape Subirat or Malvasía Riojana (Rioja's Viura is the same as the Macabeo of Catalonia, therefore permitted),Chardonnay and, to add a tinge of colour to sparkling *rosados*, Garnacha and Monastrell. While some scorn the Chardonnay as untraditional, a number of *bodegas* in the Penedés region of Catalonia are finding that a touch of Chardonnay in their tradi-

tional blend adds much needed body, fruit and flowery aroma, and one, Mont-Marçal, recently started selling a pure Chardonnay *cava*. Sparkling Raimat from the soon-to-be DO Costers del Segre near Lérida (see pages 78-9), also a pure Chardonnay – is another strong contender for the top spot among Spain's Champagne method sparklers.

The *cava* DO also controls other aspects of production. No more than 12,000 kilos of grapes may be harvested from each hectare of vineyard, and only the first portion of free-run or lightly pressed juice may be used, up to 100 litres of juice from 150 kilos of grapes (the rest must be used for other wines or sent for distillation). Non-vintage *cavas* have to be aged for a minimum of nine months, vintages for a minimum of three years, in bottles containing the yeast of their second fermentation. A tasting panel in the Penedés checks the quality of each Spanish brand twice every year – though up till now the standard has had to be extraordinarily low for a wine to be rejected.

In September 1987, Spain had 174 recognised *cava* producers, but this figure will rise as the authorities have been handing out permissions at the rate of two a month for more

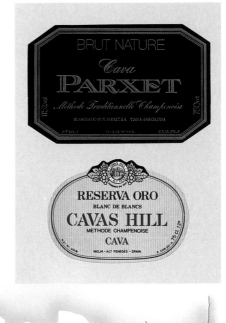

Key to map

1 Rioja.	8 Penedés; Conca de
2 Rioja Alavesa.	Barberá; Tarragona;
3 Mendavia.	Costers del Segre.
4 Gravalos.	9 Artes.
5 Ainzon.	10 Alella.
6 Cariñena.	11 Blanes.
7 Raimat.	12 Ampurdán- Costa Brava.

Styles of Fizz

Cava	115,347,000 bottles*

Sparkle comes from a second fermentation in bottle, and the wine stays in the same bottle throughout the process. Aged for a minimum of nine months from second fermentation. The label will also say *cava* or *vino espumoso natural*, and perhaps *Método Champañes (Tradicional)* or *Méthode*. Look for the four-pointed star symbol under the cork.

Granvas	11,268,000 bottles*

Sparkle comes from a second fermentation in a large pressure tank. Filtered and bottled under pressure after a minimum ageing period of 21 days. The label may say *granvas, grandes envases* (large tanks, hence the name) or *vino espumoso*. Look under the cork for a ring symbol.

Vino gasificado	8,324,000 bottles*

Simple base wine pumped full of carbon dioxide. The label must say *vino gasificado* and the base of the cork bears an equilateral triangle.

* (1986 production figures)

producers within the permitted areas to sell their wines as *cava*. *Cava* sales are booming, and the *bodegas* of the Penedés in particular have found it easy to attract investment – as well as grants from the EEC and the Spanish government – to expand or build new *cava* cellars.

Another EEC decision will affect the labelling of *cavas* by 1994. A great many *cavas* are still labelled with the French term *Méthode Champenoise* indicating that the wines are made by the Champagne method. However, the Champagne producers, keen to safeguard the prestige of their name, recently obtained a ruling from the European Court that no region (even other French regions) may use the term after that date. At least Spain is fortunate in having a well-established native word as an alternative: *cava*, derived from the Catalan for the cellar where such wines are made.

How Sweet Are They?

Brut Dry, containing less than 20 grammes per litre of sugar
Seco Fairly dry, between 20 and 30 grammes per litre of sugar
Semiseco Semi-sweet, with 30 to 50 grammes per litre of sugar
Dulce Sweet, with more than 50 grammes per litre

Below: *The entrance to Spain's second largest* cava *company, Freixenet. Nine layers of underground factory-warrens are stacked below this attractive reception and office building. Visitors trundle through caverns and passages full of bottles and* girasoles *on a little electric train.*

Alella

*D*riving north-east from Barcelona up the coast towards France, you will come across few vines. The only *Denominaciónes de Origen* in the north-eastern section are tiny Alella, almost a suburb of Barcelona, about 16 kilometres further up the coast, and Ampurdán-Costa Brava, right up by the French border.

In the 'seventies, the coastal motorway sliced through the vineyards of Alella. Indirectly, it destroyed many more vineyards than those in its immediate path, because Alella's rolling hills and seascapes suddenly became accessible to commuters. Today, when vineyard land fetches one million pesetas per hectare, a building plot of the same size would go for 15 million. Who can afford to be sentimental about a few vines in such circumstances? There are now around 590 hectares of vines – a huge drop from the 1,400 hectares under cultivation at the end of the 'sixties.

Alella's vineyards fall into two distinct sections, some facing eastwards towards the sea and growing Garnacha Blanca in the warm Mediterranean climate, the rest further inland on west-facing slopes and terraces in a more continental climate. Here, traditionally, the major grape has been the white Pansa Blanca (local name for the Xarel-lo) with a little Garnacha Tinta, Tempranillo and Pansa Rosada for *rosados* and reds, but successful trials have been run with the other two Penedés varieties, Parellada and Macabeo, as well as some foreigners, Cabernet Sauvignon, Pinot Noir, and the white Chardonnay and Chenin Blanc.

First to fall to the property developers were the highest vineyards of this inland area, those capable of producing the region's most delicate wine, but difficult or impossible to work by machine on steep slopes or terraces. If they escaped the bulldozer, many such vineyards were simply abandoned as uneconomical. Some have recently crept back into production, however, under the influence of Alella's main private *bodega*, Marqués de Alella, which has made contracts with about 50 owners of small vineyards. By paying for the vines, necessary treatments and small crates to keep the grapes in fine condition at harvest time, the *bodega* has secured for itself a supply of top class grapes.

Marqués de Alella have a super-modern, stainless steel-equipped *bodega* up in the interior in Santa María de Martorelles, where they make about 40 per cent of the region's wines, exclusively white. (Alella grows few reds.) They have been known so far for their medium dry white Marqués de Alella, but far more interesting are the latest (dry) additions to the range: attractive, appley-fresh Marqués de Alella Seco, in which the Pansa Banca is helped along by the sharper, fruitier

Pick of Alella

Alta Alella Marqués de Alella Seco and Chardonnay. The *cavas* from sister company **Parxet** are also excellent, fresh and fruity.

Above: *Wines on sale to the public at the Garriguella Co-op in Ampurdán-Costa Brava. Almost all the region's wine starts life in a co-operative such as this one. Conditions in most co-ops are still fairly primitive.*

Macabeo and some Chenin Blanc; and a very attractive, light, pineappley Chardonnay – as well as their delicious sparkling wine, whose fizz is inserted by sister company Parxet in the town of Alella. All their wines are made for drinking fresh and young.

Not so the wines of the Alella Co-operative, who makes almost all the rest of Alella's wine. So far, they have continued ageing their *semi-seco* wines for a year in wooden barrels, and have been trying to sell the tired, old fashioned result at high prices. Their dry white is sold young, but is disappointing. The region's other private firm, Jaume Serra, recently moved to Penedés, keeping just one tiny Alella *bodega*, whose wines are dull.

Ampurdán-Costa Brava

The other northern DO, Ampurdán-Costa Brava, is less advanced. Bordered to the north by the Pyrenees and to the east by the Mediterranean, it consists of about 5,000 hectares of hot, windswept vineyards. Most are owned by small-scale growers, who almost invariably have other interests, pigs or sheep, olives or cereals. Co-operatives have therefore grown until they account for nearly 95 per cent of production. Only one, at Pau, has proper temperature control at fermentation time. Much of the equipment is old fashioned, too, and the resulting wines are often coarse.

Above: *Family team spraying vines at Garriguella. Most Ampurdán grape-growers are general farmers, with livestock or cereals as well as vines.*

Almost three-quarters of Ampurdán-Costa Brava's wines are fairly alcoholic *rosados* – the principal grapes are Cariñena and Garnacha (known locally as the Lledoner). Then come the sweet, fortified, often rather astringent Garnachas, made by fermenting the juice for three days then fortifying it with grape spirit up to 15 or 16° of alcohol. There are some heavy reds, a smaller proportion of improving but unexciting whites, semi-sparkling (*agujos*) and sparkling wines, and rough, sherry-style *rancios*. A new arrival in recent years is *vi novell* or *vi del any*, a fruitier, Beaujolais-ish style red wine for early drinking, and perhaps the best bet among the region's offerings, though rarely good.

Biggest and best of the commercial firms is Cavas del Ampurdán, sister of the sparkling wine company Cavas del Castillo de Perelada (housed in the impressive *castillo* in the region's principal town, Perelada). The firm has some vineyards, and is experimenting with a wide selection of French grapes, but most of the wine is supplied by co-operatives and blended by the company with sound but unexciting results.

Tarragona

As you travel south-west from Tarragona city, parallel to the Mediterranean along the flat plain of the Campo de Tarragona which is full of irrigated fruit trees and dusty vineyards, a range of granite mountains rears up, blocking the way south. This marks the end of El Campo de Tarragona, biggest of the three Tarragona sub-zones. With a light, chalky soil and a Mediterranean climate, this is white wine country, growing the Penedés trio of Macabeo, Parellada and Xarel-lo, plus a little red Sumoll and Tempranillo.

Up and over the mountain range to the west lies hilly, cooler Conca de Falset, its mixed granite and limestone terrain more suitable for red grapes, principally Cariñena and Garnacha. In the far west is Ribera de Ebro, chalky, pebbly land along the banks of the Ebro (the same Ebro that flows, much earlier in its course, through Rioja). The climate here is more continental, with roasting summers, cold winters and low rainfall. Despite this, Ribera de Ebro is also white wine country, growing the Macabeo and Garnacha Blanca. Seventy per cent of all the grapes grown in Tarragona are white.

Tarragona is a land of co-operatives, who sell much of their wine in bulk to blending companies within and outside the region. Apart from fairly alcoholic table wines, there are *rancios* and *generosos*, known as *Tarragona clasicos*.

Worth seeking out are the wines of Pedro Rovira, whose *bodega* in Ribera de Ebro has an efficient combination of old fashioned and modern equipment. By picking early and cool fermenting, they make full, fragrant, characterful (and cheap) whites and pleasant reds. Also above average are the wines of De Muller, made in their imposing 18th century warehouse-*bodega* down by the port in the city of Tarragona.

Terra Alta

Both these firms also make wines from Terra Alta, a separate *Denominación de Origen* in the province of Tarragona, geographically a continuation up into the hills of the Ribera de Ebro region. Terra Alta is wilder country than Ribera de Ebro, with strong winds, hotter summers and colder winters, and one of the lowest rainfall levels in Spain. Vineyards compete for space with almonds and olives, and because there is so little rain, the bushy vines have to be pruned very close to the ground so that no water is wasted in

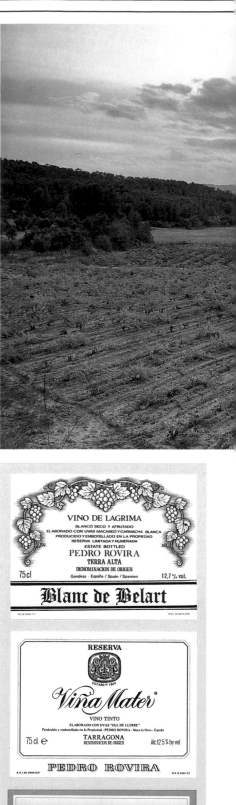

excess foliage. Yields are tiny. As in Tarragona, whites are most important, principally Garnacha Blanca, with some Macabeo, and for the reds, making up around a quarter of the production, Cariñena, Garnacha Peluda (a hairy-leaved local mutant of the ordinary Garnacha) and a little Tempranillo.

Traditionally, the white wines of Terra Alta weighed in at a thumping 16° of alcohol, but most *bodegas* (here, too, overwhelmingly co-operatives) now usually manage to keep them between 12° and 15°. The reds are a little less alcoholic, but usually rather coarse, and Terra Alta also produces *rancios* and *generosos*.

Sacramental wine for use in church services (*vino de misa*) is Terra Alta's other speciality. Pedro Rovira and De Muller both make them from Terra Alta as well as Tarragona whites, usually Garnacha Blanca and

Above: *Young vines north of Flix in Terra Alta. The vines here have to contend with low rainfall and very strong winds.*

Macabeo picked ulta-ripe to cut down on the amount of grape spirit needed later to fortify them. Sacramental wines form, in fact, about a third of De Muller's business. They are the world's biggest supplier, exporting them to 49 different countries, including the Vatican. These are strictly "organic" wines, made without chemicals, and De Muller, a good, Catholic company, obtain their seal of approval from the Bishop of Barcelona.

Like their other white wines, the sacramental wines are now cold fermented before being fortified and aged for two years in big oak barrels, as opposed to the traditional four years.

Pick of Tarragona and Terra Alta

Pedro Rovira *Bodegas* in Tarragona and Terra Alta. Best from Tarragona are the characterful, dry white Viña Montalt Blanco Seco, and in the reds the soft, fruity Viña Mater Tinto Reserva at about four years old, and savoury, pruney, bottle-aged Gran Vino Tinto Reserva, sold perhaps a little too old at around eight or nine years. Best from Terra Alta are the lovely, herby, characterful Vino de Lagrima, and an extraordinary, light, sweet, musky-lemony Alta Mar.

De Muller *Bodega* in the city of Tarragona. Their best white Tarragona wine is an unusual and delicious Moscatel Seco, a lovely dry, floral, lemony wine from a freak plantation of Moscatel grapes near the village of Montbrió. They have a pleasant, young red Tarragona, Viña Solimar Tinto.

Priorato

PRIORATO

S tunningly beautiful the mountains of Priorato may be, but their precipitous slopes provide a hard living for the inhabitants. It is often impossible to use machines, and in places the vineyard workers have to hang on to ropes to tend the vines. And after all the effort, a vine here can be expected to produce as little as half a kilo of grapes in an average year, compared with five kilos or more in the Penedés. The population has dropped so alarmingly in the last decades that the Catalan government has had to provide financial support to keep agriculture and viticulture going at all.

Priorato lies in the mountains to the north of Falset, the central section of Tarragona. The narrow roads follow ancient cart tracks, winding up between wild, rocky hills to eight remote villages. Terraces here and there allow for mechanisation, but most of the vines simply cling to the steep slopes in dark, slaty soil, their roots working deep into the fissures of the rock in search of water. Little else but a few olive trees will grow.

It rarely rains in Priorato, and dry, northeast winds scoop up most of the little moisture that does fall. Summer day-time temperatures are very high, easily up to 40°C, but falling at night to as little as 10 to 12°C, which helps to preserve the grapes' flavours and aromas. The tiny yields concentrate the juice, too, so that the wines of Priorato have the potential of incredibly intense flavour and deep colour when young. With the high temperatures accentuated by the sun reflecting off the slate, alcoholic degrees are inevitably high. The DO rules call for a *minimum* of 13.75° of alcohol, but Priorato wines can shoot up to 18° or more in the hottest years.

Two red types of Garnacha, Garnacha Tinta and hairy-leaved Garnacha Peluda, have traditionally been the principal varieties, but Cariñena now makes up about a third or even half of most blends. A few whites (Garnacha Blanca, Macabeo and Pedro Ximénez) are also grown to make a small proportion of dry or semi-dry white wines, but most of the wines are young reds, bottled early for drink-

ing young in their first three or four years. Garnacha wine has a natural tendency to oxidise, so these are not wines for keeping, but Priorato has a tradition of mature wines, too: the alcoholic, medium-sweet or sweet *generosos* and dry *rancios*, which develop penetrating, nutty, raisiny flavours when left to age for five years or more in large oak barrels. These have between 14 and 20° of *natural*

Pick of Priorato

Cellers de Scala Dei Good, fresh, alcoholic *rosado*, Rosat Scala Dei; fruity, fresh, raisiny and fairly alcoholic young red, Negre Scala Dei; wonderful wood- and bottle-aged red made in the best years, Cartoixa Scala Dei.

De Muller Good, intense, youngish table wines in the traditional style at about 15.5° with flavours reminiscent of tea, figs and damsons. Also wood-aged Priorato; especially good are their Aureo, Priorato Muy Viejo, rich, sweet, nutty and raisiny; and delicious, dry, concentrated Priorato ''Dom Juan Fort'' Extra Rancio, Solera 1865.

Masía Barril Private estate with good, dark, alcoholic wines.

alcohol, but, at best, extraordinary concentration of flavour to balance it.

Each village has its own co-operative, whose wines tend to be heavily alcoholic, tannic and astringent. They now bottle some at a joint bottling plant, but sell most wines in bulk for blending.

One important customer is the Tarragona firm of De Muller, who also have a small ageing *bodega* in the village of Scala Dei, perched up in the north of Priorato. By advising the co-operatives on their winemaking, they manage to buy softer, less astringent wines, good drunk young or aged to the *rancio* or *generoso* styles.

Scala Dei is the point of pilgrimage for the few tourists who venture this far from the coast, since it houses the ruins of the famous 12th century Carthusian monastery that gave Priorato its name. Fine wine worshippers should make a pilgrimage there, too, to visit Priorato's most famous *bodega*, Cellers de Scala Dei.

With its gleaming stainless steel equipment, designer glasses and labels and num-

Above: *The little village of Scala Dei, right up in the northern Priorato peaks, has been painstakingly restored by escapees from Barcelona. It is the home of the region's finest* bodega.

bered bottles, it could easily pass as a California "boutique" winery. It belongs to five Barcelona families, who have set up home in Scala Dei. Their wines come only from their own grapes, and, continuing in the California style, they have terraced and wired their vineyards. Garnacha is their main grape, with as little as ten per cent Cariñena, but they are also conducting trials with Cabernet Sauvignon, Chardonnay and other varieties foreign to the region. They pick their grapes early, barely scraping the minimum 13.75° of alcohol, and employ a university-trained winemaker. From their young *rosados* and reds to their top wine, Cartoixa Scala Dei (aged for about 14 months in small oak barrels, then a few more years in bottle), these are extraordinary, rich, complex wines.

*I*n 1988 the Costers del Segre should become the most westerly of the Catalan DOs. "Costers" is Catalan for "costas", so the region is called "banks of the Segre". At the time of writing, it is recognised by the Catalan government, but not by the central Spanish government or the EEC. Even with this partial recognition, exact statistics have been hard to come by, probably because vinegrowing in much of the possible DO area is in decline, and there is little point in dignifying an area with a DO if it is interesting only from a historical point of view. One thing is certain, however: if the Costers del Segre does achieve full DO status in anything like its present suggested form, it will be extremely fragmented.

Wines from the areas Las Garrigas (in the south-east corner of Lérida province) and Segría (to the north-east of the city of Lérida) are seldom seen outside Catalonia. Predominant grape varities in both are the Macabeo and Parellada for white wines, and the Garnacha, Sumoll and Cariñena for reds. There are no outstanding wines.

Each of the other two wine regions within the provisional DO has one notable property. To the west of Lérida lies Raimat, a vast modern oasis of vines set in virtual desert, while the historic (but rather dilapidated) Castell de Remey is in Urgell, about 35 kilometres north-east of Lérida. Both owe their agricultural existence to the canals that carry water down from the Pyrenees, which in both cases were brought into full operation during the 1960s. Were it not for irrigation (forbidden for vines except by special dispensation in Spain), the flourishing plantations of cereals and fruit trees would not be there. Neither would some of the vines.

The wine made on the Raimat estate has been almost solely responsible for the proposal of the Costers del Segre DO. Raimat was bought by the Raventos family (owners of the Codorníu *cava* company) in 1914. Since then, the 13th century castle has been restored, a village built (complete with railway station, sports centre and school) for the estate's employees, and a 3,000 hectare agricultural estate prepared and planted with fruit trees, cereals and vines.

Latest expenditure has been on a magnificent new winery dug into the side of a hill, connected by a tunnel to the original, early 20th century, cathedral-like cellars. This would give Raimat the capacity to expand from the 1,025 hectares of vineyard planted at present to a maximum of 2,000 hectares, if permission is forthcoming from the EEC. Such permission is by no means out of the question, as Raimat has already been classified as a "model agricultural estate" by the Spanish government, both for its resurrection of the traditional agricultural community of Raimat and its innovative programme of research. The company has been advised in this programme of research (into varietal experimentation, vine rootstocks, clonal selection, training of vines, methods of irrigation and mechanical harvesting) by experts from

Below: *California State University advised on the planting of the Raimat vineyards. Trained on wires and irrigated, imports like Cabernet and Chardonnay flourish.*

Pick of Costers del Segre

Raimat Raimat Chardonnay has a lively, grassy acidity balancing honeyed, buttery fruit. Raimat Abadia is a blend of 50 per cent Cabernet Sauvignon, 35 per cent Tempranillo and 15 per cent Garnacha with a good, savoury Tempranillo and blackcurranty Cabernet character enhanced by a touch of oak. The Raimat Cabernet Sauvignon (with ten per cent Merlot and five per cent Tempranillo) has more concentration of stylish blackcurrant fruit, and can be kept for up to ten years.

Above: *Recently opened, the new section of the Raimat winery is inspired by Egyptian temple architecture and combines white marble, mirror glass and stainless steel.*

Davis and Fresno Universities in California.

The "experimental" nature of the Raimat plantation – vines are principally Chardonnay and Parellada with some Macabeo and Xarel-lo for white wines, and Cabernet Sauvignon, Tempranillo, Merlot, Pinot Noir and Monastrell for reds – has meant that Raimat has been able to circumvent many of the rules as regards irrigation and training of vines. This in turn has made the vineyards very profitable, giving grape yields twice or even three times the average for other near-desert areas like La Mancha.

The aim of this massive project is to produce wines of a consistently high quality. The climate of the region is severe, hotter than is recommended for most grape varieties) with almost unbearably hot summers and low winter temperatures. Indeed, the ostensible purpose of Raimat's sophisticated system of thermostatically-controlled irrigation is to rescue the vines when extremes of temperature would otherwise cause damage.

At Castell del Remey, where there are also plantations of Cabernet Sauvignon, the owners say it would be impossible to obtain financially worthwhile yields *without* irrigation. The vineyard at Castell del Remey was originally planted with Cabernet Sauvignon and Sémillon by French winemakers brought over from Bordeaux at the time of the phylloxera epidemic at the end of last century.

Although the *bodega* the French built was modern *then*, little had changed when the estate was bought by the Cusiné family in 1982, and they had to instigate a programme of renovation. So far, they have planted five hectares of Cabernet Sauvignon (the rest of the 20 hectare vineyard has Macabeo), and installed a modern press and temperature-controlled fermentation tanks. Much of the wine on sale at present is from old stock bought with the *bodega*.

*I*n Spain, the wines of Galicia are highly prized – but not all of them. There are four officially demarcated areas, two of which, Ribeiro and Valdeorras, have DOs, while the others, Rias Baixas and Valle de Monterrey, are two of the regions whose wines have been recently classified as *Vinos de la Tierra*. Ironically, it is for the wines from Rias Baixas that there is most demand.

The best of the Rias Baixas wines are made from the Albariño grape, and regularly command the highest prices for young wines in Spain, while the best white wines from Ribeiro fall much more into line with the young whites of Rioja. As for the wines of Valdeorras, they are Galicia's also-rans. Three-quarters of them are poor quality reds, and hardly conform to the popular concept of Galician wine.

Galicia is famed as the wettest and coolest part of Spain, but in fact this applies only to the coastal Rias Baixas region, where vines are trained on pergolas or high supports to protect them from rot and endemic mildew and oidium. Ribeiro is higher and drier, in Valdeorras the climate is nearly continental, and Valle de Monterrey is hotter and drier than all the rest of Galicia.

Rias Baixas

The Rias Baixas region consists of three zones, El Salnes (round Cambados, traditional home of the Albariño), El Rosal and Condado de Tea. After phylloxera had devastated northern Spain, much of Galicia was replanted with hybrid crossings between phylloxera-proof American vines and native European varieties. Most of these hybrids produced much more than the original European vines, and vastly in excess of the miserly yield of the Albariño. So, although more quality-conscious growers began to replant with European vines grafted on to American rootstock, many hung on to the hybrids.

It was not until the early 1980s that the Galician government decided to encourage a programme of Albariño replantation, and to

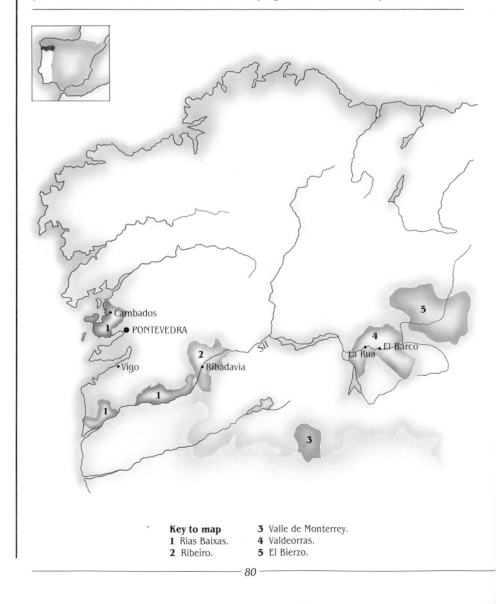

Cambados

1 ● PONTEVEDRA

2

●Vigo   ●Ribadavia

Sil

4
La Rua ●El Barco

5

1

1

3

Key to map
1 Rias Baixas.
2 Ribeiro.
3 Valle de Monterrey.
4 Valdeorras.
5 El Bierzo.

Pick of Galicia

Agrupación de Cosecheiros Albariño do Salnes (Rias Baixas) Medium-sized, immaculate, modern *bodega* making fresh, apple and peach scented Albariño Dom Bardo.

Bodegas Cardallal (Rias Baixas) Tiny, exquisitely-equipped *bodega* set in fields of kiwi fruit and maize. Their Albariño was the best we tasted, fresh, perfumed, soft and complex.

Co-operativa Pazo Ribeiro (Ribeiro) Largest producer in the region. Top brand Bradomin made only in good years. Viña Costeira is next best, off-dry, clean and honeyed.

Bodegas Santiago Ruiz (Rias Baixas) Top El Rosal *bodega*. Wine is not pure Albariño, but mixed with Loureira and Treixadura, and very good, light, appley-peachy, with a steely acidity.

Bodegas de Vilariño-Cambados (Rias Baixas) Medium-sized, ultra-modern *bodega* producing excellent, balanced Albariño Martin Codax, with flavours of apple, pear and peach kernel.

withold a full DO from the area until a vineyard register had been completed, so that it would be possible to control production. The programme has progressed quite well, but because the register is not complete, Rias Baixas has only so far made it to *Vino de la Tierra* status. And as Rias Baixas lacks the controlling apparatus a DO region would have, it is unfortunately relatively easy to pass non-Albariño wine off as the real thing.

Of course, there are *bodegas* provided with the latest in gleaming stainless steel equipment making excellent wines from pure Albariño grapes. But on the whole, the wines of Rias Baixas are no more reliable than those of the other two regions. In El Rosal the main grapes are the Caino Blanco, Godello and Loureira, and in Condado de Tea, the Treixadura and Loureira. Both areas have Albariño in small quantities, and growers are being encouraged to plant more.

Ribeiro

Although Ribeiro is much sunnier and drier than Rias Baixas, with altitudes varying between 100 and 250 metres above sea level, on a hot day a haze still clings to the forests and hills. Some vineyards lie in the river valleys, but most are on the hill-sides.

Almost half of the total production is of the white Palomino de Jerez, a grape that gives very high yields, but wines of little quality unless made in the sherry style. The indigenous white varieties, Treixadura, Torrontés, Godello and Albariño, can make wines of tremendous character (as wines made by the local *Consejo Regulador*'s experimental *bodega* clearly demonstrate). Even the red

grapes, Souson, Brencellao and Caino, which account for about a third of Ribeiro's output, give red wines of a pleasantly herbaceous nature, although the *Consejo Regulador* is trying to effect a move from red to white wines within the DO.

Ribeiro is clearly a region where the wines are improving, led by the renovation of old vineyards by weekenders from the cities. When more of the vineyards have been changed from Palomino to good local grapes, Ribeiro should yield white wines to rival any others made in Spain.

Valdeorras

The winemakers of Valdeorras, however, are gloomy. There used to be five or six privately-owned *bodegas* in this mountainous region, but they failed, and now there are only three co-operatives. The terrain is difficult to cultivate, and people make very little money from their vineyards.

Ninety per cent of the production is white Palomino de Jerez or red Garnacha Tintorera, neither of them suited to quality wine. The white Godello and Doña Blanco and the red Mencía and Mouratom make much better wines, but account for a tiny proportion of vines planted. And there is no prospect of replantation, as growers make so little from the vines they already have. Valdeorras seems trapped in an inexorable downward spiral.

Valle de Monterrey
Right in the south of Galicia, by the Portuguese border, this former *Comarca* turned *Vino de la Tierra* makes mostly heavy, dark red wines or *claretes* from the Alicante grape, the most alcoholic wines of Galicia, tending to be rough and bitter.

O utput of top-quality wine in the provinces of Castilla-León is dominated
by Ribera del Duero and Rueda, but
three other regions whose wines are less well-
known are worth mentioning.

Toro

Ribera del Duero's western neighbour, Toro,
became a full DO in 1987. Though a little
lower than Ribera del Duero at 620 to 750
metres above sea level, it has an equally
extreme climate, with frosts from October to
May, and hot summers with not quite such
cool nights. It is much drier than Ribera del
Duero, and yields are even smaller.

Seventy per cent of Toro's wine is red, the
rest mostly white (also DO) from the Malvasía
grape. The red grape, Tinto de Toro, is yet
another manifestation of the Tempranillo or
Tinto Fino, which tends here to give more
highly coloured, more tannic wines, lower in
acidity than the well-balanced wines of
Ribera del Duero. Reds must be made from
at least 75 per cent Tinto de Toro (the rest
being Garnacha), though the best are 100
per cent Tinto de Toro.

The wines have improved a lot in the last
few years, with earlier picking, cooler temperatures and shorter contact of juice with
skins during fermentation making the wines
finer and softer. Bodegas Fariña (Bodegas
Porto renamed, since the EEC will not allow
the name of one of its regions to be used for a
winery in a different region) is far ahead of
the rest of the area in quality.

El Bierzo

Between the last mountainous recesses of
Galicia and the predominantly flat province
of Castilla-León lies El Bierzo, a *vino de la
tierra* region of some 8,100 hectares, almost
entirely shielded by mountain ranges from
the more extreme effects of Atlantic and
Continental climates.

Wine-making centres on the old pilgrim-
route towns of Villafranca del Bierzo and
Cacabelos, which boast the region's most
important co-operatives and the impressive
Bodegas Palacio de Arganza.

Eighty per cent of Bierzo wine is red, and
most of that made from the Mencía grape,
sometimes optimistically identified with the
Cabernet Franc. The wine has a herbaceous
quality when young, with a characteristically
bitter note to its flavour, but needs the help
of oak ageing to develop into more than a
pale, fragrant red for early drinking.

The Cacabelos co-operative solves the
problem of inadequate colour by using a
thermo-vinificator (to heat the grapes prior
to fermentation and extract more colour
from their skins). This is frowned upon by
INDO, the central Spanish regulatory body,
however, and may have to stop now that El
Bierzo is a *vino de la tierra*.

Above: *Primitive* bodegas, *tunnelled into
the baked red earth, are still used by
peasant farmers around León villages
such as here near Benavente.*

Quite what will happen at Bodegas Palacio
de Arganza, far the grandest of the Bierzo
privately-owned producers, is anyone's
guess. Their skill lies in blending and maturing Bierzo wines with wines from other parts
of Spain, particularly neighbouring Ribera
del Duero, but also Aragón, Jumilla, Rioja
and Tarragona.

León

The cluster of wine-making villages to the
south of León, historic capital of the province, finds its best expression in the wines
blended at Vinos de León (usually known as
VILE, an unfortunate acronym). This large
bodega on the outskirts of León was founded
to update the local wine-making methods
that still exist in primitive *bodegas* tunnelled
into the baked red earth round villages like
Valdevimbre, Los Oteros, Ardón and Villa-
mañan. VILE has over one million litres capacity of oak barrel storage for the maturation
of the best reds, as well as an ingenious
system of water running through channels in
the cellar floor, to lower temperature and
raise humidity.

The *bodega* supplements the local produce (in this case mostly the black Prieto
Picudo, and a small quantity of Mencía, Garnacha and white Palomino) with wine from

throughout the province. They are putting the finishing touches to a new *bodega* in Nava de Roa, near Peñafiel in the Ribera del Duero DO, scheduled to open in 1988.

Cigales
Cigales was proclaimed *Denominación Especifica* in October 1986 only to be converted to *Vino de la Tierra* when the new regulations were published in December. Though it is best known for its *claretes* and *rosados*, it makes quite good reds and could potentially make fine reds, both young wines and *crianzas* – Ribera del Duero is only a few kilometres to the east, and conditions here are similar. Reds must have 75 per cent, *rosados* 50 per cent of Tempranillo, the rest being largely Garnacha.

Cebreros
It is hard to believe that this remote country with its narrow, pot-holed roads is only 100 kilometres from Madrid. Winemaking here is as behind the times as the rest of life, and the raisiny, alcoholic Garnachas do not merit their new title of *vinos de la tierra*.

Madrid
Winemaking is still so primitive and the wines so universally poor in this large, hot, dry area around Madrid that it is hard to understand how the region came by its *vino de la tierra* qualification. The sector around the town of Arganda grows whites Airén and Malvar, and Tinto Fino; Navalcarnero has Malvar and Garnacha, and San Martín de Valdeiglesias has Albillo and Garnacha.

Pick of Toro, El Bierzo and León

Bodegas Fariña (Porto), Toro Medium-sized family *bodega* making very good, rich, soft, fruity and sometimes oaky, modern reds, Tinto Colegiata and Crianza Gran Colegiata.

Bodegas Palacio de Arganza, El Bierzo Privately-owned blending and maturation *bodega*, specialising in excellent red Reservas and Gran Reservas sold under the Señorio de Arganza and Palacio de Arganza labels.

Bodega Comarcal Co-operativa Vinos del Bierzo, El Bierzo Best of the Bierzo co-operatives, with good, oak-aged Señorio del Bierzo red.

VILE (Vinos de León), León Relatively modern blending *bodega*, with good Palacio de Los Guzmanes range: the white Verdejo from Rueda, the Rosado Tinto Fino from near Salamanca, and the oak-aged red Prieto Picudo and Tinto del Pais.

Rueda

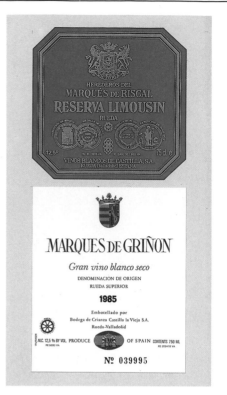

"We have the best white wines of Spain" is no idle chauvinistic boast from the winemakers of Rueda. Not only have they kept their ideas and their equipment abreast of the times, but they have a natural advantage over most of the rest of Spain: a white grape that actually has some character.

The native Verdejo makes a fresh, fruity, nutty wine, not too alcoholic if picked early, and with plenty of body. Winemakers measure a wine's body by its "dry extract", the solids left after boiling the wine dry in the laboratory and the Verdejo's extract is as high as that of some red Riojas. Fortunately, it is the most abundant vine in the area. The DO also authorises Viura, Palomino (for fortified wines only) and, since 1985, Sauvignon Blanc.

Rueda's entire white crop used traditionally to be made into sherry-style fortified wines, but today only a couple of *bodegas* still make them. There are two basic types, both dry: a *fino*-style Palido Rueda, fortified up to a minimum of 14°, rather less tangy than a Jerez *fino* but matured, like a *fino*, in cask under a veil of *flor*; and Dorado Rueda, fortified to a minimum of 15°, and allowed to age longer in cask after the *flor* has gone, like a proper Jerez *amontillado* but without its intensity of flavour. They age in a single cask, rather than passing through a Jerez-type *solera* system.

Nowadays, such wines have fallen out of favour with the younger generations of local drinkers as well as the once thriving export markets, and producers have turned to young white table wines. When Rueda's table wines were granted their DO in 1980, the rules were that a simple Rueda should have at least 25 per cent Verdejo and between 11.5 and 14° of alcohol, while a Rueda Superior should have a minimum 60 per cent Verdejo and six months' wood ageing followed by six months in bottle before sale.

With the public clamouring for younger and fresher whites, the ageing regulation for

---

Pick of Rueda

Marqués de Griñon White Marqués de Griñon is a Rueda wine, made 100 per cent from Verdejo grapes at Bodegas Castilla la Vieja, a full, soft, fresh, aromatic wine that gets our top marks. (The delicious red Marqués de Griñon is oak-aged here, but grown in Toledo, south of Madrid.)

Marqués de Riscal, Vinos Blancos de Castilla A fine, modern *bodega* founded in 1972 by Marqués de Riscal of Rioja, who considered the Rueda wines to be much better than their white home produce. It is Rueda's principal exporter. Pleasant Rueda; good, fresh, oaky Reserva Limousin Rueda Superior; and soft, flowery Sauvignon Rueda Superior.

Alvarez y Diez Technically well-equipped *bodega* making all its wines by "organic" methods, without even using sulphur in the winery. Good, soft, nutty Mantel Nuevo Rueda; and pleasantly sharp, fresh, nutty Mantel Blanco Rueda Superior. Mantel Palido and Mantel Dorado are the region's best *generosos*.

Castilla la Vieja Good, light, soft Rueda Superior. (Excellent, flavourful *cava*-method sparkling wine, which has the DO neither of Rueda nor of *cava*.)

Vinos Sanz Good Rueda and Rueda Superior.

Bodegas Angel Rodriguez Very good single estate wines, fragrant and fresh, labelled Martinsancho Rueda Superior.

Bodegas Cerro Sol Very good, fresh Doña Beatriz Blanco, with honeyed and limey flavours.

Rueda Superior has now sensibly been waived, so that Superior generally indicates simply a wine with a high proportion of Verdejo and therefore more body, flavour and character. Treated with care and aged in new or newish oak, the Verdejo *can* respond well to wood ageing, however. The Rueda *bodega* of Marqués de Riscal makes a delicious, oaky Reserva Limousin, and Alvarez y Diez (who have more wooden barrels than the rest of the region put together, and are rather peeved at the recent turn of the rules) still age their Superior wines in oak, to pleasant effect.

The switch to young, light wines has meant changes in the vineyards as well as the cellars. Winemakers at the region's big cooperative Agricola Castellana explain how, over the past ten years, they have encouraged their members to pick early, aiming for the lowest permitted alcoholic degree, as well as controlling the fermentation temperatures, installing new, gentler presses, modern bottling lines and, this year, stainless steel tanks.

The co-op serves all the 71 towns and villages of this flat or gently sloping, sprawling region, where visitors might even be forgiven for thinking that the wines are made from wheat or barley rather than grapes, so scattered are the vineyards, tucked away on the least fertile land, far from the main thoroughfares. There is little difference, according to the co-operative winemakers, in the grapes of the different parts of this large area. Most important for the quality of the grapes is the considerable altitude of the whole region: big drops in temperature between day and night in summer and autumn make for better aroma and flavour in grapes throughout Rueda.

Above: *Antonio Sanz Moro at Castilla La Vieja. Besides the* bodega's *own wines, he makes the excellent white Marqués de Griñon here, and ages the red, brought up from Toledo, in new oak barrels.*

Below: Rancios, *sun-matured wines in the* oloroso *style for local consumption, age here in huge glass jars at Castilla La Vieja. The best of Rueda's traditional, sherry-style fortified wines are aged in wooden barrels, as in Jerez.*

Ribera del Duero

Cosecha 1984

Ribera del Duero means "Banks of the Duero", and although the river is rather better known as the Douro, the famous port river, once it crosses the Portuguese border, this central Spanish section has also made a fine name for itself at home and abroad, especially in the USA, and most especially for the region's star wine, Vega Sicilia. High demand for relatively small quantities of this wine has sent prices soaring.

The reputation is well founded, because this is perhaps the region of Spain with the greatest potential for making fine red wines. Even if only a few enlightened producers are really getting the best out of their grapes so far, the raw materials are excellent, and a sparkling new government-financed research station should shortly begin to make a greater impact on the level of quality in the region as a whole.

The secret of the high quality of the red wines of the Ribera del Duero is altitude. At 800 metres above sea level, it is at the limit of vine cultivation. In May, when the tourists are already lapping up the sun on the Costas, vine growers here are likely to be up half the night lighting fires to combat the frost among their newly budding vines. Although the temperature during an average summer's day may be as high as 32°C, the night can be a chilly 6°, and, as explained at the beginning of the book, cool nights work wonders for the quality of the grapes. Good acidity, plenty of fruity flavour, and above all wonderful aroma mark out the Duero's produce. Small yields on the poor, fairly chalky soil also mean that what grapes there are on the vine get more than their share of concentrated flavour.

The DO includes *rosados* as well as red wines, but no whites. By far the principal grape is a local strain of Tempranillo, known here as Tinto Fino, Tinto Pais, Tinta del Pais or Tinto Aragonés, but there are also plantings of Garnacha, Cabernet Sauvignon, Malbec and Merlot. (The Vega Sicilia estate began to plant these Bordeaux vines at the beginning of the century.) Cabernet Sauvignon here makes big, full-bodied, blackcurranty wines, especially good when blended with Tinto Fino.

Vega Sicilia is unusual in the region in respect of the proportions of "foreign" grapes it uses: Tinto Fino accounts for just 60 per cent of most of its blends, with 25 per cent Cabernet and the rest made up of Malbec and Merlot, and there are even plans to increase the Cabernet proportion to 40 per cent as the vineyards are gradually extended to cover more of the huge estate. Vega Sicilia makes three wines, Unico, at prices vying with the fine wines of Bordeaux, and two younger wines, called Tinto Valbuena, more affordable though still expensive. Depending on the vintage (and vintages vary a lot in this extreme climate), the top Vega Sicilia wine may stay in large wooden vats and barrels new and old, French and American, for up to ten years before bottling: too long for many modern tastes, though the wine is so big and intense that such long wood-ageing fails to subdue it. Valbuena is rich, concentrated, complex wine, too, like a very good Rioja.

Above: *Alejandro Fernandez, producer of Tinto Pesquera, amidst year-old Tinto Fino vines. His prices soared when his wines made headlines in America.*

Down the road at Peñafiel is the region's other best known *bodega*, the co-operative Bodega Ribera Duero in a maze of tunnels below the town's imposing castle. Expensive as they are, the "better" wines of the *bodega*, the Reserva and Gran Reserva Protos, have been very unreliable, generally exhibiting a musty flavour from excessive ageing in the dank cellars. However, the young Vino Tinto, bottled the year after it is made, shows the fine potential of the co-operative members' grapes. It remains to be seen what improvements their first qualified winemaker will make following his recent appointment.

Less well known than these two famous

Above: The house at Ribera del Duero's most famous bodega, *Vega Sicilia. True to reputation, the wines are incredibly big, rich and intense in flavour.*

names are two excellent small family *bodegas*, Alejandro Fernandez and Pérez Pascuas, who have installed gleaming modern equipment and begun to make their wine in a modern way, with extremely good results. More wines aspiring to this standard are gradually coming to light, and will continue to do so over the next few years, as more producers wake up to modern methods.

Pick of Ribera del Duero

Vega Sicilia Fine estate growing the red Bordeaux varieties as well as Tinto Fino to make intense, complex wines with long wood ageing. Extremely expensive, long-lasting Vega Sicilia Unico, and expensive, also excellent, Valbuena Third and Fifth Year.

Alejandro Fernandez, Viña Pesquera High demand puts these fine, oaky, aromatic wines at steep prices. Crianza and Reserva, from Tinto Fino and a little Garnacha, are both very good.

Bodegas Victor Balbas Fairly small family firm, with vineyards of good Tinto del Pais, making some of their crop into elegant, oak-aged red wine.

Bodegas Mauro Excellent, rich red (soon to be included in the DO), made by the winemaker of Vega Sicilia.

Hermanos Pérez Pascuas, Viña Pedrosa Immaculate small family *bodega* with an excellent, light, aromatic Tinto Joven from Tinto Fino grapes with a little Cabernet, and delicious, perfumed, oaky Crianza. Good value.

Bodegas Vivaza As this family business bottles its wines in Rueda, its red Viña Irvina from Ribera del Duero is not entitled to the DO. It is quite rich, firm and plummy.

Yllera Though made in Ribero del Duero, the excellent, raspberry-fruity, attractively oaked reds are bottled outside the region, and so not yet allowed to bear the DO. The DO is soon to be extended to the west, however, taking in the bottling plant.

La Mancha

Heading south from Madrid across Spain's vast central plateau or *meseta*, surrounded for hundreds of kilometres by grain fields, olive groves and vines fading away into distant, flat horizons, it is easy to understand how the La Mancha region can yield 40 per cent of all Spain's wine. In the south-eastern part of the *meseta*, La Mancha sprawls over the four provinces of Cuidad Reál, Cuenca, Toledo and Albacete. La Mancha DO is Europe's biggest quality wine area, bigger than any other DO, AOC or DOC, yet the denominated sector of the region makes only a tenth of La Mancha's huge production.

The name Mancha comes from the Arabic for "dry", but despite its hot, arid summers, this is white wine country. Prop up any Madrid bar, and you will see the locals downing countless glasses of La Mancha's traditional produce, deep yellow, alcoholic and *rough*. In Britain and the USA, however, any bottle of La Mancha is likely to be new-style, pale, fresh, lower in alcohol (11.5° or 12°), bland but fruity – so long, that is, that the vintage is the most recent one, because these are wines that fade quickly.

This viticultural divide is just as plainly to be seen in the *bodegas*. On one side the old concrete Ali-Baba *tinaja* jars stretch from floor to ceiling, their narrow tops just protruding through to the second storey, and covered like jam pots with tie-on plastic caps. Alongside, temperature-controlled stainless steel vats, vacuum filters and modern bottling lines take up more space year by year.

It was not until 1979 that the first pioneer thought of chilling his fermenting wine to retain its freshness, and the modicum of aroma of which the uncharacterful Airén grape is capable. Now, a quarter of all the *Denominación de Origen* wine is made along modern lines – 75 million litres out of the total 3 million hectolitre DO La Mancha production. And the grapes for the new-style wines are picked in early September rather than being allowed, in the traditional way, to reach their maximum sugar potential in October before they are gathered.

The local authorities have had the foresight to help finance modern winemaking equipment and bottling lines – and in helping to promote the resulting lighter, fresher wines. With the equipment subsidised, there is a good price incentive; though still cheap, the new-style whites fetch much higher prices than the traditional brews.

La Mancha's whites, 90 per cent, that is, of all the wine made, are the product very largely of Airén grapes. The Airén is found in a

Key to map
1 Madrid.
2 Méntrida.
3 La Mancha.
4 Valdepeñas.
5 Almansa.

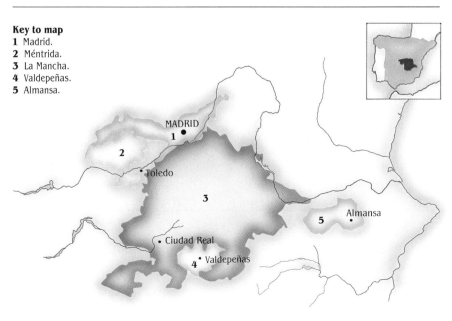

Pick of La Mancha

Bodegas Julian Santos Aguado Good, fresh whites and light, soft, fragrant reds called Don Fadrique.

Fermin Ayuso Roig Well-made, balanced whites and reds, Estola and Viña Q.

Co-operativa del Campo Nuestro Padre Jesus del Perdón Huge, half ancient, half modern. Fresh, fruity white Lazarillo, Yuntero and Casa La Teja are the best wines, surprisingly fragrant when young. Recent vintages of red Casa La Teja have also been good, soft and fruity.

Vinicola de Castilla Large *bodega*, one of Spain's most modern, formerly owned by Rumasa. Very well-made whites and reds Castillo de Alhambra and Señorio de Guadianeja. Best reds contain some Cabernet.

Co-operativa del Campo Nuestra Señora de Manjavacas Part old, part new vinification, all scrupulously clean. Good, light, fresh white and *rosado* Zagarron.

Rodriguez y Berger Part antique, part super-modern vinification. Good white Viña Santa Elena.

Above: *On the flat La Mancha plain the foliage of the low-pruned vines trails along the ground to provide shade for the grapes from the scorching sun.*

few of the surrounding provinces, but it is almost exclusive to La Mancha. Yet, because of La Mancha's vast expanse, it is the world's most planted variety, red or white. In volume terms, however, it comes nowhere near the top of the list. Because of the hot, dry climate, it produces some of the tiniest yields of any vines in the world. Controlled irrigation would give higher yields, but Spain forbids irrigation in her vineyards. The local solution has been to space the wines in a wide, square pattern (called Marco Reál), with 2.5 metres allowed between rows each way, and to prune the bushy vines in such a way that the vegetation hangs down close to the ground, shading the grapes from the blistering sun.

Fungal pests would go wild at such a prospect in most vineyards, but La Mancha is so dry that farmers rarely need to spray their vines against rot. Rainfall is very low, and usually confined to the months of March and April, and October to December. The temperature swoops from summer maxima of over 44°C to winter frosts of -22°C, because notwithstanding the continental climate, it must be remembered that this is high land despite its deceptive flatness.

The La Mancha DO also authorises three other minor white grape varieties, Macabeo (Viura), Pardilla and Verdoncho, as well as, for reds and *rosados*, the Cencibel, Garnacha and Moravia, though the Cencibel (alias Tempranillo) is by far the most frequently planted vine after the Airén.

As much as 60 per cent of La Mancha's wine is made in co-operatives, some of them enormous, but there are plenty of private *bodegas*, too, occasionally rivalling the co-operatives for size.

Valdepeñas

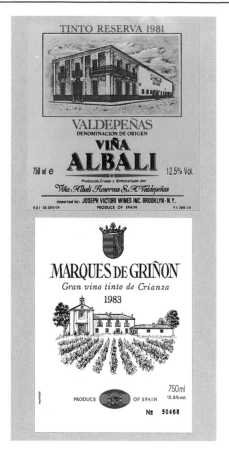

TINTO RESERVA 1981

VALDEPEÑAS
DENOMINACION DE ORIGEN

VIÑA
ALBALI

750 ml e · 12.5% Vol.

Producido, Criado y Embotellado por:
Viña Albali Reservas S.A. Valdepeñas

Imported by: JOSEPH VICTORI WINES INC. BROOKLYN · N.Y.
R.E./ 50.2015/CR · PRODUCE OF SPAIN · R E 2920-CR

MARQUES DE GRIÑON
Gran vino tinto de Crianza
1983

750ml
PRODUCE OF SPAIN 12.5%vol.
Nº 50468

V aldepeñas, an enclave of undulating land in the south of the flat La Mancha DO, grows principally the white Airén grape, like La Mancha, yet it is for its red wines that it is famed. Only around 15 per cent of the land is planted with red Cencibel, but the proportion is increasing, since only red grapes may now be replanted in the region. This was, in fact, a region of black grapes until the phylloxera louse devasted the vineyards at the beginning of the century.

Today, the red or *clarete* Valdepeñas that swamps the bars, restaurants and dining tables of Spain comes largely from *white* grapes, with about 20 per cent (the legal minimum) red Cencibel to provide the colour. Containing so much of the short-lived Airén, these *claretes* are wines for drinking young. So, too, are many of the actual *tintos*, deeper coloured reds, made in smaller quantities; for frequently these also contain a proportion of white wine, which fades quickly and detracts from the freshness of the red wine in the blend. However, most of the Valdepeñas exported to Britain and the USA is fuller-bodied, longer lasting wine made 100 per cent from the Cencibel. There are *rosados* and white wines, too, like those of La Mancha, but these are far less important in Valdepeñas than in the rest of the great La Mancha plain.

Prices are low in Valdepeñas, and the full-bodied, 100 per cent Cencibel reds are often very good value. Even the new wave of oak-aged Valdepeñas reds arrive on our shelves at very modest prices. Bodegas Los Llanos and Félix Solís in particular have impressive cellars for oak ageing. Their Reservas and Gran Reservas are excellent value, but from the other *bodegas*, stick to the young reds.

The many *bodegas* of Valdepeñas are clustered together in the main town of that name, which is undermined by over 200 cellars. The region was known as Valle de Peñas (Valley of Stones) in the 16th century. At between 600 and 705 metres above sea level, it has a similar, though not quite so extreme,

Below: *Lorries queue to have their loads weighed and sampled outside the Los Llanos bodega, where nearly a million kilos of grapes can be handled each day.*

climate as La Mancha, with little rain and temperatures in summer reaching 40°C, while in winter they may drop to -10°C. In the autumn heat, Valdepeñas grapes can easily reach a potential 15° of alcohol, but the better modern wines are now nearer 12.5°.

Almansa

Off to the east of La Mancha, Almansa has the same climate and soil, but grows the grape varieties of the Alicante and Valencia regions further to the east, along with a little of La Mancha's Cencibel. Three-quarters of the wines made are red. The principal red grape is the Garnacha Tintorera, also known as the Alicante, the only Spanish variety with red flesh. Monastrell is also a native of Almansa, and the best reds have a higher proportion of this grape. The whites, made from the Merseguera grape, are bland and dull.

Méntrida

Up on the La Mancha plain just to the north-east of the La Mancha DO area, Méntrida makes basic, dark, alcholic *rosados* and reds, often bitterly tannic, which end up as rough house wines in the bars of Madrid or, even more ignominiously, at the distillery. Reds are made mainly from the Garnacha (sometimes known here as the Aragonés), with a back-up of the common local grape Tinto Madrid and, increasingly, Cencibel, which is being introduced in an attempt to improve quality. Winter temperatures are less severe here than in the La Mancha DO, only dropping to just below freezing, but the summers are just as roastingly hot. The result is *rosado* wines of between 13° and 18° alcohol, and reds between 14° and 18°. The reds come in two basic styles, ordinary "*tinto*", and "*tinto doble pasta*", made by running off about half of the juice before fermentation begins, so that the double quantity of skins makes a darker, tougher, more concentrated wine.

Marqués de Griñon
The Marqués de Griñon estate, near Toledo on the La Mancha plain, turns out some of Spain's most exciting red wine. It is, however, not admissable within the current rules of the DO, as the Cabernet Sauvignon is not a permitted grape variety, the vines are trained on wires and they are irrigated. The young wine is currently sent for ageing in new wood to the *bodega* in Rueda that makes the Marqués de Griñon white wine.

Left: *The traditional clay or concrete tinajas, seen here at Bodegas Canaveras, are used for fermentation and storage.*

Pick of Valdepeñas, Almansa, and Toledo

Marqués de Griñon (non-DO) Immaculate modern estate making fine, rich, new-oak-aged Cabernet Sauvignon.

Bodegas Los Llanos (Valdepeñas) Sparklingly clean, well-equipped cellar with a lot of oak casks. Among the region's very best reds, especially strawberry-herby-tasting Gran Reserva, and good, fresh white Harmonioso.

Bodegas Félix Solís (Valdepeñas) Good producer with a lot of oak casks, making good reds under the brand name Viña Albalí.

Bodegas Luis Megía (Valdepeñas) Big-volume *bodega* making light, fresh, fruity whites; fresh, tangy *rosados*, and adequate reds (good when young), under the brand names Duque de Estrada, Marqués de Gastanaga and Monte Gaudio.

Bodegas Piqueras (Almansa) Small family concern making light, savoury Castillo de Almansa Crianza and a flavourful Gran Reserva.

Dionisio de Nova Morales Small-scale organic producer, making good, light, soft, fruity reds.

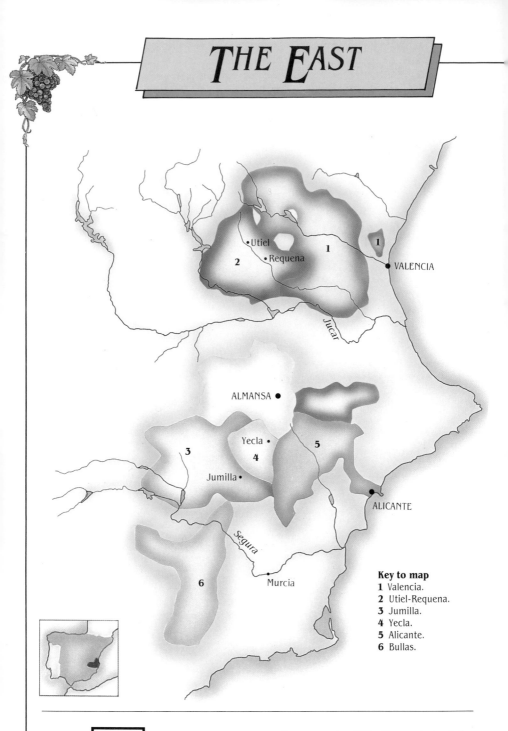

THE EAST

Key to map
1 Valencia.
2 Utiel-Requena.
3 Jumilla.
4 Yecla.
5 Alicante.
6 Bullas.

Valencia

The fact that four out of five of the main exporting Valencian wine *bodegas* have Swiss shareholders – two of them, Schenk and Egli, wholly Swiss-owned – is an indication of how the Swiss view the potential of the Valencian wine industry. Valencia is one of Spain's most important seaports, and the Valencians have been traders for generations. The Swiss appreciate the flexibility of the trading mentality. Locals sometimes compare their life-style with that of San Francisco in the USA, easy-going but innovative. With regard to wine, they do not seek to impose particular wine-styles on their customers, but try to interpret what the customer wants within the context of the wines of the region. On the whole, this means less experimentation with "foreign" grape varieties, and more technical expertise.

Most Valencia DO wine is white, usually dry and made from the Merseguera grape, an adequate rather than exciting variety. Some red wine is made, principally from the Garnacha and Garnacha Tintorera ("dyeing Garnacha" – so named because of its unusual red flesh), and from Monastrell in the south of the region. A decreasing amount of Moscatel is grown, too, sometimes to add aroma to dry Merseguera wines, sometimes made into lusciously sweet Moscatel de Valencia, a mixture of Moscatel grape juice with wine alcohol.

The DO region is divided into three separate areas, the most northerly and highest being the Upper Turia, at an average of 600 metres altitude, producing white Merseguera

C Augusto Egli Swiss company, with a modern *bodega* and a 150 hectare estate, Casa Lo Alto, high in the hills of Utiel-Requena, with plantings of nearly 40 varieties "foreign" to Valencia. Casa Lo Alto red is made from Cencibel and Garnacha, rich and meaty, with good strawberry fruit and a hint of new oak.

Vincente Gandía Pla Gandia's immaculate, new 600 million peseta *bodega* at Chiva, bristling with stainless steel and the latest technology, is the most impressive large winery in Spain. The Castello de Liria range has pleasant red and white, and excellent *rosado*.

Bodegas Schenk Swiss-owned (traditionally, the head of Schenk is the Swiss consul in Valencia), with pleasant Cavas Murviedro white, *rosado* and red *crianza*. Las Falleras red is a blend of herby Bobal rounded out by strawberry-like Cencibel fruit. San Terra is a strong, characterful red, made from Monastrell.

Cherubino Valsangiacomo Smallest of the *Grao* exporters, with a traditional *bodega*, filled with wooden vats. Arnoldo Valsangiacomo, Swiss national (but Valencia-born) head of the firm, is one of the most highly regarded wine dealers in the region. The Vall de Sant Jaume wines are all reliable, and the Marqués de Caro red, white and *rosado* among the best wines of the region.

Vinival Largest of the Valencia exporters, with well-equipped modern *bodega* just outside the Grao. Best of their Torres de Quart range is the soft and almondy *rosado*. Casa de Calderon is their up-market brand, with a fresh, lemony white and meaty, herby red. Their Vival d'Oro is a pleasant, light, sweet wine with a touch of fizz and real Moscatel fragrance.

wines with good levels of acidity. These are useful for blending with wines from Valencia's largest sub-area, Valentino, and Clariano, the Valencia DO's most southerly area, bordering the vineyards of Alicante.

Although much of the wine in Valencia is made in co-operatives, the export of Valencian wines is dominated by five large *bodegas*, Vinival, Vincente Gandía, Schenk, Egli and Valsangiacomo. In the past, these companies did their business in Valencia's *Grao* (Valencian for "port"), but most have moved out of the area as they have expanded and modernised. Gandía is the only one to have moved right away from the city, to a magnificent new *bodega* in Chiva. The group of exporters is a remarkably co-operative bunch. There cannot be many wine regions whose exporters have pooled resources to fund exhaustive market research into a new range of products destined for the USA, as the Valencians have done.

fragrant, as well as reds with a strong, herby character.

The five big Valencian exporters would love to see a Valencia DO that embraced all the DOs within the autonomous region of Valencia, since it makes no sense for them to invest in new bottling plants in either of the two little towns of Utiel and Requena, only 20km at most from their current bottling lines. (Without doing so, they are not entitled to the DO, under Spanish law.) Officialdom turns a blind eye to the fact that much Utiel-Requena wine is bottled as Valencia DO.

Alicante

Most of Alicante's vineyard areas lie well back from the coast, in the hills of the Upper Vinalopo, adjoining Yecla in the neigbouring autonomous region of Murcia. With the exception of the sweet Moscatel wines made from grapes grown in La Marina, (an area including several miles of coastline about 30km north of Benidorm), most Alicante wine is red, made from the Monastrell variety, and usually highly-coloured with lots of alcohol. A little white wine is made from Merseguera and Airén grapes.

Utiel Requena

Whether or not the label on a bottle of *rosado* or red wine made in the autonomous region of Valencia says "Utiel-Requena DO", that is where the wine is likely to have come from. The principal variety of this remote, mountainous region (average altitude 720 metres) is the Bobal, which can make one of the best *rosados* in Spain, light, fresh and

The local curiosity is Fundillon, a liqueur Monastrell, with at least 16 per cent alcohol (sometimes aged in *solera* for up to ten years before bottling), which is one of Spain's best *rancios*, full of nutty, toffee'd flavour.

Yecla

To the west of the highest part of the Alicante DO lies the region of Yecla, at an average altitude of 650 metres. Life for owners of the chalky, stony vineyards here is hard: yields are among the lowest in Spain, and the prices for what grapes they *do* manage to grow make it hardly worth their while to tend the vines at all. Not surprisingly, the vineyard area is shrinking. Most wine is high alcohol, low acid red, made from Monastrell, though there is some white wine, made from Merseguera and Verdil.

The DO is dominated by two producers, the Co-operativa La Purisima and Bodegas Ochoa, a company that also has interests in Alicante. The level of export is remarkably high, with Ochoa exporting 90 per cent of its production, much of it in bulk.

Jumilla

It hardly rained at all in Jumilla between 1982 and 1986, but on our last winter visit, there was a rare morning of downpour, which turned the streets of the little town of Jumilla into rivers, and left black dots of leafless vines in the plain looking like birds that had settled on the ground in startlingly regular formations.

Usually in winter, the dusty vine-stumps blend into the background, hardly showing against the sun-bleached soil of the plains. Many of the vines have never been grafted on to American rootstocks, and whole areas of vineyard have been dying of phylloxera. Now, however, grants are available from the EEC to renew the vineyards with grafted vines. Some producers think this may change the character of the typical Jumilla wines, almost all strong, dark reds made from the Monastrell grape (a little white is made from Airén, Merseguera and Pedro Ximénez, and *rosado* from Monastrell). A change might not be a bad thing from a commercial point of view, since lighter wines are more fashionable both in Spain and abroad. Not that Jumilla has ever really had problems in selling its wine. But much of the trade has been in bulk, and producers are keen to upgrade profitability by shipping wine in bottle.

The locals are emphatic that their region is an excellent one for vines. Apparently, two French companies have recently bought vineyards in Jumilla. The only problems have been the lack of rain and old-fashioned vinification methods. The first of these is unlikely to change, but winemaking in Jumilla has improved dramatically, and several of the large producers have enough refrigeration equipment to cool-ferment a large proportion of their wines.

Jumilla reds have always been popular as blending wines for other wine-producing countries in less sunny parts of Europe because of their high alcohol, deep colour and concentration of flavour. Switzerland, Austria, West Germany and Hungary remain faithful customers, as do the wine producers of Galicia in the north-west of Spain. Jumilla even did good business with some Bordeaux companies in 1987 after a disappointing Bordeaux vintage.

Particularly popular for beefing up feeble reds are the *vinos de doble pasta* (double-pulp wines). This is a style of wine that has evolved in all the regions of Spain's Levante, and is strictly for blending, not drinking. The process is basically the same in Jumilla as in Yecla, Utiel-Requena and Alicante, where *tinto doble pasta* wines are also made. First the crushed grapes are macerated for two days. Then between 50 and 60 per cent of the juice is run off (to be made into ordinary red wine). More crushed grapes are added to

Pick of Yecla and Jumilla

Bodegas Bleda, Jumilla Wine comes from a well-equipped, new winery (INDUVASA) in which Señor Bleda has a third share. The Castillo Jumilla range is modern and well-made, with a fresh, fruity Airén white, an almondy, redcurranty *rosado*, and a rich, strawberry-fruity, herby *crianza* Monastrell red.

Bodegas Ascensio Carcelen, Jumilla Experimental plantations of over 30 foreign grape varieties on over 1,000 hectares of own vineyard. All ageing is done in oak vats, though fermentation is temperature-controlled. Acorde Blanco Semi-Seco is made from Airén, Riesling and Pedro Ximénez, clean and fresh, with fruity perfume. Con Sello red is half Cencibel, half Monastrell, with herby, liquoricey flavour. Sol y Luna (Sun and Moon) is a delicious liqueur Monastrell, with 15° of alcohol, a rich, vanilla nose, and flavour of vanilla and coconut.

Bodegas Ochoa, Yecla Recently revitalised private company run by former technical director of Co-operativa La Purisima. Reds are best, Barahonda, rich and curranty; Cuvée Prestige, soft, plummy and pruney; and Vino Tinto Ochoa, rich with strawberry fruit and vanilla oak.

Bodegas Juvinsa, Jumilla Family-owned company with good reds under various labels: Pedro Gil Tinto is young, fruity and curranty, and Incunable is oaky, with round, cherry and berry fruit.

SAVIN, Jumilla Second largest winemaking plant of SAVIN, Spain's largest producer. Señorío de Robles *Rosado* and Tinto are light and fresh.

Co-operativa San Isidro, Jumilla Spain's *largest* co-operative (and third largest in Europe), with a huge *bodega* built in 1976. A financial crisis caused real problems in 1982, but things are better now, though the gigantic winery is still not working at full capacity. Best wine is Casa Alta Vino Nuevo, with young cherry fruit, Jumilla's answer to Beaujolais.

Co-operativa La Purisima, Yecla Fourth largest co-operative in Spain, making wine and olive oil. Most wine is kept too long before sale, but CALP Reserva Tinto has good, rich, figgy fruit.

bring the total volume back to the original level, and the fermentation is allowed to start. With a much higher ratio of skins to juice than would normally be the case, the resulting wines are *very* deep in colour, with extremely high tannin and acidity.

Below: *A neatly pruned vineyard in Jumilla, after a rare late winter downpour. Many of Jumilla's vines have never been grafted on to American rootstock, and whole areas of vineyard have been dying of phylloxera.*

Condado de Huelva

Twenty years ago, the sherry country's north-westerly neighbour, Condado de Huelva, sold a good half of its produce to the *bodegas* of Jerez, whence it would re-emerge as sherry. But demand from the east has all but died over the last couple of decades. The farmers of Huelva have resourcefully turned at least part of their attentions to other crops: the province grew 130 million kilos of strawberries in 1987, and more strawberries, sugar beet, grain and olives are still replacing vineyards, so weak is the demand nowadays for the traditional sherry-style Condado wines.

Sensibly, too, some of the region's grapes are being turned into a new product: light, simple, fruity white wines. Condado de Huelva was the first Andalucian *Denominación de Origen* in 1979 to admit young white table wines. In the early 1980s, a small group of private *bodegas* got together to set up a high-tech winery, the Sociedad de Vinos del Condado, to make modern, fresh table wine. And in 1986, the biggest co-operative, in the large town of Bollullos, equipped itself with modern presses, vacuum filters and computer-controlled cooled fermentation tanks to join the action.

Making light, fresh wines in Condado is no easy matter. The grapes have to be picked a month earlier than normal, in the first few days of September and transported gently in small plastic crates. The producers suffer not only from the usual hot-country problems, but their main grape, the bland-flavoured Zalema, easily oxidises and spoils unless extreme care is taken. The Zalema used to occupy over 90 per cent of space in the vineyards, but, where it has not given way to strawberries, it has now often been replaced by Palomino Fino (known here as Listán) so that it currently accounts for only about 75 per cent. (There is also a little Moscatel, Garrido Fino and Palomino de Jerez.)

Neither the Zalema's blandness nor its tendency to oxidise are a problem if the Zalema is to be turned into the *oloroso*-style Condado Viejo. Made just like a dry *oloroso* sherry, but much less intensely nutty and complex, these must have between 15° and 23° of alcohol, and may be sold dry to sweet *(seco, semiseco, demidulce or dulce)*. As in Jerez, *flor* grows on the more lightly fortified barrels of Condado wine, turning it into a rather fatter style of *fino* than the Jerez versions. Until recently, however, the producers of "Condado Palido", as the local version of *flor*-affected wine is called, were prohibited from calling their wines *fino*, as by law this could be used only for Jerez wines. But in 1985, a Condado producer successfully argued in the High Court that *fino* is a

Above: *Cork trees recently stripped of their bark. The type of oak that produces cork bark is found from western Andalucía right up through Extremadura as far as Toledo and Salamanca; it grows even more extensively in southern Portugal. The bark can be cut off every nine or ten years, and a cork tree can be expected to live for up to 200.*

generic name, and can be used to describe *flor*-affected wines from anywhere in Spain. In Condado, *finos* must have between 14° and 17° of alcohol. All the fortified wines must age for a minimum of two years in oak casks, a year less than the minimum in Jerez.

Apart from producing similar wines, Condado de Huelva's climate is much like that of Jerez, including (for Spain) quite high rainfall. Its soil is rich in calcium (not the whiter-than-white *albariza*, but with a higher content of sand and clay) – and therefore capable of fairly high yields, if not quite as

exceptional as those of Jerez. Its vineyards are much more traditional, however, pruned into wide-spaced, straggly bushes.

Much of the winemaking is as primitive as the vineyards. Whereas in Jerez only 30 per cent of the winemaking is done in co-operatives, here the figure is 85 per cent, as most of the grape-farmers are small-holders. Much of the co-operatives' equipment is antique. Until recently, the 19 co-operatives sold all their wine in bulk, either to *bodegas* outside the region or to the private maturation *bodegas* in Condado itself, whose produce is very mixed in quality. Touring the town, you might fall one minute upon a well-run, small *bodega* complete with neat *soleras* and modern bottling equipment, the next into a scruffy courtyard housing mules, Ali-Baba jars festooned with drying onions and garlic, and some of the world's filthiest casks, pipes and filters.

Fortunately for the future of the region's wine, the Bollullos co-operative has suddenly launched itself into modern winemaking, and it accounts for as much as 65 per cent of all the co-operative wine of Condado. Though they still make 140,000 hectolitres a year of old-style wine, warm-fermented in *tinajas* and still mostly sold in bulk, they now make 30,000 hectolitres of fresh, light, fruity wine at a mere 11.5° of alcohol, as opposed to the region's more typical 14° mind-blowers.

Extremadura

A lot of wine is made in Extremadura, alongside the Portuguese border, but very little is ever bottled under its own name for the simple reason that the quality is almost universally execrable. There are no DOs, and a large part of the production goes to brandy distillers. Most of the wines are made in Badajoz in the south of the region, north of Huelva, where highly fertile soil brings huge yields. Just ten per cent of the region's wines are made in ancient, run-down vineyards in the area round the city of Cáceres. Apart from PX, Viura, Garnacha, Tempranillo and Mazuela, the Extremadura region grows a variety of obscure grapes. The results are big, coarse, alcoholic white wines and tannic and astringent reds.

Pick of Condado de Huelva

Sociedad de Vinos del Condado Pleasant, fresh, fruity white Viñaodiel – excellent by local standards.

Vinicola del Condado Good, fresh white (top of range) Privilegio del Condado and quite good Par de Condado.

Villarán Small private maturation *bodega* with good examples of the region's fortified wines, especially their Oloroso Solera 34, fairly dry, nutty, rich and pleasantly austere, available only in Spain in Corte Ingles department stores.

Jerez-Xérès-Sherry

Travellers to the sun-drenched south will be surprised to learn that the rain in Spain falls more than anywhere else upon the town of Grazalema, just 30 kilometres from the borders of the Jerez region. Jerez itself has a much higher average annual rainfall than Rioja. The sherry country's vast expanses of chalky-white vineyards and sunflower fields may *look* dry and dusty in the summer heat, but take a spade to them, and modestly hard digging will reveal moisture.

Jerez's rain falls from autumn through to spring, carried inland by south-westerly winds from the Atlantic. It falls on to vineyards broken up and ploughed in such a way that the water soaks in rather than washing down the gentle slopes. The *albariza* (predominantly chalky) soil and sub-rock has remarkable, sponge-like qualities, and holds the water in reserve for the long, hot summer. Summer sea dew also helps the grapes to mature.

The results are the same for sunflowers as for grapes: enormous yields. Jerez tops Spain's grape production figures. The main grape, the Palomino Fino, is a very productive grape anyway, and the abundance of subterranean water and sunshine (but temperatures of never over 40°C in July and August) accomplishes the rest, even with fairly strict pruning. The region's best vineyards, 70 per cent of the total and classified as Jerez Superior, are allowed to produce up to 80 hectolitres per hectare, the rest, known as Jerez Zona, as much as 100.

Nine towns and villages fall within the sherry production area, but over half the vineyards are planted on the gently undulating land around Jerez itself. Most of those are on the crumbly-white *albariza* soil, which contains between 60 and 80 per cent chalk – the chalkiest soils produce the finest, most elegant wines – and which ripens the grapes more thoroughly by reflecting light up from below. (The other constituents of *albariza* soil are sand and clay). The other two famous sherry towns of Sanlúcar de Barrameda and Puerto de Santa María are on flatter land by the sea, Sanlúcar also blindingly white with *albariza*, plus a little of the two inferior soil

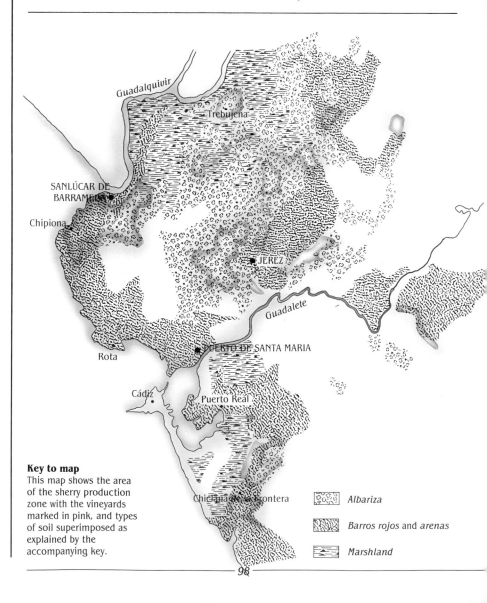

Key to map
This map shows the area of the sherry production zone with the vineyards marked in pink, and types of soil superimposed as explained by the accompanying key.

Albariza

Barros rojos and arenas

Marshland

Above: *Huge advertising signs are a common sight on the hilltops and roadsides of the Jerez region. Tio Pepe is by far the biggest-selling* fino.

Above: *In the autumn, Jerez's vineyards are ploughed into steps, which catch the winter rain so that it soaks in rather than washing down the slopes.*

types, *barros rojos* (up to 30 per cent chalk) and *arenas* (sandy soil with only ten per cent chalk); Puerto de Santa María lies mostly on *barros rojos* and *arenas* by the sea, with a little *albariza* further inland.

Whichever town they are in, the sherry *bodegas* are allowed to use grapes from throughout the sherry region. A wine qualifies as a *manzanilla* by having been *matured* in Sanlúcar, not because it was grown in the surrounding vineyards. The *bodegas* own about a third of the sherry vineyards themselves; another third is owned by small-scale co-operative members, the remainder by farmers large and small who sell directly to the *bodegas*.

It is principally these independent farmers who have been responsible for an enormous and much-needed reduction in land under vine in the last few years. By the mid-'eighties, the *bodegas* were so awash with wine as a result of over-production and fall-

ing demand that prices were being squeezed to suicidally low levels. A combination of market forces and grants stepped in to encourage farmers to uproot their vines and plant other crops instead – sunflowers, sugar beet and wheat. It was more often than not the larger-scale farmers with mixed farms, often, sadly, on *albariza* soil, who made the switch: many of them began to grow grapes only in the sherry boom years of the 'seventies and to tear them up was no great sentimental wrench. Growers with tiny patches of land, often cultivated at weekends after a working week in the *bodegas* or factories, were far more attached to their land and have stuck to their vines, even though many of these small plots are on the poorer *barros* and *arenas* types of soils.

Jerez is well ahead of most of Spain in the modernisation of its vineyards. Practically all vines planted since the mid-'sixties are trained on wires, with a high density of vines per hectare in line with modern trends, rather than the widely-spaced systems often misguidedly preferred in other parts of Spain. Many *bodegas* invest in and safeguard the quality of the grapes supplied to them on long-term contracts by providing growers and farmers with rootstocks, trellising and any necessary herbicides, as well as advice and regular vineyard news bulletins. The quality of the vines themselves has improved. Two strains of Palomino used to be grown extensively in Jerez, Palomino Fino and the coarser Palomino de Jerez, but Palomino Fino now accounts for 98.5 per cent of all Palomino in the area. Both Palominos together make up 93 per cent of all vines grown, with four per cent Pedro Ximénez (PX) and three per cent Moscatel. Healthier plants and wiring have, however, increased yields still more, resulting in wines lower in alcohol at their ripest than used to be the case, so that more fortification is necessary once the wines are made.

The English-speaking world understands the terms *amontillado* and *oloroso* quite differently from the natives of the sherry towns. In Jerez, both are bone dry, but for the export markets, the convention has grown up that *amontillado* means medium dry, *oloroso* dark and sweet.

There may be little or (more likely) no real *amontillado* sherry in a medium dry branded version of that name. It takes eight years for sherry to turn into the real thing, and by that time it would be too expensive for the price tag customers expect to pay for the familiar sweetened sherries. Medium dry "*amontillado*" sherries tend to be blends of cheap, second-rate *finos* with fairly young and therefore cheap *oloroso*-style wines, sweetened up with fortified Palomino grape juice. Basic sweet *olorosos* are young *oloroso*-style wines sweetened with PX, a dark *mistela* made by fortifying the syrupy juice from Pedro Ximénez raisins, and they are sometimes also darkened with *vino de color* – boiled-up, caramelised grape juice. These wines might also be labelled "cream" or very occasionally "*amoroso*".

Pale creams have emerged as a new, popular trend of the past decade. They are made

Above: *Most of Jerez's vineyards are gently sloping or on the flat. This is an example of the best* albariza *soil.*

Below: *Home of* manzanilla; *the seaside town of Sanlúcar de Barrameda, cooler and more humid than inland Jerez.*

The Authentic Sherry Styles

Manzanilla	Delicate, pale, dry sherry matured in the seaside town of Sanlúcar de Barrameda under a thicker veil of *flor* than is found in the other two sherry towns. The result is a finer, crisper, more pungent and aromatic wine in the *fino* style, sometimes called *manzanilla fina*. By law, its alcohol should be between 15.5° and 17°, and it should be at least three years old, but it is generally sold older. Best chilled. (Beware if ordering in other parts of Spain: *manzanilla* also means camomile tea.)
Manzanilla pasada	After about seven years' ageing, a *manzanilla's flor* gradually dies, and the wine gains in strength, slowly turning amber and taking on some of the characteristics of dry *amontillado*, yet maintaining its crisp, aromatic and slightly pungent character. This is the Sanlúcar equivalent of the *fino amontillado* of the other sherry towns. The final stage of maturity is called *manzanilla amontillada*.
Fino	Light, elegant, pungent, pale wine matured under a veil of *flor* in towns of Jerez and Puerto de Santa María. The latter may be labelled *fino del Puerto* and may be slightly lighter in style than *fino de Jerez*. Best served chilled.
Fino amontillado	*Fino* that has slowly lost its *flor* after about six years and gradually turned amber-coloured, slightly nutty-flavoured, and more alcoholic.
Amontillado	The next stage of *fino* maturation after *fino amontillado*, a deeper amber, richer and nuttier than *fino amontillado*, though still with something of the pungent tang left by the *flor*.
Oloroso	Oloroso in Spanish means richly fragrant, not the sharp, pungent fragrance imparted by *flor*, but a rich, nutty, raisiny aroma. These are strong, dry sherries, ranging from dark gold to a deep brown as they age. They are fortified to too high a degree before maturation for the *flor* yeast to grow on their surface, and they thus never have the sharp pungency of *flor* sherries, but they can be just as impressive.
Palo Cortado	Just as *bodegas* differ on the dividing line between a *fino amontillado* and an *amontillado*, the precise nature of a *palo cortado* varies according to its assessor. In theory, it is a wine that started out as a *fino*, completed its maturation under *flor* and began to develop quite normally as an *amontillado*, then veered off towards the more richly, fragrantly oxidised style of an *oloroso*, while still retaining the elegance of an *amontillado*. In colour and alcohol content, it should be similar to an *oloroso*. However, one *bodega's palo cortado* might easily have been classified by a neighbouring *bodega* as an *amontillado*. Among sherry connoisseurs, this style is in great demand – an incentive for producers to stretch their imaginations.
Pedro Ximénez and Moscatel	Extremely sweet, dark, syrupy wines, low in alcohol, made from raisins of these two grape varieties. Rare, and more often used for blending than for drinking straight.

by sweetening fairly young, cheap *finos* with pale grape juice concentrate or even, as was common in the earlier days of pale creams, with ordinary liquid sugar.

Even some brands of *finos*, authentically bone dry, are slightly sweetened to soften their austere edge. Supermarkets are particularly prone to sweeten their *finos*, though not all do. But most branded *finos* on the export markets are completely dry, as in Jerez.

The sad fact is that these basic, low-priced sherries rarely offer more than a hint of in-teresting flavour. The quality of some is appalling, though their sweetness helps them go down. Among the lower-priced sherries, *manzanillas* and *finos* can be the exception: even though sometimes astonishingly cheap, they may have piercingly tangy, pungent flavours, and can be excellent value.

It is surprising, too, that really fine dry *amontillados* and *olorosos* often cost little more than the cheap, sweetened brands. You simply do not find sherry at extortionate prices.

*P*ractically all the sherry we see in export markets comes from the big *bodegas* in the three towns authorised to mature sherry: Jerez inland, and the glistening white seaside towns of Sanlúcar de Barrameda and Puerto de Santa María. A *bodega* must have a minimum of 1,000 hectolitres of sherry ageing under its roofs to qualify for the *Denominación* of sherry or, in the case of Sanlúcar, *manzanilla*. The biggest *bodegas* are concentrated in Jerez itself, with just a few large ones in the seaside towns. Until the Spanish government confiscated the vast sherry empire of the Rumasa group in 1980 for fraud and malpractices, nearly half the *bodegas* belonged to the group. Now the companies have been sold off to the private sector.

Apart from sherries of the big companies, a few fine *almacenista* sherries have made their way abroad in recent years, shipped by the firm of Emilio Lustau. *Almacenistas* are tiny to small-scale wine maturers who buy in young wine from small producers or co-operatives, age it and generally sell it to the big *bodegas* for blending, though selling perhaps ten per cent direct to local wine connoisseurs, who bring their own containers and draw straight from the butt. To register

Below: *Domecq's El Alcade vineyard which is some 8 kilometres north-west of the town of Jerez. Half of Jerez's* *vineyards are planted, like these, on wires in closely-spaced rows, and cultivated with tractors.*

and trade as an *almacenista*, one needs 200 barrels, but the average is 300, and some have 1,500 or more. Years ago, when the *bodegas* used to buy large quantities of mature wine rather than making and maturing it themselves, the sherry region was bursting with *almacenistas*. Today, there remain no more than 50, and most of the owners employ people to run their *bodegas* while getting on with some other principal profession. The owners of the biggest *almacenista bodegas* include doctors, builders, a pharmacist, a cattle breeder, a land owner, a tax specialist and the head of one of Spain's largest printing firms.

Emilio Lustau's ingenious idea was to sell these delicious, often extraordinarily complex, individual wines unblended, as the produce of a single butt. They may be labelled with a fraction such as 1/5 or 2/8 – indicating that the sherry has been bottled from one butt out of five or two out of eight bought by Lustau from a particular *almacenista*, whose name will also be on the bottle. These, along with the small-scale top blends of a few of the major *bodegas*, are the sherry country's finest wines, yet still a very affordable snip for the consumer, and especially so compared with the prestige wines of other famous wine regions of the world.

Pick of Sherries

Antonio Barbadillo (Not to be confused with Bobadilla.) Superb *bodega* in Sanlúcar, sharing a super-modern fermentation *bodega* with Harveys out in the vineyards. Excellent, delicate Manzanilla Fina, and Eva, and Fino de Balbaina; Principe, a delicate, nutty-tangy *manzanilla amontillada*; salty-nutty Solear Manzanilla Pasada; salty-honeyed, rich but lean Oloroso Seco; and sweet but elegant Sanlúcar Cream, made from real raisiny-savoury, aged sherry.

Luis Caballero Family firm in Puerto. Burdons Heavenly Cream Rich Old Oloroso, sweet, raisiny wine backed up by really good, raisiny, nutty old sherry.

Delgado Zuleta Old family company in Sanlúcar with good, almondy La Goya Manzanilla Pasada and serious, concentrated, nutty-salty Amontillado Fino Zuleta.

Diez Merito One of the biggest sherry companies. Very good, oily-flavoured, austerely tangy, well-aged Don Zoilo Fino; very rich, nutty and saltily concentrated Victoria Regina Oloroso.

Domecq One of the biggest selling, yet one of the very finest *finos*, La Ina; elegant, dry, austere Botaina Amontillado Viejo.

Garvey Large Jerez company with very good San Patricio Fino. Rich, nutty Palo Cortado and wonderfully treacly, raisiny Pedro Ximénez.

Gonzalez Byass The biggest selling, yet one of the very best *finos*, Tio Pepe, comes from this huge *bodega*. Also excellent top range Mathúsalem Oloroso Muy Viejo, big, deep, pruny *oloroso* sweetened with PX; Apostoles Oloroso Viejo, medium-dry, nutty and grapy; and Amontillado del Duque Seco y Muy Viejo, a fine, *dry*, austere wine, nutty and pungent.

Harveys Very large, British-owned company. Good light, tangy *fino* Tio Mateo; full, soft, nutty-savoury *oloroso*-style "1796" Palo Cortado; and slightly sweetened, lighter, curranty-nutty "1796" Fine Old Amontillado.

Hidalgo Family firm in Sanlúcar making sherries only from their own vineyards. Fine, salty, softly nutty but concentrated Manzanilla Pasada; softly concentrated, nutty Jerez Cortado.

Emilio Lustau Excellent quality, often own-label wines for supermarkets etc. Exciting range of *almacenista* sherries from single butts of top quality wines. Under the Emilio Lustau label, very good, rich, nutty Dry Oloroso Solera Reserva "Don Nuño" and excellent, bone-dry Principe Pio Very Rare Oloroso with salty-nutty richness.

La Riva Small *bodega* with very good, austere Fino Tres Palmas.

Sandeman Owned by international giants Seagram. Lovely, pungent, hazelnutty, honeyed Bone Dry Old Amontillado; soft, concentrated, richly walnutty Dry Old Palo Cortado; dark, savoury Dry Old Oloroso.

de Soto Good Fino Soto.

Tomás Abad Subsidiary of Emilio Lustau, making excellent *fino*.

Valdespino Old fashioned, top quality family *bodega*. Excellent *fino* Inocente; *oloroso*-style Palo Cortado Cardenal, packed with flavour; dry, dark, powerful Amontillado Coliseo; magnificent, dry, concentratedly nutty-tangy Don Tomás Amontillado; complex, malty, raisiny, fairly sweet Don Gonzalo Old Dry Oloroso; wonderfully dense, concentrated demerara-and-raisins flavoured Pedro Ximénez Solera Superior.

Williams & Humbert Fine, dry, nutty Dos Cortados Very Old Dry Oloroso.

Montilla-Moriles

Montilla has set itself up in Britain (its main market) as poor man's sherry. It may even be cheaper than the sorry brews sold as "British sherry". Montilla is able to undercut the Jerez competition for several reasons, but largely because the type of Montilla sold in Britain is unfortified (though made otherwise in a sherry-like way) and is classed for duty purposes as a light wine (under 15°), so avoiding the higher duty sherry pays. Besides the saving on duty, there is no fortifying alcohol to buy, the grapes are cheaper and the wine is aged for a shorter period.

The wealthy Jerez neighbours have given Montilla producers a hard time over the years. They succeeded for a while in preventing Montilla from using the terms "*fino*", "*oloroso*" and even "*amontillado*" (which originally meant "made in the style of Montilla"). After a series of law suits, Montilla has now retrieved its rights to these terms, but only for *finos* over 15°, and *amontillado* and *oloroso* over 16°. Montilla is therefore sold in Britain as Montilla Dry, Medium or Sweet (Cream), though it appears (fortified) as "*fino*" etc in the USA, Canada and other export markets where duty is less prohibitive.

The new DO regulations of 1985 make a clear distinction between two categories of "light" wines and the strong, wood-aged wines. The first category of light wines is made from early-picked Pedro Ximénez grapes, cold fermented to an alcoholic degree of between 10° and 12°, and with no wood ageing. (So far such wines have been unimpressive.) The second is the British style of Montilla, wood-aged wine of natural strength of 13° and over.

Only around half the Montilla-Moriles wines are fortified, but the unfortified wines are quite strong enough to be made into a sherry style. The baking-hot climate of the production area south of Cordoba produces sweeter grapes than those of Jerez, making wines with a higher natural degree of alcohol (typically 14.5° compared with 11° in Jerez) and, once mature, a more raisiny, less complex flavour.

The main grape here is not the Palomino, but the Pedro Ximénez (PX). Also grown are the Lairén (the Airén of La Mancha, to the north), Moscatel, Baladí (a local grape) and the Torrontes of Galicia. Montilla has been and still is to a certain extent an important supplier of Pedro Ximénez to Malaga, and to Jerez, where it grows less successfully but is needed as a sweetening wine.

As in Jerez, Montilla-Moriles' finest, most delicate wines are grown on white, chalky soil, known here not as *albariza* but *albero*. It is found on two patches of undulating, higher ground called the Sierra de Montilla (or Montilla Albero) and Moriles Alto (or

Above: *Checking the specific gravity of wine fermenting in the traditional* tinajas *at the Alvear* bodega.

Above: *A cellar worker at Alvear pumps wine out of one stage of the* solera *system ready for feeding into the next.*

Pick of Montilla-Moriles

(In Britain, most Montilla-Moriles is sold under supermarket names.)

Alvear Montilla's biggest producer and exporter, a modern *bodega*.

Carbonell Well-equipped *bodega*, also a major producer of olive oil. Good Fino. Honeyed, buttery Moriles Solera Fina with soft, salty *flor* character.

Gracia Hermanos Company making wines of unusual style and concentration for Montilla, including really nutty Medium Dry and Cream.

Moriles Albero), around the town of Montilla and the small village of Moriles. Heavier, fuller wines are made from grapes from the lower-lying, sandy *Ruedos*, surrounding these two "Montilla Superior" areas. (*Ruedos* is also a name given to fortified Montilla-Moriles wines that have not undergone ageing. They can be sold as DO if mixed with a minimum ten per cent aged wine, resulting in a minimum 14° of alcohol.)

Wines from Moriles are generally much lighter and more elegant than those of Montilla, with greater depth and length of flavour. It is rare to find Moriles sold unblended in export markets, however, though one British supermarket chain now sells it. It is sold in Spain in dark brown hock-type bottles, whereas Montilla or a Montilla-Moriles blend is sold in sherry-type bottles.

Finos are ideally made from the *albero* grapes, the first, free-run juice being reserved for *finos*, the following pressings for *olorosos*. The wine-making processes are the same as in Jerez (see pages 24-29), except that it is not always necessary to fortify the young wines. However, fortified Montilla-Moriles *finos* can reach 17.5°, *amontillados* 22.5°, and *olorosos* 20°, particularly if they are very old wines.

The finer wines, destined to be *finos*, are aged in partly-filled casks and kept fairly cool, between 15 and 18°C, to encourage the growth of *flor* yeasts on the surface of the wine. The casks containing the heavier *olorosos*-to-be are completely filled and kept in warmer conditions. Ageing here for fortified wines is for a minimum of two years, through a system of *criaderas* and *soleras* as in Jerez. But the wines that are sold to Britain only have to be aged for a minimum of a year. For export, both wood-aged categories of wines are then generally sweetened with varying quantities of concentrated grape juice.

Though exports of Montilla have recently been rising healthily, cashing in on low price, supply still far exceeds demand in Montilla-Moriles, to the extent that over half the production goes for blending or distillation. As elsewhere, one solution has been a partial switch to young, light table wines. Thousands of acres have also recently been taken out of production and turned over to bush olives or cereals with the aid of local and EEC subsidies, and 600 hectares of ancient, ailing vineyard have been replanted with healthy new vines.

Below: *Barrels of* oloroso-*style Montilla ageing in the heat outside the Alvear* bodega. *The finer wines,* finos *and* amontillados, *are kept cool inside.*

Málaga

*M*álaga is among the down-and-outs of Spain's wines. Towards the end of the last century, when the Málaga (or Mountain) market flourished in Britain, Russia and Eastern Europe, the region could boast 112,000 hectares of vineyard and an annual production of 30 million litres. Now it makes only six million litres, far less than many individual *bodegas* in other parts of Spain, and of 16,000 hectares still under vine, only about 3,000 hectares grow grapes for winemaking.

Málaga was never properly replanted after the vineyards were devastated by the phylloxera vine louse late last century, but its decline was sealed by the loss of the important Eastern Bloc markets, and more recently by the worldwide disfavour with heavy, sweet, high alcohol drinks. Most of the few companies that remain in Málaga find it hard to break even on the low prices they are able to charge – with the exception of the huge gin company of Larios, with its tiny Málaga sideline, and López Hermanos, whose lighter,

Below: *Picking PX in vineyards near Mollina in the hot inland district of Antequera. Most of the big* bodegas *make their base wines in a jointly-owned* bodega *not far from here.*

uncomplex style of Málagas are still popular in Spain, where they are promoted with the aid of heavy advertising.

Despite the declining sales, the principal grape of Málaga wine, the Pedro Ximén (PX – the Pedro Ximénez of Jerez), is in short supply, and the local authorities have permitted ten per cent of a *bodega*'s wine to be bought in from Montilla-Moriles, a little way to the north.

The problem has been aggravated by a gradual replacement over recent years of Pedro Ximén grapes by the neutral-flavoured Lairén (the Airén of La Mancha, also known here as Vidueño). In the Málaga vineyards, the Lairén can produce three times the yield of Pedro Ximén, and PX prices do not make it worth the farmers' while. Theoretically, Lairén grapes are not permitted in the Málaga

Pick of Málaga

Scholtz Hermanos Best for rich, characterful Málagas: Málaga Semi-Dulce, rich, intense and black treacly; Málaga Dulce Negro, very dark, complex, and sweetly treacly; Lágrima Delicioso, an extraordinary mix of pungent, raisiny, treacly and nutty flavours; and Solera 1885, fine, intense, raisiny and nutty.

Larios Spain's largest gin distiller has a small Málaga *bodega*. Best of their wines is Seco Benefique, fairly dry, nutty with reasonable concentration.

DO, but they *are* being used (some unscrupulous firms even buying Airén from La Mancha). There is a proposal before the government of Andalucía that they should join with the EEC to subsidise a PX replanting programme, and, for speed, the grafting of PX vines on to established Lairén roots.

The other grape permitted for production of Málaga is the Moscatel Fino. The small amount of Moscatel used for wine comes from smallholders and co-operatives in the rugged, precipitously steep hills of the coastal Axarquia district in the south-east, with its mild, Mediterranean climate. The PX grows in hotter country inland to the north-east, on slightly undulating land bordering the plateau of Antequera, among fields of olives, maize and wheat, and oceans of sunflowers.

Before the new road linked Antequera with Málaga town, transport was a long and bumpy business, and the winemaking became concentrated up in the mountains. This is still where the wine is made, most of

the principal firms obtaining much of their wine from a fairly basic *bodega* which they own jointly. Because of the excessive summer heat, the rule evolved that all Málaga wine was to be matured within the confines of Málaga town, to which it is taken some time after fermentation. But in Málaga itself, there is little of the old tradition to be seen – a Corte Ingles department store now stands on the site of the Scholtz Hermanos *bodega*, and it, like nearly all the others, has moved out into a characterless brick building on the outskirts of the town.

Málaga is generally a curious blend of wines and juices – a bottle may, for instance, contain a mix of dry wine, fortified grape juice and juice *boiled* up to sweet, treacly concentration. The basic PX and Moscatel wines are made in varying degrees of sweetness from dry to cloyingly sweet and aged for at least two years in a *criadera* or *solera* system (see page 26). The other blending ingredients, added before or after maturation, may include:

Arrope – a dark, thick, treacly, caramelised grape juice concentrate, made by boiling grape juice down to a third of its original volume (as opposed to a fifth in Jerez).

Vino de color – like **arrope** but even more concentrated.

Vino tierno – dark golden, raisiny, immensely sweet wine made from grapes dried in the sun, and partially fermented before fortifying up to 16° of alcohol.

Vino maestro – juice fortified to 7° with wine alcohol before a very slow fermentation up to 15 or 16°.

Mistela – grape juice fortified with wine alcohol to over 13° to prevent it from fermenting.

Málagas may be named according to their sweetness (*seco* to *dulce*), their colour *blanco, dorado, rojo-dorado, oscuro* or *negro* (white, golden, tawny, dark and black) and sometimes according to the grape juice used, Moscatel, Pedro Ximén, and Lágrima, a term which describes wine made from only free-run juice squeezed out by the weight of the grapes, without any mechanical pressing being employed. Most common in the region itself is Dulce Color, dark, sweet, treacly wine containing about ten per cent *arrope*, while smallholders often make their own *vino de paso*, raisin wine, for home consumption as well as to sell to appreciative locals. If a *bodega* has fine old wines, they may be sold under "Solera" names. All have to have between 15 and 23° of alcohol.

*I*t may not be immediatey obvious to holi-
daymakers in Mallorca, Menorca and Ibiza
that there *are* any local wines. Some
restaurants list one or two among a host of
mainland wines; some shops stock the odd
bottle; but there is very little wine left once
the locals have bought their domestic supplies. Many of the vines have been ousted to
make way for villas and hotels, and many that
remain are now practically abandoned – their
owners now find the tourists far more profitable than cultivation of their land.

Mallorca, with 2,600 hectares of vineyard,
is now the only island with a wine industry
worth mentioning. (There are 73 hectares on
Ibiza, 30 on Formentera and a tiny plot not
even amounting to a hectare on Menorca.)
The smaller of Mallorca's two regions, Binisalem, was declared *Denominación Específica
Provisional* in March 1986, only to be
lumped in the catch-all secondary denom-
ination of *Vinos de la Tierra* when the new
regulations were introduced in December of
the same year. It seems unlikely, however,
that it would ever have reached full *Denominación* status; the whole island can boast
only three producers of anything like quality,
all making wines of a completely different
style, and one of those is in the other region,
Felanitx.

On a central plateau 150 metres above sea
level, protected from the cold north wind by
mountains, Binisalem has the potential to
make good wine. Its main grape, occupying
about half of the 600 hectares, is the fruity
red Manto Negro; other major red grapes are
the fairly high quality Callet and the boring
Fogoneu, along with whites Prensal and Moll,
and there are experimental plantations of
Cabernet Sauvignon and Tempranillo. This is
hot country, but the best *bodegas*, Jaume
Mesquida and Franja Roja, manage to keep
the alcohol level to a reasonable 12.5° or
under. There are barrel-aged red wines,
young reds, and whites fairly low in alcohol
and coarsely fruity.

The other Mallorcan region, Felanitx,
extends from the border with Binisalem out
to the coast on the southern side. Here, the
principal grape is the Fogoneu, with Callet
and Manto Negro making up a third of the
vineyard. The reds here are lighter in colour
and body than those of Binisalem, and lower
in alcohol, (usually around 12 to 14°). They
are mediocre and usually blended with wines
from Valencia on the mainland.

Canaries

Little has changed for centuries in the
vineyards and wine cellars of the Canary Isles.
The grapes are still crushed by foot, and most
of the rough wine is drunk at home by the
producers, or sold in bulk to the locals. The
few bottled wines that exist are hard to track
down even on the islands themselves.

Tenerife has the most extensive vineyards
and had been granted the only *Denominación Específica Provisional* (since reclassi-
fied as *Vino de la Tierra*) for the hilly, sometimes terraced 2,460 hectares of

Tacoronte-Acentejo, up towards the north-
eastern tip of the island. More than 80 per
cent of the vines are the white Listán Blanco,
supported by the red Listán Negro and
Negramoll, which are often vinified together.
The resulting reds, foot-pressed and fermented in outdoor troughs or *lagares*, are
generally light in colour and body, with mer-
cifully little aroma and an astringent, herbaceous flavour. They are best drunk, if at all,
during their first year. (One or two good,
fruity examples are to be found.) There is
even less to be said for the other winegrowing
areas of Tenerife, all clustered in the northern part of the island, whose wine tends to be
harsh and turbid.

Lanzarote's Malvasía is the most famous
wine of the Canaries. Vines grow all over the
island – 2,000 hectares in all – in amazingly
inhospitable terrain. In this dry, dark, volcanic land, the vines often have to be planted
in cone-shaped holes up to three metres
deep shielded by low stone walls from the vio-

lent winds. Malvasía vines take up 70 per cent of the vineyards, Listán Blanca 15 per cent, the rest being Negra Commún, Diego and Moscatel.

Winemaking methods are mostly as backward as on the other islands, though modern technology is slowly arriving. At their best, the Malvasía Secos are straw coloured with a delicate aroma and full, musky flavour, and the semi-sweet wines, known simply as Malvasías, are fragrant, soft and amber coloured after brief wood ageing.

The island of Hierro makes wine in its northern section, but none is bottled. There are ill-kempt vines and primitive cellars in the south of La Palma, and farmers in La Gomera and Gran Canaria make wine only for their own consumption.

Below: *Vines in the black Lanzarote soil, protected by low walls of volcanic rock. In the windiest parts, vines are planted in walled, cone-shaped holes.*

Pick of the Balearics and Canaries

Jaume Mesquida (Mallorca) Dynamic producer with modern cellar, stainless steel and new oak barrels. Plantations of Cabernet Sauvignon, Pinot Noir and Chardonnay as well as vines from the mainland. His dark, curranty "Cabernet Sauvignon" in fact contains 70 per cent Monastrell, Tempranillo, Cariñena and Alicant Bouchet.

Franja Roja, Jose Ferrer (Mallorca) Binisalem *bodega* with cooling equipment and some stainless steel, all scrupulously clean. Trial plantations of foreign varieties. The young Tinto is best of the reds, with a flavour like raspberry jelly cubes. Whites are pale and fruity if drunk young.

Vinos Oliver (Mallorca) High, arched cellar with rudimentary equipment. Red Mont Ferrutx is a powerful, peppery, curranty wine with plenty of tannin.

Bodegas El Grifo (Lanzarote) Good Malvasías.

Mi Bodega (Tenerife) Best producer of Tenerife, Miguel Gonzáles Monje. The 13-degree Tinto, made of Listán Negra and Negramoll, is cherry-red and fresh with a blackberry-like aroma.

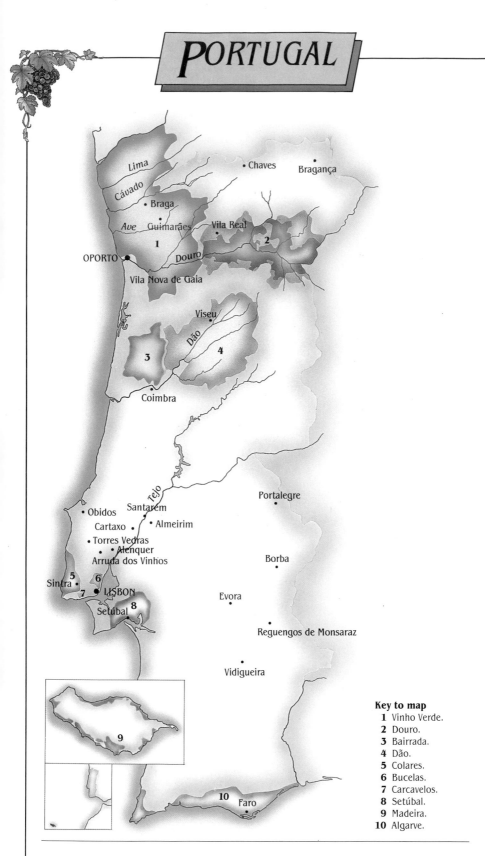

Key to map
1 Vinho Verde.
2 Douro.
3 Bairrada.
4 Dão.
5 Colares.
6 Bucelas.
7 Carcavelos.
8 Setúbal.
9 Madeira.
10 Algarve.

Portugal's best-known wine, port, represents less than six per cent of the country's average wine production. Port has achieved its fame through consistent quality and an attention to consumer tastes, evolving in different styles to serve different markets, and the result has been steadily successful sales at home, as well as increasingly flourishing exports.

The potential for producing fine table wines in Portugal is enormous, and the pro-

duction from its 363,500 hectares makes Portugal the seventh largest wine-producing country in the world. But most of the Portuguese table wine industry has been behind the times for years, and traditional domestic market demand has meant that Portuguese winemakers have had no need to adjust to the outside world. The Portuguese knew what they liked and drank it all.

Recently, the Portuguese have realised that many of their table wines are prime can-

Above: *Picking grapes on a farm near Amarante in the Vinho Verde district of northern Portugal. This is by far the largest of the* regiões demarcadas.

didates for export, and have started to spruce up their image. Tight controls on quality are only really possible within the framework of clearly-defined wine regions. At present, Portugal has only 11 *regiões demarcadas* (demarcated regions): Algarve, Bairrada, Bucelas, Carcavelos, Colares, Dão, Douro (for port *and* table wine), Madeira, Setúbal (for its fortified Moscatel wines) and the Vinho Verde region. Of these, Carcavelos has only one vineyard still planted; production of Bucelas, Colares and Moscatel de Setúbal is minute; and no one has a good word to say about the wines of the Algarve.

Between them, these demarcated regions produce only 15 per cent of Portugal's wine, and not always the best ones. The Portuguese Government has therefore agreed to the formation of 26 new demarcated regions (see map on pages 150-1), which will encompass roughly a further 15 per cent of wine production. Statistics on these demarcated regions-to-be are scarce to non-existent, mainly because, at the time of writing, the local committees are still scratching their heads and haggling over boundaries. Until these are finally decided, information will be hard to come by and of questionable value.

The only set of rules that already applies to the whole of winemaking Portugal specifies which grape varieties may be planted in which regions, demarcated or not. Otherwise, rules apply solely to the existing demarcated regions. While many of these rules are admirable, relating to yields, density of plantation and the like, several regions still have ageing requirements that do little to further the export cause.

When challenged on this, officials tend to bluster about the importance of not losing the typical character of the wines of the region. If this philosophy were applied throughout the winemaking world, we would still be in the vinous equivalent of the Dark Ages, and some of Portugal still is.

It would of course be tragic to lose some of Portugal's extremely characterful grape varieties, but there is no suggestion that this is happening. Indeed, Portugal is one of the few countries in southern Europe that is *not* experimenting wholesale with Cabernet Sauvignon, Chardonnay and other foreign imports. There are healthy pockets of varietal experimentation, but the Portuguese vine-grower is a cautious man. The Tinta Barroca, one of the top five port grapes, is thought of as new because it arrived in the Douro only a century ago.

However, out-of-date winemaking methods do not merit preservation notices. Money must be found to help refurbish old-fashioned winemaking installations in promising regions. Seventy per cent of Portugal's wine is made in co-operatives, occasionally glittering with the latest in stainless steel, but more often crumbling with down-at-heel concrete. Nevertheless, the very existence of the co-operatives is an improvement on every farmer making wine in his back shed. Whether made in co-operatives or by smallholders, most Portuguese wine is still bought, blended and marketed by large merchants, and it is at their wineries that most of Portugal's modern equipment is to be found.

The emergence of a sprinkling of quality-conscious, single estate wines has recently challenged the merchants' near-monopoly. Realistically, it will be a very long time before these represent anything more than a tiny fraction of Portuguese wine production, but the standards the best have set are salutary for the rest of the industry.

Portugal is rich in grape varieties, many of them unique, but the same grape can masquerade under many different names. Even the most respected grape growers and winemakers contradict each other over the identities of their raw materials. The official government study still leaves many questions unanswered, while perpetuating a few myths. The best attempt so far to sort out the muddle is a study of 85 varieties carried out in 1982 by a Frenchman named Truel. What follows is an attempt to sift Truel's report, the official list and all the information garnered during our travels.

White Grapes

Alvarinho Portugal's finest white grape, grown in quantity only around Monção and Melgaço in the north. The Alvarinho is low-yielding, and makes wine with good acidity, high alcohol for the Vinho Verde region, and complex aromas and flavours.

Arinto Principal grape of Bucelas, making up at least 75 per cent of the blend, and also grown in Alenquer, Alentejo, Bairrada, Colares, Carcavelos, Douro, Setúbal and, alias the Pedernã, in the Vinho Verde region. The Arinto has high acidity and a neutral flavour when young, but develops some complexity with age. Its high acidity makes it a good base for sparkling wine in Bairrada.

Arinto do Dão Quite different from the Arinto of Bucelas and elsewhere in Portugal. Officially, it is said to be a synonym for Assario Branco, but other authorities disagree. It is a recommended variety in the Dão, where it makes rather alcoholic wines.

Assario Branco Officially said to be the same as the Arinto do Dão, (qv). A grape of this name is also grown in the Alentejo.

Avesso *Vinho verde* grape grown principally in the south-eastern corner of the region, nearest the Douro. Even in the baking Douro climate, it is capable of retaining both acidity and aroma and makes soft, "winey" wine. This is the Jaen Blanco of central Spain.

Azal Branco Grown throughout the *vinho verde* region to boost acidity. Azal ripens very late, and makes neutral, acidic wine.

Barcelo Recommended but rare in Dão.

Bical Good acidity and fine fruit aroma. Grown in Bairrada and Dão (where it is known as Borrado das Moscas – fly droppings).

Boal It seems that five different grapes go under the name Boal in Portugal – and no one has yet made a serious attempt to discover which grows where and is related to what. Most famous is the Bual (the English form) of Madeira, which makes full-flavoured, sweetish fortified wines. Another, the Boal de Alicante, is grown in the Ribatejo and Oeste, where it is also known as the Farana. Yet another version grows in the Douro.

Borrado das Moscas Dão name for Bical.

Cerceal (do Dão) *Not* the Sercial of Madeira. It can make wine with good acidity, and aromatic, greengagey fruit. Because of confusion with the Sercial of Madeira (found quite widely on Portuguese mainland) it is not yet clear how widely planted this vine is.

Diagalves One of the main white grapes of the Alentejo, although of no great character. Also grown in Setúbal.

Encruzado This must make up at least 20 per cent of white Dão blends. Quite high in alcohol, but of reasonable quality.

Esgana Cão Whether this grape is named "dog strangler" because of its high acidity is not clear. It is important in white port blends, and less so in Bucelas and most of the *vinho verde* region. This is the Portuguese name for Sercial in Madeira, which, according to Truel, is in fact the Cerceal, Cercial or Sercial of Bairrada, Bucelas, Carcavelos and the Douro, but quite different from the Cerceal do Dão.

Fernão Pires Portugal's most cultivated white grape, small, highly flavoured and slightly reminiscent of Muscat, makes wines with high alcohol, reasonable acidity and sometimes good fruit in Arruda, Alenquer, Torres Vedras, the Douro, the Setúbal Peninsula, and the Alentejo. As the Maria Gomez, it is the predominant grape in white Bairrada.

Gouveio *see* Verdelho.

Loureiro The most aromatic of the white *vinho verde* varieties, with good acidity. Used throughout the region, but especially in the central part, to add a musky-grapey perfume to blends, and sometimes on its own.

Malmsey *see* Malvasia.

Malvasia As elsewhere in the world, the name "Malvasia" is applied to a variety of grapes. Best known as Malmsey in Madeira, but even there different types of Malvasia are found. The best is Malvasia Candida, with musky, apricotty flavour, very fine if well made. The Malvasia Corada of the Dão is the Vital of the Oeste and the Malvasia Fina of the Douro. The Douro also has a Malvasia Rei, making pale, light, neutral wine, which some consider to be a variant of the Palomino of Jerez. At least 80 per cent of white Colares must be "Malvasia", but this version is unlike Portugal's other Malvasias.

Manteudo One of the Alentejo white grapes.

Maria Gomez *see* Fernão Pires.

Moscatel This sweet, *grapy*-flavoured grape appears in many guises in Portugal (Moscatel do Douro, Moscatel Galego, Moscatel Roxo, Moscatel de Setúbal . . .) but it is thought that almost all Portugal's Moscatel vines are strains of the Muscat of Alexandria, less fine than the Muscat à Petits Grains.

Pedernã *see* Arinto.

Perrum Grown widely in the Alentejo and Algarve. Some claim that it is the same as the Palomino of Jerez, but this is not true.

Rabigato *see* Rabo d'Ovelha.

Rabo d'Ovelha High-yielding grape grown all over Portugal. It means "ewe's tail". Sometimes called Rabigato in the north.

Roupeiro Characterful, honeyed grape of the Alentejo and Setúbal Peninsula, also grown, alias Codega, in the Douro. The Tamarez of the Algarve is possibly the same vine.

Sercial da Madeira *see* Esgana Cão.

Talia (or **Thalia**) None other than Italy's Trebbiano, grown in the Ribatejo and Setúbal Peninsula. Neutral with good acidity.

Tamarez Grown from the Beira Littoral and Interior (south of Bairrada) down through the vineyards of the Ribatejo and Oeste as far as the Algarve (but it is thought that the Algarve version may actually be the Roupeiro). In the Alentejo, it is known as the Trincadeira das Pratas.

Terrantez Rare Madeira grape, now being replanted. The variety known as Terrantez in Dão is not the same.

Trajadura Early-ripening, fairly aromatic variety grown throughout the *vinho verde* region. Loses acidity if not picked early.

Verdelho One of the ''noble'' grapes of Madeira, high in alcohol. Some authorities, including Truel, are convinced that this is the Gouveio of the Douro, where it is sometimes also called Verdelho. It appears that the Verdelho of the Dão is different, making acid, boring wine.

Vital Makes decent, fairly fruity wine with good acidity in the Ribatejo, Oeste and Setúbal peninsula. Sometimes known as the Boal Bonifacio or Malvasia Corada.

Black Grapes

Alfrocheiro Preto (or **Alfrocheiro**) Major grape in Dão, and grown widely throughout the country. It provides plenty of colour.

Aragonez see Tinta Roriz

Azal Tinto High acid, late-ripening *vinho verde* grape with little colour.

Baga This accounts for 90 per cent of all Bairrada vines. It has great potential for rich fruit and fragrance, along with tannin and highish acidity, but has traditionally been fermented with the stalks, making tough and astringent wine. A little is found in the Ribatejo, Alentejo and Douro, sometimes alias Tinta Bairrada.

Bastardo This early-maturing variety used to be a highly-regarded grape in port production, but modern viticultural research has downgraded it. Its wines are high in alcohol, often low in acidity. Bastardo was traditional but now little seen in Madeira. One of the major grapes of Dão, and authorised for Bairrada. This is the Trousseau of the Jura.

Borraçal Early-ripening *vinho verde* grape with good colour and low alcohol. Thought to be the Caino of Galicia (Spain).

Camarate Red grape of the Oeste.

Castelão Frances see Periquita.

Espadeiro Tinto Late-ripening *vinho verde* variety with high acidity, pleasant fruitiness reminiscent of cherries and redcurrants, but very little colour. In the Setúbal Peninsula and Carcavelhos, the name is given to the Tinta Amarela of the Douro.

Jaen *Not* the Jaen of Spain, this is grown in Dão and Bairrada, making wines low in acidity with reasonable colour and alcohol.

João de Santarém Excellent grape also known as Santarém, Castelão Frances, Periquita, Trincadeira Preta and Mortagua. The most planted grape in the southern part of Portugal, predominant red grape of Oeste (where it is called the Mortagua), Ribatejo (Mortagua and Trincadeira Preta) and Alentejo, and also found in Carcavelos, Bairrada

and Douro table wines. In the Setúbal Peninsula it is known as the Periquita.

Moreto Very widely grown grape (in Douro, Beiras, Oeste, Ribatejo, Setúbal peninsula, Alentejo and Algarve), but not highly thought-of. Truel believes that a quite different grape bears the name in Dão.

Moreto do Dão Dark wine, low in alcohol.

Mortagua Confusingly, this is the local name for the Touriga Nacional in the Ribatejo, but for the João de Santarém in the Oeste.

Periquita see João de Santarém.

Ramisco Found only in Colares, where it must make up at least 80 per cent of the red wines. It makes tough, tannic wines.

Tinta Amarela Lesser grape of the lower reaches of the Douro, also grown in Dão. Goes under several names including Rabo de Ovelha Tinto, Trincadeira and Espadeiro.

Tinta Barroca A very regular and reliable port grape even under extreme conditions, making big, full, fruity, tannic wine.

Tinta Miuda Minor port variety, more widely grown in Oeste and Ribatejo. Said to be the Graciano of Rioja.

Tinta Negra Mole Principal grape of Madeira, making wine of deep colour and highish astringency, and not a lot of character. It is encouraged in the Algarve, and permitted in Carcavelos.

Tinta Pinheira Grown widely in the Dão, but also found in the Douro, Bairrada, Alcobaça in the Oeste and the Alentejo. The wine is dull, low in alcohol and light in colour.

Tinta Roriz (or **Aragonez**) Spain's Tempranillo, an important port variety, and under increasing surveillance by Douro winemakers for its table wine potential. It has a good, deep colour, firm structure and good length. Also recommended in Dão.

Tinto Cão One of the five highly recommended port varieties, of excellent quality but almost extinct until recent moves to encourage replantation, as its yield is tiny. Also allowed in Dão and for red *vinho verde*.

Touriga Francesa Important port variety, making softer and lighter wine than Touriga Nacional. Fine, delicate aroma and flavour.

Touriga Nacional Considered best of the port varieties, with rich colour, a powerful aroma with a hint of blackcurrants, a full, individual flavour of liquorice and ripe berry fruits and plenty of tannin. Better-yielding clones are now being produced to counter the very low production. It performs best in the hotter areas of the upper Douro. In red Dão, alias Tourigo, it must account for at least 20 per cent of blends, and is also grown in the Setúbal Peninsula. In Bairrada it is called the Mortagua.

Trincadeira Found in the Oeste, Ribatejo and Alentejo, and permitted in Bairrada. Trincadeira Preto, however, is a synonym for Santarém in the Ribatejo.

Vinhão Good, late-ripening *vinho verde* grape remarkable for its deep colour. It has rich damson and blackcurrant-like flavour, and adequate acidity and tannin. Several authorities, including Truel, claim that this is the Souzão of the Douro.

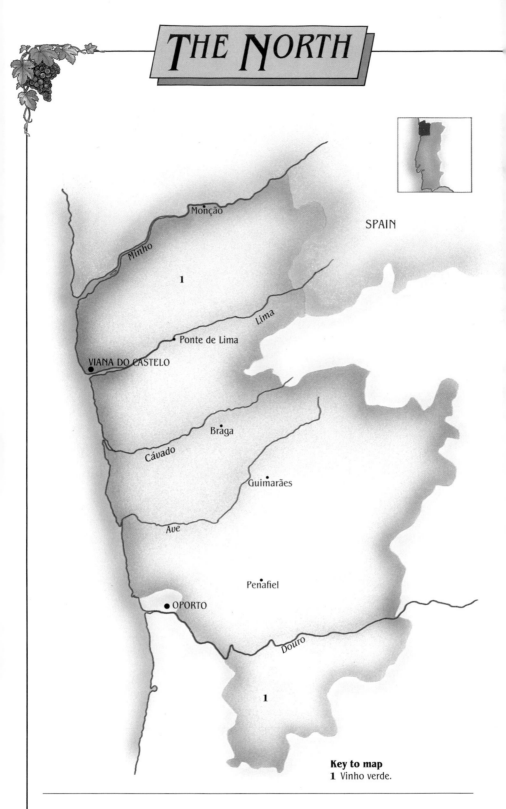

THE NORTH

SPAIN

Monção

Minho

1

Lima

Ponte de Lima

VIANA DO CASTELO

Braga

Cávado

Guimarães

Ave

Penafiel

OPORTO

Douro

1

Key to map
1 Vinho verde.

Travel round the *vinho verde* region in the height of summer, and you could be forgiven for thinking that the wine takes its name from the countryside where it is grown. Everything is luxuriantly green, from the vines rampaging up trees and canopies to the lush grass verges and long-stalked, spindly cabbages that surround every farmhouse.

But the wine is called "green" because it is young, not because of the landscape, or because it is made from unripe grapes, or because it is itself green in colour. In fact, *vinho verde* can be white or red, and there is still twice as much red made as white, although the proportion of white is on the increase. In 1983, the ratio was three red to one white, but even in Portugal itself red *vinho verde* is waning in popularity. It is little drunk in Lisbon or the south, only in the northern half of Portugal.

This is the Minho region, famed for its young wines, which has come to be known as the *vinho verde* region, and demarcated accordingly, the *Região Demarcada dos Vinhos Verdes*. To call it by the name of the river that runs along its northern border is a little misleading, since the area stretches

Above: *Friends and neighbours arrive with their ladders and buckets at harvest time to pick the grapes for* vinho verde. *Traditionally, different varieties have been grown in a jumble, and it is virtually impossible to pick each at its perfect stage of maturity.*

from Portugal's northern border with Spain down to (and indeed south of) the Douro a few miles east of Oporto, from the coast to more than 60 miles inland at its widest point.

It is a region of hills, trees, vines – and industry. Eighty per cent of Portugal's exports come from the region north of Lisbon, and the small, diamond-shaped chunk of land between Braga, Barcelos, Vila Nova de Famalicão and Guimarães, Portugal's ancient capital, contains most of the country's textile industry. The road from Guimarães to Famalicão is so built-up that there is no break between towns: "the road has become a street", as one local put it.

But everywhere you see vines, in trees, on pergolas and in the fields themselves. They are always trained well above the ground, to avoid the rot endemic in this hot but humid part of the country. The weather is usually hot and dry through the summer, but often breaks in September and October, just at the time when the grapes are ready for picking. The predominantly maritime climate is reinforced by the five rivers, the Minho, Lima, Cávado, Ave, and Douro, that traverse the region, acting as perfect conduits for the moist sea air.

Vine-growers discovered that if they grew the vines up trees, the grapes rotted less easily in the better-aerated conditions. So began the traditional system of *enforcado* training ("hanged", so called because the vine hangs from the tree).

After the discovery of maize on the American continent, a royal decree was passed, forbidding the cultivation of vines in fields except around the edges, to clear the way for plantations of the new wonder-cereal. In many parts of the *vinho verde* region, particularly where the wine is intended only for family consumption, this is still how the vines are grown, usually three of them, up a poplar, willow, chestnut or plane. The natural progression from this was to link one tree with the next by extending wires, and train the vines along. After that came the trellis, or *ramada* system, in which the vines lean out over the field, although their roots are still on the edges. Many of these are still in place, because 20th century legislation reimposed the old edges-only ban (lifted only after the 1984 revolution), and decreed that vines might only be grown for "decorative purposes". The present owner of one *vinho verde* estate remembers, though, how his father could make up to 75,000 litres of wine from the fruit of "decorative" vines.

Now, however, growers have realised that both these traditional ways of training vines are far from perfect. Sometimes the blanket of leaves over a pergola is so thick that you wonder how the sun can possibly penetrate to the grapes underneath. Often, it does not, and the grapes are green and unripe. Or the air cannot flow freely through the bunches, and they rot in the humid October air. Pergola-trained vines are fine as canopies over picnics on sunny days, but pretty inefficient for growing good grapes.

Most of the wealthier growers have planted new vineyards with vines trained on *cruzeta* supports (see pages 12/13). The best (and newest) of the vineyards have moved on from this to a higher version of the classic French *cordon* system, sometimes known here as *barra*, now favoured as the method that permits the best exposure to the sun.

The farmers of small estates (and the average size of a *vinho verde* property is less than half a hectare) cannot afford new systems of vine training, or expensive chemical fertilisers. They have to stick with *ramada*, pergola – and cows, which both eat the maize grown in the fields, and fertilize the vines round their edges.

Most *vinho verde* grapes are grown by hard-pressed farmers of small plots, who cultivate vines as well as kiwi fruit, maize and vegetables; average grape quality is far from great. On such farms, vines grow up the trees and pergolas in a jumble of different varieties – over 100 different grapes are grown in the *vinho verde* region, although only about a quarter of these are recommended, or even authorized. Yields can reach 80 hectolitres per hectare in a *good* year, less than most other parts of Europe, although high for Iberia.

Different grapes ripen at different times, but most farms cannot afford to hire workers to pick each variety at the right moment. Harvesting has to be done by members of the family, or neighbours who will expect the same favour in return, and many grapes are unripe or actually rotten when picked.

The worst grapes tend to be sold to the co-operatives, who can rarely offer more than a 5 escudos (2.5p) supplement per kilo of grapes as an incentive for better quality. If a grower cannot sell his best grapes to one of the large, privately-owned wine producers like Sogrape or Borges & Irmão (who offer better prices and quicker payment than the co-operatives), he will keep them to make wine to drink at home.

However, even the large commercial producers have pretty unpromising material to convert into wine. Anyone who has stood beside one of their grape reception areas at harvest-time and watched the clouds of rot and swarms of flies that rise from many a load of grapes might well wonder how they do it. For the good producers, the answer is some very sophisticated technology, particularly the centrifuges and vacuum filters used to clean the must before fermentation.

The virtual monopoly of the *vinho verde* market by the large producers is now being challenged by an association of single estates. Their rules oblige them to bottle only the wine made from grapes grown in their own vineyards, and these dry, characterful wines are very different from the often sweetened mass-market *vinhos verdes,* which hardly represent the potential of the region.

APEVV (the association of producer-bottlers of *vinho verde*) is a welcome ginger group on the *vinho verde* scene, although their production represents less than five per cent of the region's wine. From the imposing Palacio da Brejoeira estate right up by the border with Spain down to half a dozen estates clustered round the westerly reaches of the Douro, the APEVV properties are working hard to turn out wine that is a credit to the region. Not all have entirely succeeded, but their appearance has galvanised some of the large companies into coming up with their own single vineyard wines, some of them first-class. Quality encourages more quality.

The rules for the making of *vinho verde* mean that all of them have a highish acidity, and the climate means that most will be fairly low in alcohol (perhaps around eight degrees). Those containing Avesso, Trajadura, and especially Alvarinho and Loureiro grapes are most aromatic (see pages 112/3 for more details of *vinho verde* grapes). Romantics would have us believe that the prickle of fizz in *vinho verde* comes from CO_2 generated during the secondary, malolactic fermentation. This is rarely the case: most is added just before bottling. Because of the high level of acidity required by law, the majority of producers do not allow the malolactic fermentation to happen, as it would lower the acidity too far. Practically all the red wines also have added CO_2, which results in a curious wine to a non-Portuguese palate, red, acidic *and* slightly fizzy. *Vinho verde* should be drunk young, and it is worth scrutinising labels (front or back) to make sure a bottle is as young as possible.

Right: *Women in traditional head-dress prepare tubs of* vinho verde *grapes for transport to the local co-operative. The best grapes are often taken home.*

Pick of Vinho Verde

Adega Cooperativa do Ponte de Lima Only reliable co-operative in the *vinho verde* region, with good, lemony-grapy Loureiro white.

Casa de Cabanelas Typical, well-made, dry *vinho verde*, with lemony acidity and Loureiro and Trajadura perfume, from an estate north of Penafiel.

Casa de Compostela Large, modern estate, with stainless steel winery built to cope with planned expansion of their 36 hectare vineyard to become one of the biggest in Northern Portugal. Good, attractive, lemony *vinho verde*, with grassy, honeyed scent.

Casa dos Cunhas One of the most northerly estates, near the river Lima, whose wine is made from the Loureiro grape, rich, appley-lemony, with a hint of mint.

Paço d'Anha Property just south of Viana do Castelo, making clean, fresh, lemony wine.

Paço de Teixeró Near-Douro estate belonging to the Champalimaud family, making attractive if untypical wine, creamy, lemony and soft.

Paço do Cardido Estate in the valley of the river Lima whose excellent wine is made and marketed by João Pires & Filhos. Mainly Loureiro, with delicious perfume and lemony-grassy zing.

Palacio da Brejoeira Portugal's most expensive white wine, with unusually complex flavours and more alcohol than most *vinhos verdes*, made from the low-yielding Alvarinho grape in an immaculate winery housed in an impressive 18th century palace outside Monção.

Quinta de Vila Nova (Tormes) Home of the wife of the famous Portuguese writer Eça de Queiroz, and setting for his novel *The City and the Mountains*. Tiny two hectare vineyard making wine dominated by the Avesso grape, dry and savoury.

Quinta da Quintão Soft wine, made predominantly from the Loureiro grape, with honeyed, grapy character, from hillside estate south-west of Guimarães.

Quinta do Tamariz Better of the wines from two estates owned by Vinagre family near Barcelos. Pure Loureiro, with perfumed, grapy aroma and characterful, lemony bite.

Solar das Bouças Another wine mainly made from Loureiro, perfumed floral and rounded, in immaculate winery north of Braga.

Although we know port as a sweet, fortified wine, this was not always the case.
Fortifying port with brandy was
originally designed to protect the unstable
young wine on its shipment overseas. The
practice is said to have begun towards the
end of the 17th century. Two young English-
men from Liverpool were sent out to Viana do
Castelo in northern Portugal to learn the
ways of the wine trade, but found the local
wine (red *vinho verde*) in short supply. They
decided to travel further inland in search of
supplies, and came across an exceptional
wine in a monastery in Lamego (in the south-
eastern corner of the present demarcated
region of the Douro). It was rich and sweet,
and they learned that it had been fortified
during fermentation rather than afterwards
as a preliminary to shipping. They bought all
they could, and shipped it back to England.

It took about 50 years for fortification
during fermentation to become normal
practice. Meanwhile, the good name of port
was being subjected to widespread abuse –
inferior wines were being brought into the
region (mainly based at that time around the
river Corgo) for blending with true Douro
wine, as demand outstripped supply. The
Prime Minister of the day brought in strin-
gent laws to safeguard the quality of the
wines sold as "Factory" wines (probably
because they were shipped by the foreign
"factors", or merchants), and to demarcate
the region in which they could be made.

These laws laid a basis of port legislation
that has only ever been adjusted, rather than
changed outright. At the beginning of the
20th century, after the triple scourge of
oidium, phylloxera and mildew in the second
half of the 19th century, the rules were tight-
ened again. New boundaries were fixed for
the region, and it became obligatory to ship
port for export only from the *entreposto*
(warehousing area) of Vila Nova de Gaia. In
1986, this law was relaxed (as was that obliging all shippers to hold minimum stocks of
300 pipes of port), enabling port to be
exported from single estates in the Douro by
farmers who did not possess warehouses in
the congested town of Vila Nova de Gaia.

One rule that has remained in this latest
round of liberalisation is the "three to one"
stock rule: simply expressed, a shipper is
allowed to sell no more than a third of his
total stock in any year. The logic behind this
is to back up the rule that port may not be
sold, either in Portugal or abroad, until it is
at least three years old, but it is a severe
financial burden on the port industry.

It is fortunate, then, that sales of port are
booming as never before. For a wine that
seems to go against most of the current
trends in drinking – it is very alcoholic,
sweet, and most of it is red – its success is
phenomenal. The last decade has seen the
greatest growth in port export since port's
earlier heyday of 1924 and 1925, and the last
three years have been the best ever.

The pattern of port sales has changed considerably. The UK was displaced as top export

Above: *Emptying an autovinificator at
Bomfim. The "shower head" acts as a
sieve, as well as aerating the wine.*

Port's Regulatory Bodies

*E*ach year, the minimum prices payable for grapes and wine and the proportion of total production allowed to be made into port in the different areas of the Douro (see box on pages 122-3) is announced by the Government after consultation with the following three associations that represent the interests of the growers, shippers and state.

Casa do Douro Otherwise known as the Federation of Winegrowers of the Douro Region. All farmers have to belong to the Casa do Douro, the body that controls plantation of vineyards, viticulture and vinification. The Casa do Douro also holds a buffer stock of wine bought in plentiful years, and released in years of shortage.

Associaçao dos Exportadores do Vinho do Porto The Port Shippers' Association handles the interests of the shippers, particularly matters concerning the storage and maturation of wines at Vila Nova de Gaia.

Instituto do Vinho do Porto This, Port's overall controlling body, is a quasi-governmental organisation, although only the chairman is a directly political appointee. The inspectors of the IVP (as it is usually known) have power of entry into any shippers' premises in Vila Nova de Gaia, and keep close control over all stocks of port held there. It also has a technical department that carries out research on behalf of the whole industry and a financial department that can help growers and shippers in difficulties.

market in 1963, although Britain still buys more vintage, late-bottled vintage and ruby than anyone else. France is easily the leading export market, with over a third of total sales, followed by Belgium and Luxembourg (taken together). The French and Belgians prefer the lighter style of tawny port (the British have stronger livers, according to one Portuguese port shipper), and buy a lot of cheap wine in bulk, as do the Dutch, fourth in the export league.

Below: Barcos rabelos *used to deliver port from the Douro. Now, moored at Gaia, they advertise the port firms' wares.*

*T*he valley of the river Douro has changed enormously in the last 30 years. The river used to be dangerous, with fast-flowing currents and treacherous rapids, but it was nevertheless the only link with Oporto and the outside world until first roads, then the railway, penetrated the wild, mountainous country where wine was made.

Then, in the late 1950s, they started to build dams. With the completion of the first, the Douro scenery changed. Parts of the river that had been little more than an exhausted trickle at the height of summer became vast, still expanses of water. Not only did the look of the Douro change, so did the sound. The river used to crash and tumble down the valley, sometimes through narrow granite gorges and rapids, sometimes through more peaceful stretches, but always with the noise of water flowing vigorously towards the sea.

Now the flow is harnessed, and the Douro valley, particularly in the upper reaches beyond Pinhão, has become a place where the prevailing stillness is broken only by signs of human occupation, the shriek and rattle of a train as it shuttles up the predominantly single-track line to or from Oporto, the crowing of cocks, or just the blare of a transistor radio from a *quinta* on the other side of the valley.

Even the terraces carved out of the schistous rock are changing. The hanging vine-gardens of the Douro, one of the most extraordinary testaments to the determination of farmers to overcome almost insuperable natural difficulties of terrain, are gradually giving way to vineyards that require less labour. The existing, narrow terraces are being converted into wider ones that can be tilled by small tractors, or even replanted with the rows of vines vertical to the slope.

Creating a new vineyard is no easy matter. The soil of the Douro is not really *soil* at all, but slaty, schistous rock that becomes workable and soil-like only after years of digging and tilling. While this is undoubtedly one of the most fundamental influences on the very nature of port, it makes the Douro almost impossible to cultivate. To plant a new vineyard on previously unused land is not just a matter of bulldozing the ground flat. You have to dig down to a depth of 1.2 metres, and either cart large stones away or bury them. The characteristic stone terrace walls of traditional Douro vineyards were largely a means of ridding the ground of large stones in the days before tractors and roads made removal easier.

The schist has its uses, though, and not just in providing long slate stakes to tether the wires along which vines are trained in most modern vineyards. Companies experimenting in the new, vertical (or "up-and-down") plantations have found that the very stoniness of the Douro vineyards prevents the problems of erosion forecasted by all the pundits. Combined with cultivation by tractors driving *down* the slope (so throwing earth back *upwards*), erosion is less of a disadvantage than the problems of picking and pruning on a slope, and loss of water.

Traditional terraces were built so that the level of the ground sloped back in towards the hill, encouraging the precious winter rainfall to run back along this slope and soak into the ground until the vines really needed it in the blazing heat of summer. In the "up-and-down" plantations, the rain runs forward and down the slope, lost to the vines.

Below: *Harvest time at Pinhão is hard on the feet as well as the back – slaty, schistous rock passes for soil in the Douro valley. The Quinta do Bomfim is one of the Symington family's top estates.*

Above: *The new terracing at Quinta de Vargellas has done away with the traditional stone banks and walls and allowed space for tractors to cultivate the double rows of vines. Some new plantations elsewhere have been made vertically to the slope rather than hugging the contours, changing the Douro landscape even more drastically. The rocky character of the soil prevents the erosion many experts feared would result.*

Manual work on the steep slopes of the Douro hill-sides is hard at the best of times, involving endless clambering up and down stone steps between terraces, while picking and pruning (both done by hand) on a steep slope are very tiring for anyone not born with one leg shorter than the other. However, the saving in labour from mechanical cultivation is tremendous, although some companies have found that modern equipment provided for *quintas* is ignored in favour of the tried and trusted ways as soon as the owners' backs are turned.

Some of the most impressive vineyard developments clearly visible on a river-ride are those sponsored by the World Bank. This was a scheme to revitalise the Douro (defined as a depressed area) by encouraging plantation of new vineyards, up to a total of 2,500 hectares in all. Plots were to be between three and ten hectares in size, allowed only in A and B (and a few C) areas (see pages 122-3), and had to be planted in "premium" grape varieties. Loans to finance these plantations were below market rates and repayment terms easy.

The varieties now recognised as being superior to all others for red port are the Touriga Nacional, Touriga Francesa, Tinto Cão, Tinta Roriz and Tinta Barroca. Current research (and there is a programme of research jointly funded by 11 different companies) now suggests that perfect port can be made from these grapes alone, in varying proportions. "The revolution has to start in the vineyard" was the way one young Portuguese viticulturist put it – but this is a revolution that will take at least 20 years to come to fruition.

Soil and grapes are both very influential in determining the nature of port. The third crucial factor is the climate of the demarcated Douro region. Although there are huge differences from east to west, the whole region is sheltered from the damp Atlantic climate that envelops Oporto for much of the year by a spectacular range of mountains, the Serra do Marão, which rise to 1,400 metres above sea level.

Broadly speaking, though, the weather becomes hotter and drier from the west to the east. On average, there is more than twice as much rainfall in Regua, ten kilometres from the region's western limit, as at the easternmost point on the Spanish border. The mid-point in terms of both rainfall and temperature occurs somewhere between Pinhão and Tua, and this is the area most highly thought of by the majority of shippers, as representing an ideal balance between the cool, damp Atlantic and hot, dry Mediterranean climates.

The shippers' historic hierarchy of vineyard qualities is enshrined in the system of "*beneficio*" ratings (see box), a means of calculating which vineyards in the region may make the largest proportion of their annual production into port. For although theoretically any wine from within the demarcated region may be made into port, in practice the proportion of production to be fortified is fixed each year by the IVP, depending on stocks held by the industry and fluctuations in market demand.

Inevitably, there is some dissent from those farmers whose vineyards are not as highly rated by the *beneficio* system as others. The most vocal of these is Miguel Champalimaud, of the Quinta do Côtto, one

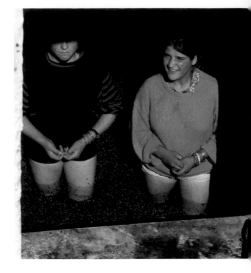

Above: *All the grapes actually grown at Quinta de Vargellas are still crushed by foot and fermented in* lagares.

of the few estates both to make and export its port since the removal in 1986 of the obligation to ship all port from Vila Nova de Gaia. His criticism of the vineyard rating system as "the most stupid in the world" must be motivated partially by frustration at the fact that however well he makes his wine he will be prevented from turning as much into port as some farmers whose commitment to quality winemaking is less, but whose vineyards happen to be in the right place.

Research into vinification techniques is well under way, however, and since 90 per cent of farmers in the Douro have long-term contracts with port shippers to supply either grapes or wine, the shippers have every incentive to ensure that whatever wine is not made in their own wineries is *well* made. Technical staff spend long hours at vintage-time buzzing up and down the Douro and its tributaries in boats, visiting and advising farmers.

Below: *Grapes from Quinta do Bomfim form the basis of Dow's top ports, but Bomfim is soon to be launched as an off-vintage, single* quinta *wine. About half the Symington group's wines are made here.*

The Vineyard Rating System

*E*ach vineyard in the demarcated region is rated according to 12 different factors, and the total of points obtained decides whether a vineyard is classed as A, B, C, D, E or F. In the last decade or so, A and B vineyards and C and D vineyards have been lumped together, and allowed to make, say, 60 and 40 per cent of their production respectively into port. This has led some to question the necessity of splitting the vineyards of the region into six different categories, when only four are in use.

Vineyard rating factors
(potential percentage of total points awarded)

Altitude (20.6) Most points are awarded for low-lying vineyards.

Productivity (20) Over a certain limit of production, the more wine obtained from a particular area, the lower the quality will be. Top marks go to vineyards producing up to 600 litres per 1,000 vines. Anything over this is marked correspondingly lower.

Geological composition of the soil (13.7) Schist is acknowledged to be the best soil for port. There are penalties for soil that is either wholly or partly granite, and for vineyards liable to flooding.

Locality (12.7) This takes into account particular micro-climates, as well as general totals of rainfall and temperature.

Methods of training vines (11.8) Vines trained along relatively low wires are marked more highly than those trained on high pergolas.

Grape varieties (8.8) Only those varieties rated as Very Good and Good receive any points.

Vineyard gradient (3.9) The steeper the slope in a vineyard, the more points awarded.

Aspect and exposure to the sun (2.5) Based on the questionable principle that the ripest grapes always make the best wines, vineyards with a southerly aspect are awarded most points.

Density of plantation (1.9) On the basis that a lower density of vines per hectare means higher degree of mineral extract per plant and lower productivity, points are won by low density vineyards.

Stoniness (1.6) The stonier the better in the Douro, because of water retention and stored heat.

Age of vines (1.3) Older vines make better wine, and vineyards with vines over 25 years old win most points.

Shelter (1.2) Vineyards sheltered from cold winds make higher quality wine, and are awarded more points.

*T*he *entreposto* (or *entrepôt*) of Vila Nova de Gaia has changed less than the port winemaking region itself. The old, steep, cobbled streets climb sharply away from the river, skirting huge "lodges" (warehouses, from the Portuguese "*loja*"), where the wines sit maturing in wooden vats and barrels under red, clay-tiled roofs. But nowadays vast tanker lorries inch their way up the narrow streets originally designed for nothing wider than an ox-drawn cart.

The term, *entreposto*, refers to this cramped assortment of lodges and offices in Vila Nova de Gaia (Gaia New Town) just across the Douro river from Oporto. "*O porto*" is Portuguese for "the port", but the place is usually referred to by the Portuguese just as "Porto". Gaia has been used for at least 200 years for the storage and maturation of port wine, and its status as an extension of the winemaking region of the Douro was finally ratified by law in 1926.

From then until the law was rescinded in 1986, it was illegal to ship port abroad from anywhere but Gaia. The limits of Gaia were firmly fixed, even marked by symbolic sentry-boxes at intervals round the perimeter. Anyone who did not own property in Gaia 100 years ago had little chance of buying any in the 1980s, and this was thought to be unfair to some farmers who wished to export, so the new law permits wine to be exported from *anywhere* within the demarcated Douro region, including the *entreposto* of Gaia, miles away from the actual winemaking region. The very closed area of Gaia enabled the authorities to keep a tight control on everything to do with the maturation, blending and bottling of port for the export market, however, vital for a wine whose reputation had taken some hard knocks over the centuries.

The next big step in legislation should be

Port Measurements

Pipe "Pipa" is Portuguese for a cask, or barrel. As a unit of volume, a pipe varies considerably. In the Douro, every farm's yield is measured in pipes, in this case of 550 litres. Pipes in the Gaia lodges can be any size between 580 and 630 litres. A shipping pipe, however, has a precise measurement, 534.24 litres.

Almude One almude is 25.44 litres. There are 21 almudes in a pipe.

Canada One canada is 2.12 litres. There are 252 canadas in a pipe, and 12 canadas in an almude.

In his book *Rich, Rare and Red*, Ben Howkins gives an explanation for these strangely interlinked measures: "One oxcart could pull a pipe; an almude could be carried on one's head, and a canada was the optimum measure that a man could drink". Those were the days!

in place by 1994, the obligatory bottling of all port in Portugal. Everyone has agreed in principle, but the shippers are insisting that the limits of Gaia be extended to allow them to build new bottling plants (so far only the Symington group of companies and Sandeman have large, modern bottling lines in Gaia).

Despite the relaxation of the Gaia-only export law, new bottling plants in the Douro region itself would not provide the answer:

Below: *By now, this 1985 Grahams vintage port is in bottle – vintage ports are bottled two years after picking. The best 1985s have fine aroma and excellent balance of tannin, acidity and colour.*

Port Vintages

A shipper does not "declare" a port to be worthy of the name "vintage" until after he has watched its development for two years. Even the best years vary, so it is important to know your way around port vintages. Some shippers sell vintage port in half-bottles, but these mature more quickly than full bottles, and never to the same peak of development. Historically, the "first-growth" vintage ports have come from Taylor, Warre, Dow, Graham, Cockburn, Fonseca, Croft and Sandeman.

1945	The great post-war vintage, and one of the best of the century. Rich, powerful wines, still magnificent, if you can find them.
1948	Not many shippers declared a vintage, but those who did made sweet, concentrated wines after a blazing summer. Taylor, Fonseca and Graham are still excellent.
1950	Rather a delicate set of wines, as vintage ports go, most past their best.
1955	Pleasant wines from a good season, sun and rain at the right times. Almost all shippers declared, and the wines are still smoothly fruity, though should be drunk soon.
1960	Good, middle-of-the-road vintage. Potentially perfect weather conditions were spoiled by rain during the latter half of the harvest. Now at its peak of maturity.
1963	The best vintage since 1945. All authorities describe it as "classic", and most wines still need more time to develop – if there are any left.
1966	Very hot summer weather made sweet, firm wines. Most are excellent now, though a few need longer.
1970	Ideal weather gave fine, balanced wines. They are still quite closed, and should not be drunk until 1990 onwards.
1975	Light, early-maturing vintage, though welcomed by the shippers as the first with real vintage potential since 1970. Pleasant drinking already, though should last until 1995.
1977	The vintage of the 70s, picked after a perfect growing season. The wines are big, alcoholic and packed with flavour. Keep until the turn of the century.
1980	A small vintage of good, elegant wines, for drinking from 1995 onwards.
1982	Soft, easy wines that will mature fairly fast. Only a few shippers declared. Drinkable from 1993 onwards.
1983	Most who had not declared in 1982 did so this year, which made rounder, richer, longer-lasting wines than 1982. Drink from 1995 onwards.
1985	First universal declaration for a decade. The top wines are near-classic, and have the concentration to last for years, but some lesser wines are almost ready for drinking already.

shippers hold most of their stocks at Gaia because it has a near-perfect climate for maturing wine. Together with Istanbul, Oporto has the most humid climate in Europe. Wines matured in hot, dry Douro lodges evaporate and mature at a rapid rate, leaving them with a sweet, almost cooked character known as "Douro bake", desirable in aged tawnies, but not suitable for other types of port. Gaia-matured wines age more slowly in the high humidity (boosted if necessary during the summer by watering the earth floors in the lodges).

Finally, after ageing and blending, most wines are submitted to processes of filtration, refrigeration and sometimes pasteurisation to stabilise them before bottling. Basic tawny and ruby, and premium versions up to Vintage Characater and most Late-Bottled Vintage, are all treated this way to ensure there will be no unsightly deposits when bottles are poured undecanted. Actually, some deposit in the bottle should be a welcome sight, as it means the wine has *not* been subjected to exhaustive filtration processes, which remove some character.

*I*n May 1986, England and Portugal cele-
brated the 600th anniversary of the Treaty
of Windsor, an alliance of political and
trading interests that has bound the two
countries together since the 14th century.
There have been British traders based in
Oporto for centuries supervising the import
and export of wool, fish, oil, corn – and wine.

For many years, the selection and shipping
of port was the province of the British, and
cultivating the Douro vineyards and winemaking was left to the Portuguese. Gradually, the distinction blurred. The British,
seduced by the wild beauty of the Douro
countryside, bought farms, and the Portuguese realised that blending and shipping

port wine was a profitable business.

Some of the choicest estates now belong
to the British (or "international") shippers,
most of them equipped with increasingly
modern wineries, while a few distinguished
Portuguese port shippers can trace their ori-
gins back over 200 years.

Several of the major shippers have
changed hands, in most cases moving out of
family control into ownership by large, international drinks organisations, but the old,
familiar names of the port trade survive. The
Warre, Graham, Guimaraens, Sandeman and
Delaforce families still have members who
work in the trade, though they no longer own
the port houses that bear their names.

Pick of Port

Churchill Graham Lda The only new port shipper founded in recent years, by Johnny (ex-
Cockburn's) and Caroline (née Churchill) Graham. Quantity is secondary in importance to
quality, and styles are limited to rich, complex Churchills Vintage Character and Crusted
ports, and tough, traditional Vintage.

Cockburn Smithes Owned by brewing giant Allied, through Harveys of Bristol. Cockburn's are
at the forefront of research into viticulture and vinification, with extensive experimental
vineyards and nurseries at Vilariça in the Upper Douro. Vintage ports are rich and powerful,
with a dry finish, the Crusted is similar on a smaller scale, and there is a single *quinta* wine,
Eira Velha, recently launched in the USA.

Croft One of the oldest companies, founded in 1678. Their ports have a sweet style said to
come from the grapes of their flagship property, Quinta da Roeda, just outside Pinhão.
Croft is owned by the international company IDV, itself a subsidiary of Grand Metropolitan,
and many of their ports are rather disappointing, but Croft Distinction is a reliable tawny,
about eight years old.

Delaforce Also owned by IDV, and best known for their tawny, His Eminence's Choice, another
good wine between five and ten years old.

Dow's Brand name for ports from the house of Silva & Cosens, one of the three Symington
family companies. Dow's top ports are based on grapes from their Quinta do Bomfim
(shortly to be launched as an off-vintage single *quinta* wine). Bomfim also has a modern
winery where about half the Symington group's wine is made. Dow ports have a relatively
dry style, and the vintage is concentrated and long-lived. Tawnies younger than the
30-Year-Old are slightly disappointing. Dow's Crusted is meaty and serious, worth keeping a
few years.

Ferreira Serious Portuguese shippers, now owned by the Guedes family of Mateus Rosé fame.
Ferreira have done much experimental work on viticulture and winemaking, and are
pioneers of the "up-and-down" system of vine plantation, with rows vertical to the slope of
the vineyard. Their vintage ports have an elegant, blackcurrant and cedar style, but
Ferreira's greatest strength lies in their tawnies, Dona Antonia's Personal Reserve (about
eight years old), Quinta do Porto Ten-Year-Old and the delicious Duque de Braganza
20-Year-Old.

Fonseca Brand shipped by the House of Guimaraens, owned by the Robertson family (who
also own Taylor's). Quantities of Fonseca ports are much smaller than of Taylor's, and the
style is deliberately different, a little sweeter, plummier and less austere. The top wines,
based on grapes from two quintas in the Pinhão valley, Cruzeiro and São Antonio, are
uniformly excellent, particularly the aged tawnies, the vintage Fonseca wines, and the off-
vintage Fonseca Guimaraens wines. Latest developments are a rich, serious LBV and a single
quinta wine, Quinta do Panascal.

Graham Bought in 1970 by the Symington group, Grahams is a softer, sweeter style of wine
than the other Symington wines. The principal estates for the Graham wines are Quinta dos
Malvedos, overlooking Tua, and Quinta dos Lages. Quinta dos Malvedos makes one of the
best-known single *quinta* off-vintage wines, full of soft, figgy fruit.

Martinez Gassiot The Martinez lodge in Gaia is right next to that of Cockburns, and also
owned by Harvey's of Bristol. Martinez used to ship a lot of port in bulk, and matured their
wines in the Douro, giving them the sweet "Douro bake". These days the wines are matured
in Gaia, but still made intentionally sweet. Old tawnies are the Martinez speciality.

Montez-Champalimaud (Quinta do Côtto) Miguel Champalimaud, of Quinta do Côtto, was one of the most ardent campaigners for the relaxation of the Gaia maturation rule, and the Quinta do Côtto ports are now exported from the family estate near Regua. The vintage port is soft, plummy and easy, and the aged Tawny Velho Doce is wonderfully nutty.

Niepoort Independent company run by Rolf Niepoort, who has the reputation of being one of the best tasters and blenders in the port trade. Niepoort produce some fine old tawnies.

Offley Forrester Now part of Martini & Rossi, the international vermouth and drinks group, Offley still base their vintage ports on wine from the famous Quinta Boa Vista, stylish wines, sweeter than most.

Quinta da Romaneira One of the *quintas* to have taken advantage of the relaxation of the Gaia maturation rules, exporting directly from the Douro. Quinta da Romaneira is a 400 hectare estate (with 70 hectares of vines), between Pinhão and Tua, owned by the Vinagre family. They ship a plummy, almondy Ruby and *colheita* wines of various ages, made in the concentrated, nutty, minty style the Portuguese themselves prefer.

Quinta do Noval Not all the Quinta do Noval wine comes from this beautiful *quinta* high above Pinhão. Quinta de Noval is unusual in having a patch of vineyard planted with ungrafted, pre-phylloxera vines. No one knows why these have escaped the phylloxera bug, but they produce an average of 2,200 bottles of fabulously concentrated port each year, about one-third of which is bottled and offered to merchants as an incentive to expand sales of Noval's other wines. Noval LB is their most widely sold wine, rich, nutty and good for straightforward LB; tawnies are also impressive.

Ramos-Pinto Extremely quality-conscious Portuguese house. All grapes come from their own *quintas*, and all new plantings are of selected varieties grown on virus-free rootstock on the "up-and-down" system. The wines are good, made in a medium-weight, elegant style. The Vintage Character is minty and grapy and the Late Bottled rich, serious and complex. The Quinta Ervamoira Ten-Year-Old and the Quinta Bom Retiro 20-Year-Old are classic tawnies, unusual in being from single *quintas*, and the Ramos-Pinto Vintage ports are minty, penetrating and extremely elegant.

Sandeman This was a family-owned company until 1979, when they sold out to Seagram, the international distilling and drinks company. Most interesting of the Sandeman ports are their aged tawnies, Royal 10-Year-Old and Imperial 20-Year-Old, made in a dry, woody style, with good concentration of nutty, minty flavour.

Smith Woodhouse Another company in the Symington group, bought with Graham in 1970. Smith Woodhouse also ships ports under the Gould Campbell label. Particularly noteworthy are the Smith Woodhouse Late Bottled Vintage ports, wines with much more character and complexity than most LBVs. They benefit from cellaring for at least two years and can be expected to throw a deposit.

Taylor, Fladgate & Yeatman Taylor's is the smaller of the two long-established independent British companies. It belongs to the Robertson family (who also own Fonseca), and the top wines are based on grapes from two *quintas* in the Upper Douro, Quinta de Vargellas and Terra Feita. Taylor's ports are elegant rather than heavy, although the vintage wines are among the toughest and hardest when young, and often the longest-lived. The Late Bottled Vintage has good, cedary-minty complexity, the aged tawnies have the house's dry style, and the single estate Quinta de Vargellas port is often the best of the off-vintage offerings.

Warre Warre's was founded in 1670, oldest of the firms in the Symington group. Top wine comes from the Quinta da Cavadinha, in the Pinhão valley, one of the off-vintage single estate wines to be launched recently. Nimrod, a tawny about eight years old, is always reliable; there are good Crusted ports, and serious, characterful Late Bottled Vintage wines.

More than half the wine produced in the Douro is not made into port. Some is reject wine from the lowest grades of port vineyards, but much of the region's wine is never intended to be anything other than table wine. Table wines were made here long before port. English and Scottish merchants made and imported *unfortified* red wine from the Douro region for over a century before the principle of fortification was discovered. The red Douro table wine of the 1700s was a rough brew, and what progress has been made in Douro winemaking since then has been limited almost entirely to port. But there are enough good Douro table wines to show conclusively that the area is capable of great things.

Indeed, Portugal's most sought-after red table wine, Barca Velha, comes from the Douro. It was the creation of Fernando Nicolau de Almeida of the port house of Ferreira, who had visited Bordeaux to learn how the French made red wine. He devised a rudimentary cooling system. (Day temperatures in the Douro in September can reach 45°C, and at night 42°C). Lorries brought ice overnight from Oporto, and this was packed in a container round the outside of tall, Bordeaux-style fermentation vessels, then covered with sawdust.

The results were not good enough every year, and the experiments continued. He copied the French idea of maturation in new oak barrels, having his made from Portuguese oak. He tried blends of wine from higher and lower vineyards, from different grape varieties, and has now changed from oak fermentation vats to stainless steel. The dominant grape in the blend is Tinta Roriz, with smaller amounts of Touriga Nacional and Tinta Barroca, and approximately 40,000 bottles are made each year, from grapes grown at Meão in the Upper Douro.

Barca Velha is sold as such only in the best vintages. Each wine's progress is carefully monitored, and vintages deemed good enough are released under the Barca Velha label only when ready to drink, at perhaps eight years old. "Reject" vintages, still excellent wine, become Reserva Especial.

Ferreira is unusual among the major port shippers in having devoted a lot of time to the research and development of table wine. Although it seems likely that other houses will follow (Cockburns and Quinta do Noval have both admitted interest in table wine projects), the party line in the port industry has been to concentrate on the production of port, certainly as far as grapes grown in the best areas of the Douro are concerned.

However, estates in the Baixo Corgo, with land in areas graded from C to F, have been more active in their researches into table wine, since a lesser proportion of their production may be made into port. Two estates in particular are leading the field in red table wines at present, Quinta do Côtto and Quinta da Pacheca. The two properties have followed very different policies in choosing grape varieties. Miguel Champalimaud of Quinta do

Côtto has stuck with native Portuguese grapes, while Eduardo Serpa Pimentel of Quinta da Pacheca has had considerable commercial success with imported varieties.

Both estates make port, but their table wines seem likely to take over in importance. Miguel Champalimaud makes his white wines from Malvasia and Avesso (the dominant grape on his *vinho verde* property Paço de Teixero), and uses a cooling system in the tanks to ferment at 16-17°C. His reds are made in autovinificators, from a blend of Touriga Nacional, Bastardo, Touriga Frances and Tinta Roriz, and, in the best years (often

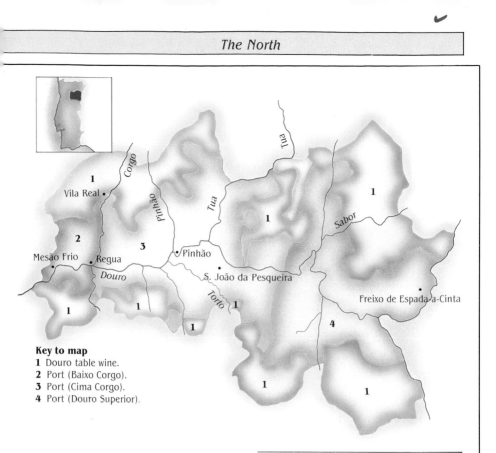

Key to map
1 Douro table wine.
2 Port (Baixo Corgo).
3 Port (Cima Corgo).
4 Port (Douro Superior).

coinciding with declared port vintages), he makes a remarkable top wine, Grande Escolha, aged in new Douro oak barrels.

Eduardo Serpa Pimentel has plantations on his two estates of Riesling, Gewürztraminer, Sauvignon and Cabernet Sauvignon, as well as Touriga Nacional, Touriga Frances, Tinta Roriz, Barroca and Tinta Cão. The white wines made from the imported varieties are very popular in Portugal, but are not yet good enough to be of real interest on the export market. His reds, however, with the native Douro grapes boosted by a little Cabernet Sauvignon, are extremely successful, with a rich concentration of flavours.

Left: *The house at Quinta do Côtto, one of the two leading Douro table wine estates.*

Pick of the Douro

Ferreira Portugal's top red table wine, Barca Velha, is a wine of considerable complexity and character, released only in the best years. It is hard to find, and sells out very quickly, but vintages to look forward to, judging by the young wines we tasted, are 1983, 1985 and 1987. Wines not good enough for Barca Velha itself are demoted to Reserva Especial, also amongst Portugal's top reds. Esteva, the young, plummy red from Ferreira, is also good.

Quinta do Côtto Watch for the wines from this property, one of Portugal's rising stars, particularly their Côtto Grande Escolha, made in the best years and aged in new oak.

Quinta da Pacheca The red Quinta da Pacheca is the best of this estate's wines, with a touch of Cabernet Sauvignon, rich and cedary-minty.

Sogrape This huge firm of Mateus fame is making reds and whites from grapes grown on a plateau south-east of Vila Real. Only the whites are successful so far, soft, fresh, fragrant Planalto, made from Viosinho with a little Malvasía Fina and Gouveio.

Caves do Raposeira Seagram-owned makers of sparkling wines, and of one of Portugal's only Chardonnays, Quinta de Valprado, buttery and honeyed.

Demarcated only in 1979, Bairrada lies south of Oporto, astride Portugal's main north-south road between Oporto and Coimbra, with the majority of the vineyards lying between the road and the coast. *Barro* is Portuguese for clay, and Bairrada's name derives from this characteristic of its soil. The best vineyards are planted on clay with a sub-structure of limestone.

It is a region of sloping vineyards stretching back into gently rolling hills. Forests of eucalyptus and cedar border vineyards in which old Baga vines (Bairrada's principal variety) stand upright like thick, gnarled walking sticks rammed into the earth. Only when the grapes grow heavy is it necessary to support these old vines, usually with a single, stout cane, although recently planted vineyards have wires stretched between metal supports.

Bairrada sometimes has to make do without rain for two or three months in the summer. But the weather changes abruptly in September, and the harvest is often interrupted or spoiled by heavy rain. In some years, this prevents full ripening of the Baga, which accounts for 90 per cent of all grapes planted. In fact, the Baga does really well only in the Jurassic clay-based soils in the centre and south of the region, and to the south of Cantanhede. These are the areas most capable of making the rich reds for which Bairrada is renowned.

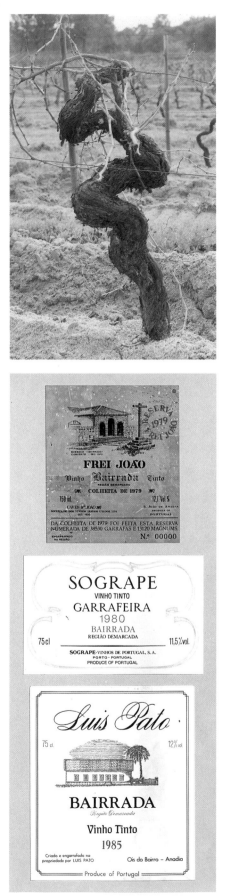

However, demand for white Bairrada, both still and especially sparkling, has risen so fast that growers have started grafting their red vines over to white. The base for these whites is the Maria Gomes grape, with help from the Bical do Bairrada, Cerceal and Arinto. More and more white wines, still and sparkling, are being cool fermented in stainless steel tanks (even in two of Bairrada's five co-operatives, Cantahede and Souzela). The most enterprising winemakers obtain additional flavour by macerating the grape skins. At Caves Aliança, California-trained winemaker Dido Mendes does this before fermentation, but estate-owner Luis Pato is even more innovative. He adds back a tiny percentage of grape skins after pressing and includes them in the fermentation, and has high hopes for the results when he is able to use grape skins from his recent plantations of Cerceal, the most aromatic of the Bairrada white grapes.

Caves Aliança, Luis Pato and Sogrape are also at the forefront of red winemaking technology in the region, believing that to succeed in international markets, red Bairrada should become a softer, less astringent wine, easier to drink when relatively young. By law, it must contain a minimum of 50 per cent of wine made from the Baga grape. However, the Baga is a difficult variety, high in the phenolic compounds that make red wine astringent; traditionally made Bairrada takes five

Pick of Bairrada

Caves Aliança Large and forward-looking company. Young red Bairrada is particularly worth trying, for its concentration of rich, buttery fruit, as is the Tinto Bruto Espumante, a Champagne method red, with delicious raspberry fruit.

Caves São João Quality-conscious medium-sized family company, mostly buying wine from local co-ops, and maturing it into dark, rich, traditionally-styled red Bairrada that needs five years' ageing for ordinary wines, and at least ten for reservas.

Luis Pato Bairrada's "boutique" winery, run by revolutionary traditionalist Luis Pato. All wines come from his and his wife's families' vineyards, and are excellent examples of the quality level Bairrada should be striving for, in reds and whites. Even his sparkling wines are delicious, especially the *rosé*, made from pure Baga, creamy, fresh, and touched with raspberry perfume.

Sogrape One of Sogrape's two big Mateus plants is here, and also makes a soft, light, fruity Bairrada as well as old-fashioned *garrafeiras*.

Left: *A gnarled old Baga vine awaits the spring pruners. Ninety per cent of Bairrada's vines are Baga, and the wines it traditionally makes are fruity and rich but also tough and astringent.*

years at least to soften into drinkability, sometimes failing to reach an attractive balance of fruit and drinkable tannin. Many producers still leave stalks behind in the fermenting wine, making the wines even more astringent.

The new-style Bairradas are softer, easier wines, fermented without stalks, though still retaining Bairrada's naturally rich fruitiness and fragrance. At Caves Aliança, Dido Mendes has tried fining and de-acidifying the grape juice to remove bitterness, and is now experimenting with a tank like a washing machine to extract colour from the grape skins for two to three days before fermentation. The ensuing fermentation will not include any skins or pips to toughen the wine. Pato ages some of his wine in new oak barrels. Sogrape remove the stalks, lightly crush the grapes, then flash-heat the juice and skins for four minutes to extract the colour, before pressing immediately; the juice has a long, cool fermentation. The resulting wines are light and fruity, for drinking young.

But such experiments cannot proceed *too* quickly. Would-be Bairrada has to be submitted to conservative official tasting panels at every stage – after fermentation, while maturing for its statutory 18 months (in tank or barrel) before bottling, and immediately prior to bottling. Luis Pato may say that "the future lies in stalk-free fermentations and new oak" but he has had wines rejected more than once for being too oaky. Nevertheless, the winemakers of Bairrada know that the Baga is a natural star (even though some have experimental plantations of Cabernet Sauvignon) and that sooner or later their wine will take its place amongst the great red wines, not just of Portugal, but of the world.

Left: *Bairrada's revolutionary traditionalist, Luis Pato, who makes softer, oaked reds from his family vines.*

*T*ucked away deep inland in Northern Portugal south of the River Douro, Dão (pronounced approximately Downg) is virtually surrounded by mountain ranges. Inside this girdle of mountains lies a hilly region of granite soil and pine forests. Looking south from the top of a hill, it is often impossible to catch a glimpse of vines, as vineyards tend to be hidden from view on the southern side, where they enjoy maximum exposure to the sun.

Many of the vineyards in the hilliest regions were literally carved out of the same granite used to build houses in the picturesque Dão villages. More recently, winegrowers have opted for gentler slopes, where the granite has been broken down to a fine

consistency, and combined with clay in some parts to form a soil that has the look of coarse sand. As is often the case, the finest wines come from the poorest soils.

Dão produces red and white wines, although its reputation is founded on its reds. Both reds and whites can be made from a large number of grape varieties, but each must contain a minimum 20 per cent of one particular variety. Encruzado for whites, Touriga Nacional for reds. Other recommended grapes for whites are Arinto do Dão (alias Assario Branco), Borrado das Moscas (or Bical da Bairrada), Cerceal and Barcelo, and for reds Jaen, Tinta Roriz, Tinta Pinheira (or Rufete, or Penamacor), Alfrocheiro Preto and Bastardo.

Pick of Dão

Caves Aliança Bairrada-based merchant blending and maturing good, rich, meaty Dão reds.

Caves São João Another Bairrada-based merchant. Their Porta dos Cavaleiros Dão brand is one of the most reliable labels for Dão reds. The wines have a delicious, raspberry, minty fruit that matures very well.

Conde de Santar Single estate in the heart of the Dão region, producing rich, cherry-flavoured reds with toffee'd depth, distributed by port company A. A. Cálem.

Vinicola do Vale do Dão (Sogrape) Wines sold as Grão Vasco. Top wines have some new oak maturation. Young red wines are the best bet, with soft, easy, blackberry fruitiness, although there are some stunning 1983 and 1985 reds still maturing in barrel, waiting to be bottled.

The white wines have a marked lemon and honey aroma when young, and a high acidity despite the hot summers. With age, the honey begins to dominate, together with a piney note and a rich, almost oily character. All white Dão has to be aged for at least six months before bottling, and *garrafeira* wines for a year (six months in vat, six in bottle).

Red wines undergo much more protracted ageing with a minimum for ordinary reds of 18 months before bottling (often extended to two to three years) and a further two months in bottle before sale. Red *garrafeiras* have to be aged for a minimum of two years in vat and one in bottle, but frequently also this requirement is substantially exceeded. The red wines often taste rather dull in the period between youth, when they can be deliciously fruity and firmly tannic, and the complex maturity of the best *garrafeiras*. Sadly, many attractive wines are left to age too long. Many producers, and their Portuguese customers,

prefer softer but less fruity, mature wines, and by the time the wines are sold, they have lost the youthful charm that would have been far more appealing to the international market. Indeed, younger, fruitier wines are frequently rejected by the conservative tasting panels at the Federation of Dão Wine Producers, who have to pass each batch of wine before it is sold.

The problem is exacerbated by the fact that two-thirds of Dão's production is handled by co-operatives with antiquated equipment. One exception is the Vila Nova de Tazem co-operative, most of whose wine is sold under the Grão Vasco label by the Vinicola do Vale do Dão, a subsidiary of the giant Sogrape wine company. The Sogrape subsidiary is not allowed to buy grapes in Dão (a universal rule intended to protect the livelihood of the small-scale Dão wine producers and co-operatives and enable them to sell their produce as wine). But it does the next best thing: Vinicola do Vale do Dão has an agreement with the Tazem co-op to buy most of its production on condition that they can supervise the winemaking and provide modern machinery to ensure quality.

A recent, additional solution for Sogrape has been to buy their own 100-hectare vineyard, and they are considering building a winery. Its viability will depend on whether the prohibition on buying grapes is dropped, since grapes from their own estate alone would not make the operation profitable.

Dão wine is cheap, considering the ageing involved. Most of the blending, maturation, sales and particularly the exports of Dão are handled by the big companies such as Sogrape, JM da Fonseca and Caves São João, from wineries outside the Dão region. Even the single estate wine (the only one till recently), Conde de Santar, is sold by the port company Cálem, while the other two estates that might one day make and bottle their wines, Quinta da Insua and Quinta do Serrado, are handled by JM da Fonseca and Carvalho, Ribeiro & Ferreira respectively. The other large companies will probably have to continue the Dão revolution started by Sogrape if this potentially excellent region is to improve the quality of its wines and upgrade its international image.

Left: Pine forests share the slopes of the Dão region with vines — and flocks of sheep and goats.

The Oeste turns out more wine than any other part of Portugal. What is more, when the next set of demarcated areas comes into force, and the Oeste has been split up into the separate regions of Arruda, Torres, Gaeiras, Alcobaça and Encostas de Aire (see pages 150-151), it seems likely that the Oeste region now known as Torres Vedras will be the largest in Portugal in terms of volume. Apparently, the name proposed for the new demarcated region is Torres, potentially confusing for wine-lovers who equate "Torres" with the famous Spanish firm from the Penedés.

At present, the Oeste (literally, "West") covers a vast area, running from the north side of the Tagus estuary by Lisbon right up to the towns of Batalha and Leiria, only 80 km south of Coimbra, and the southernmost point of the Bairrada region. Wine is made everywhere, most often on the slopes of the gentle hills that make it much more attractive countryside than the flat river valley of the Ribatejo immediately to the east.

The hills around Torres Vedras are more formidable, as the French army found during the Peninsular War, when their advance on Lisbon was halted by Wellington's entrenched position in a line of fortifications running from the Tagus river to the sea. The old castle still stands high above Torres Vedras. Below, the town bustles with traffic and activity. Down by the unspoiled coast, holiday houses are beginning to spring up overlooking some of Europe's best surfing beaches. The cool, damp, Atlantic air affects the whole of the Torres Vedras region, giving lighter, more delicate wines even than neighbouring Arruda.

The Torres Vedras whites are mainly made from Vital and Fernão Pires grapes, with some Seminario (or Malvasía Rey). They age surprisingly well. For the reds, the ubiquitous João de Santarém predominates, with help from the Tinta Miúda and Trincadeira. The Torres Vedras co-operative is by far the biggest producer in the area, and single-handed accounts for two and a half per cent of Portugal's entire wine output. Two-thirds of their production is sold in bulk, but their goal is to bottle and export a greater percentage.

Though not far away, Arruda dos Vinhos ("the road of the wines") seems remote and far more rustic. Mule-drawn carts driven by unhurried countrymen often halt the traffic flow through the main street of this little town. In the rolling hills around it, imposing manor farmhouses and villages of clay-tiled, whitewashed houses break up valleys of vineyards, and hilltops sport abandoned windmills. Arruda is dominated by its co-operative, whose 1,500 members own over a third of the 7,140 hectares likely to be included in the proposed demarcated region. Red wines, made mainly from the João de Santarém, with some Tinta Miúda, Trincadeira, Camarate and Preto Martinho, are better than the unexciting whites, made from the Vital, Arinto, Rabo d'Ovelha, Fernão Pires and João Paulo. All exports are to the

U.K. at the moment, and almost all of these are of two to three year old red wine to one supermarket, Sainsbury's, an arrangement that has provoked understandable envy from other co-operatives in the region.

Alenquer is smaller than both Torres Vedras and Arruda. Like Arruda, it is sheltered from the Atlantic by mountains to the north and west. Locals say the difference between Alenquer and Arruda is most noticeable in the white wines, although we have tasted good examples of both reds and whites. The Quinta de Abrigada, an estate with 35 hectares of vineyard, has been bottling its wines, the red made from Periquita (alias João de Santarém) and the white from Fernão Pires, Arinto and Vital, for about 20 years. Although both are light in style, they are well-made wines of distinct character, as are the wines from the Quinta do Porto Franco at Atalaia, the property of the Correia family. The family owns farms at Carregado and in Torres Vedras as well, 200 hectares in all, and bottles wine only for home consumption, selling all the rest in bulk on the domestic market. There is considerable wine expertise within the family: two sons are qualified oenologists, working for co-ops at Torres Vedras, Sobral, São Momede and Cartaxo, and another handles exports for the Torres Vedras co-op.

Further north near the coast, Lourinhã, Bombarral and Cadaval lie south of Obidos, a picturesque old walled hill town. Most of the wines of this area are white, and often quite light in alcohol, though the reds that *are* made can be successful at *garrafeira* level in good years. The Gaeiras wines from Obidos (which should soon achieve demarcated status), light and easy-drinking, have achieved popularity in Portugal in recent years, but have not yet been exported.

Wines from around Alcobaça, Leiria and Batalha rarely escape the region. Similar grapes are grown to those used in Arruda, with the addition of the Boal and Malvasía among the whites, and the Baga, Preto de Mortágua and Tinta Pinheira in the reds.

Above: *A well-groomed vineyard near the town of Arruda. Of the 7,140 hectares of vineyard likely to be included in the soon-to-be-demarcated region of Arruda, a third is owned by members of the Arruda Co-operative. The co-op is responsible at the moment for practically all the region's exports, nearly all to one British supermarket.*

Pick of the Oeste

Quinta de Abrigada, Alenquer Family-run estate making light, creamy whites and stylish, cherry-fruited reds that develop well.

Quinta da Folgorosa, Torres Vedras Property owned by Carvalho, Ribeiro & Ferreira, making rich, buttery whites that mature very successfully, and rather insubstantial reds.

Adega Cooperativa de Arruda dos Vinhos The two to three year old red wine sold to Sainsbury's is the best of the table wines, with soft, damson and cherry fruit. The co-op also makes a delicious *licoroso* from João de Santarém, with nearly 30° alcohol, richly sweet and nutty.

Adega Cooperativa de Torres Vedras Giant co-op, with limited cool-fermentation capacity for top whites, and a system of continuous fermentation for reds. The best wines are the young reds, and red *reservas* from good vintages, such as 1976, 1972 and 1969.

Adega Cooperativa de Labrugeira, Alenquer Small co-operative north of Alenquer, with good, minty, cedary red *garrafeiras*.

*T*he Tagus is over 1,000 kilometres long, the longest river in the Iberian peninsula. It rises in the Montes Universales just inside southern Aragón, winds its way south of Madrid, through Toledo and north of Cáceres before it crosses Spain's border with Portugal a few miles south of Castelo Branco. From here it flows almost due east until it turns southwards towards Lisbon by Vila Nova da Barquinha. It is just north of here that the vineyards of the Ribatejo begin.

The Ribatejo ("banks of the Tagus") includes land in the districts of Tomar, Chamusca, Almeirim, Santarém, Cartaxo, Coruche, Rio Maior, Alpiarça and Salvaterra de Magos, the first six of which should soon be individually demarcated regions. It is flattish, fertile, river valley land, with soils that vary from alluvial to sandy, with more clay to the north of Cartaxo.

The climate is quite mild, affected by the river Tagus itself, which is tidal as far as Almeirim, and the combination of a generous average rainfall of between 500 and 700 mm per year, cooling Atlantic breezes, and fertile soils gives huge annual yields. In fact, the Ribatejo is the second largest producer in Portugal after the Oeste.

The most successful grapes grown in the area are the red João de Santarém (Santarém being the region's main town) and white Fernão Pires. (The João de Santarém is sometimes known as the Castellão Francês or Periquita). Other local grapes include the Trincadeira and Mortágua, and there are plantings of other varieties such as Baga, Cabernet Sauvignon, Merlot and Alicante Bouschet. The Rabo d'Ovelha, Terrantez, Boal, Tália, Jampal and Vital are the principal other white grapes in production.

Co-operatives predominate in the Ribatejo, with the country's second largest at Almeirim, and others at Cartaxo, Chamusca, Rio Maior, Gouxa, Tomar and Alcanhões. Much of their production is sold in bulk, some locally, some to the Algarve and some to large commercial bottlers such as Caves Velhas in Bucelas (see pages 140-141). Caves Velhas, who have strong connections with the

Right: Harvest at the Cartaxo Co-op. Co-ops dominate production in the Ribatejo, and sell most of their wine in bulk.

Below: The modern Margaride winery out in the vineyards. The care lavished on the grapes is reflected in the wines.

Pick of the Ribatejo

Adega Cooperativa de Almeirim Huge, well-equipped co-operative, with cool fermentation for whites and autovinificators for reds. Whites are best, especially the Quinta das Varandas, honeyed and minty.

Casa Agricola Herdeiros de Dom Luís de Margaride Estate with two farms, Convento da Serra and Casal do Monteiro, and a modern winery and vineyards. Only about one third of production is bottled at present, under various names – Dom Hermano, Casal do Monteiro, Convento da Serra and Margaride. All are good. The whites show the aromatic, minty character of the Fernão Pires grape, and there is a good, creamy, dry rośe from Baga and Trincadeira. The Convento da Serra red is a soft, plummy mix of Merlot, Cabernet Franc, Alicante Bouschet, Baga and Fernão Pires, the other reds mainly João de Santarém, with rich, plummy and strawberry-like fruit, developing well with age.

Caves Velhas Bucelas-based company buying Ribatejo wine for many of their brands. Best are the Romeira and Caves Velhas Garrafeiras, with rich, cherry and strawberry fruit and mature flavours of tobacco and cedar.

Ribatejo, come here to buy all their non-Bucelas table wines, from the most basic plonk sold in returnable bottles to some excellent *garrafeira* wine. Carvalho, Ribeiro & Ferreira, another large commercial company, is actually based in the south of the Ribatejo region, in Vila Franca de Xira. They do not make wine themselves, but buy wines from co-operatives and blend, age and bottle them in their own cellars.

There are a few private producers who bottle and market their own wines, but only one estate of real importance, the Herdeiros de Dom Luís de Margaride, near Almeirim. Dom Luís, the father of the current owners, replanted the two immaculate family vineyards after carrying out extensive soil and grape variety studies. These vineyards now contain a wider selection of grape varieties than any others in the region, although

non-local varieties are used to add interest to blends rather than as single varietal wines. The estate grows both Cabernet and Merlot, for instance, for use in conjunction with the João de Santarém.

The immense care that goes into the grape production is inevitably reflected in the quality of the wines, and although the giant Almeirim co-operative has more refrigeration equipment than the whole of the rest of the Ribatejo put together, its wines cannot match those of the Margaride estate.

If the wines of the Ribatejo are to fulfil their undoubted potential, more producers will have to follow this estate's example. Research into the correct grape varieties for the different soils of the region is vitally important. However advanced winery technology may be, great wine cannot be made without very good grapes.

Colares is a region that has survived much, but it will need all its experience to struggle through the last years of the 20th century. Its greatest victory was over the root-munching insect phylloxera. Actually, there was not even a battle, as the pest was unable to travel across the sand dunes on which the vineyards of Colares are planted. So, while the rest of Europe succumbed to the deadly beetle, Colares escaped, perched on its dune plateau some 200 to 300 metres above the sea.

But these vineyards are very labour intensive, the style of the wine-making has obstinately refused to keep up with the times and, were it not for the curiosity value that still clings to the image of Colares, the future of this steadily-decreasing region would be in grave doubt. As it is, the Colares red wines are worth seeking out and trying, even though they are relatively expensive, for a glimpse of an ultra-traditional Portuguese style of red wine, strange though that may be to a foreign palate.

Imagine a wind-swept cliff above the sea, with groves of straggly pines and the occasional holiday development, and you will have a fair idea of the Colares region. Except that in the open, sandy spaces, vines are planted in rows between two metre high, woven bamboo wind-breaks. The vines sprawl spider-like on the sand, and have to be raised 50cm off the ground by bamboo sticks when grapes begin to form, so that the burning sand does not scorch the fruit. In the few new vineyards planted in the last five years, plastic netting screens have replaced bamboo.

The roots of the vines are not actually anchored in the sand, but in the clay soil beneath, at depths that range from one to five metres. Each time a vineyard is replanted, a hole has to be dug down to the clay. In the parts of the region where the sand

is at its deepest, there is a very real danger of the sand walls of the hole collapsing, suffocating the vineyard worker, so vineyard work is always carried out in pairs. Another man stands by the top of the hole to throw a basket over the head of the digger and keep the sand away from his face in case of emergency.

As there is no need to graft the vines on to American rootstock to repel the unwelcome attentions of the phylloxera beetle, replantation is effected by "direct propagation". This can be done in two ways. Either shoots from the vines are buried in the sand after the fruiting season, encouraging them to send out suckers which grow their own root systems and become the new vines, or cuttings incorporating some growth of more than a year old are taken from vines and stuck into the sand in the hope that they will put down roots.

Both red and white wines are made in the region (though Colares is principally renowned for its reds), from the Ramisco and Malvasia grapes respectively, with a few subsidiary varieties allowed into the blend up to a maximum of 20 per cent. *All* Colares wine is made at the Adega Regional de Colares, then

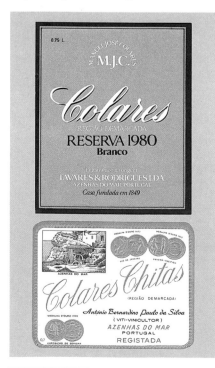

Pick of Colares

Antonio Bernardino Paulo da Silva Merchant producing good red and indifferent white table wines "from local grapes near Colares" – but outside the demarcated region – as well as red and white Colares. Current vintage of Colares Chitas Tinto is 1974, still tough and tannic, though with tremendous depth of cherry fruit.

Tavares & Rodrigues This merchant's current red, the 1976 MJC Colares Reserva, is even less ready than the Paulo da Silva 1974, very lean and acidic, with a spearminty flavour and a faint raspberry after-taste.

allocated to the three merchants who own vineyards according to the weight of grapes they delivered.

The Adega Regional pays for grapes only by weight and potential alcoholic degree. There are no different levels of quality in the wines they sell, which they do only after three or four years' maturation in concrete tanks for

both red and white wines. Wine-making is fairly basic. There is no de-stalking of the grapes before the red wine is fermented, and *all* the "press wine" is added to the free-run liquid, so Colares reds are extremely astringent, and take a long time to mature.

This is the job of the merchants still operating in Colares, A. B. Paulo da Silva, Tavares & Rodrigues and Real Companhia Vinicola. The young reds have a wonderfully rich, raspberry and cherry aroma, but the high tannin and acidity make them positively undrinkable until at least ten years (and preferably a lot longer) after they have been made.

Below: *Bamboo windbreaks are traditional in Colares, but the latest plantations, like these at Azenhas do Mar, are protected by plastic netting screens.*

Bucelas is tucked away behind mountains that shield it from the climatic influences of the Atlantic and the proximity of Lisbon. The village has only two major employers, Caves Velhas (the main producer of Bucelas wine) and a large poultry farm a few miles down the road. Otherwise, the inhabitants of Bucelas are mainly farmers of small agricultural holdings, or the shopkeepers and craftsmen who make up the intricate jigsaw of a rural community.

But Bucelas is in grave danger of becoming fashionable. It is less than 20 miles from an expanding Lisbon, whose inhabitants are cottoning on fast to the attractions of a weekend retreat so near the city and yet so sheltered from all the pressures attendant upon modern city life.

Bucelas *wine* has been in great demand in Portugal for a long time, and demand often outstrips supply. The demarcated zone covers no more than 500 hectares, and at present only about a third of that is planted with vines. Until recently, the only large-scale seller of Bucelas was Caves Velhas, most of whose shares belong to the giant state-owned beer company, Sagres. Caves Velhas have 70 hectares of their own vineyard, and buy in about 15 per cent of their grape needs from other proprietors. Their average annual production of 300,000 litres of Bucelas accounts for three-quarters of the area's production.

In the last few years, however, two new owner-producers have appeared on the scene, and locals believe that others may follow. Nuno Barba, owner of the local poultry farm, bought the 35 hectare Quinta do Avelar in 1980, and has been producing wine since 1982. A more surprising arrival has been Alcantara, a Portuguese company whose main shareholder is Tate and Lyle. They have bought a 140 hectare estate, and set about clearing land for a vineyard of 85 hectares, prior to planting, and installing a winery.

The Bucelas wine, subject of this upsurge of interest, is one of the few Portuguese white wines (Bucelas is *always* white) that improves with age. Indeed, that is how the Portuguese prefer it, as a *vinho maduro*, and it is true that the Arinto (Bucelas's principal grape variety) does develop interesting flavours in its maturity. The Arinto has to account for at least 75 per cent of any Bucelas blend, the other permitted varieties being Cercial, Esgana Cão and Rabo d'Ovelha.

Since the domestic market is the most important for Bucelas, Caves Velhas have been careful to retain a certain traditional character in the production of the wine, particularly for their *garrafeira*. So while the younger wine is mainly fermented in rather primitive, stainless steel tanks, water-cooled to about 21°C, wine destined for the *garrafeira* is fermented in cement tanks, or even wooden vats. The younger wine is confusingly labelled ``Bucellas Velho'', a long-established trademark incorporating an archaic spelling of the region (which the authorities tried, unsuccessfully, to change).

Above: *Government officials at the Caves Velhas* adega *applying wax seals to bottles to be kept in a ``sample library'' for future reference. Bucelas is one of very few Portuguese white wines that improve with age – the Arinto grape develops interesting flavours.*

Pick of Bucelas

Caves Velhas By far the largest producer, with six cellars scattered through the village. Their Bucellas Velho is mouth-filling but strongly acidic; the Bucelas Garrafeira is much more interesting, rich, soft and buttery, with strong, lemony acidity and overtones of mint, pine and nut.

Quinta do Avelar Impressively modern winery, full of stainless steel and up-to-date machinery. They do not age the wine, and it will improve with keeping. It starts with typically high, lemony acidity, but has a rich, oily depth.

Bucelas has a rich, fat texture to set against the piercing, lemony acidity of the Arinto. It is as if the area's extremes of climate come together in its wine. The mountains that exclude any cooling sea breezes in the summer heat also prevent the warmer coastal air from moderating the intense cold in winter.

Carcavelos
The recent history of Carcavelos is one of vineyard disasters and urban development. Oidium and phylloxera hit this small region very hard in the last 40 years of the 19th century, and the growth of the seaside resorts of Cascais and Estoril have all but obliterated the vineyards.

Only one estate, Quinta do Barão, is currently producing Carcavelos, a fortified wine made from a hotch-potch of grape varieties. The wine is rather coarse and raisiny, with only the faintest suggestion of the nuttiness of good tawny port. There is some hope, though, that one of Portugal's most forward-looking wine producers may be about to attempt a revival of the fortunes of Carcavelos, but the arrangement has yet to be confirmed.

Below: *Quinta do Barão and the last remaining vineyard in Carcavelos. The rest are buried beneath the seaside resorts of Cascais and Estoril.*

Portugal makes a host of sweet, fortified wines apart from the well-known port and Madeira, but among them only Setúbal and Carcavelos have so far been demarcated. Moscatel de Setúbal acquired its official stamp as long ago as 1907. It is only with the new proposed *Região Demarcada* regulations that the local red and dry white wines (see overleaf), from Palmela and Arrábida, will join this attractive, almondy-grapy sweet wine on the statute books.

However, not much Moscatel is actually grown on the Setúbal peninsula south of Lisbon. Only 107 hectares are currently planted, compared with 11,800 hectares of often very good red grapes, and 100 hectares of other, less aromatic whites. The demarcated area for Setúbal falls into two zones, the attractive hill country of Arrábida, Palmela and Azeitão in the south and south-west, and a broad, low, plain near the Sado river.

The Moscatel vine crops up in many different guises all over the wine-growing world, and growers around Setúbal will name several different strains in the vineyard. It seems likely, however, that several of these are synonyms for practically the same thing: the world's most common Moscatel, known internationally as the Muscat of Alexandria. This makes rather less fine wine than another Moscatel, the Muscat Blanc à Petits Grains, which is responsible for the French Muscats de Beaumes-de-Venise, perhaps Moscatel de Setúbal's closest rival in international terms. There is much discussion in Setúbal just now about which particular strains of Moscatel should be planted in what proportions in the future.

Production of this sweet wine is almost monopolised by the Azeitão firm of José Maria da Fonseca Successores. The fairly basic local co-operative makes about a tenth of the total, and six small *adegas* make and bottle a little. Da Fonseca buy nearly all their raw materials in the form of grapes from local growers. Of over a thousand in the region, only 35 specialise in growing Moscatel grapes, but most grow a little. At the moment, Fonseca buy some ready-made wine, but intend shortly to be making everything themselves.

At their attractive cellars in Azeitão, they de-stem and crush the grapes on arrival (approximately the 70 per cent Moscatel, 30 per cent other whites – Boal, Malvasía, Arinto, etc., – permitted by the regulations) and leave the wine to ferment, complete with its skins, until the sugar has been reduced to the required level. As in port production, grape spirit is then added to stop the wine fermenting and, remarkably, the aromatic skins are left macerating in the wine for five months before pressing some time in March of the following year. All the sugar in the wine is the natural grape sugar – no grape juice or sweetening wine is added.

The company has always traditionally sold a "young", wood-aged five or six-year-old Moscatel and a wood-aged 20 or 25-year-old

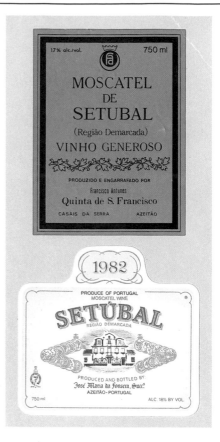

but they have recently concluded that their customers would prefer vintage wines. The younger wines, in fact, will be sold even younger. Though some 1983 is still around, the 1984 was a small vintage, and the 1985 will already be on the market by the end of 1988. This is no bad thing – young Moscatel

Pick of Setúbal

José Maria da Fonseca Successores Fine, historic family company with beautiful *adega* in the centre of Azeitão village. Fresh, grapy younger vintages and intense, raisiny, slightly spirity older vintages of Setúbal.

Quinta de São Francisco Small farm run as a hobby by a Lisbon doctor, selling good, intensely grapy youngish Moscatel de Setúbal.

Above: *Mahogany and oak vats and casks in the Vila Nova de Azeitão adega of José Maria da Fonseca Successores.*

Below: *Moscatel vines near the little town of Azeitão. Less than one per cent of the region's vines are Moscatel.*

de Setúbal is a delicious, fresh, grapy, if slightly spirity wine.

The wines are stored first in large wooden vats, then, as they reach more venerable ages, in small, old wooden barrels. 20-year-olds are rich, spirity, with a raisiny intensity, nice, fresh acidity and a long, grapy finish. Tastings of older vintages show how the grapy aroma fades some time after 20 years, transformed to flavours reminiscent of coffee, Christmas cake and caramel. The wines are regularly topped up with alcohol to around 18° during their maturation and, as with port, the spirit can sometimes be very prominent in these older wines.

Along with the switch to vintage wines, da Fonseca have also dropped "Moscatel de" from their label: Moscatel, they felt, had a down-market image for their major customers, the Americans. To call the wine plain "Setúbal" is perfectly within the Portuguese law – indeed, to have the term "Moscatel" on the label of a wine containing only 70 per cent of the grape will shortly be illegal when EEC regulations come fully into force.

Until recently, these da Fonseca Setúbals were the only ones ever seen abroad, but one small-scale producer has recently started bottling and exporting. Quinta de São Francisco, a modest farmhouse at the foot of the Sierra d'Arrábida, belongs to a doctor with a medical practice in Lisbon, who is to be found at the weekend pottering Emsworth-like among his vines. His cellar is very traditional, his production and bottling methods rather basic, but the wine is very good, though some unsatisfactory bottles have been known.

Some of Portugal's finest and best known red wines come from the Setúbal Peninsula, though few of them bear any clue on their labels as to origin. Even when the peninsula's two new demarcated regions, Arrábida and Palmela, are established in the impending legislation, many of the area's best wines will still be sold under brand names. The reputed firm of José Maria da Fonseca successores at Azeitão has built up a reputation for the local wines as up-market *brands* rather than regional wines (with the exception of the already demarcated Moscatel, as explained on the previous spread) and they intend to carry on selling them that way. Most growers sell their grapes or make wine only for home consumption and, apart from the fairly basic co-operative, the da Fonseca and João Pires *adegas* dominate fine wine production.

Details of the two new areas are still under discussion, and the official boundaries have yet to be set. The Arrábida region is attractive, hilly or mountainous country by the coast to the west of Setúbal town, where the soil is largely clay-lime. Palmela, further inland to the north-west of Setúbal, consists of a ridge of gentler, sandy hills and wide valleys. Though the peninsula is famous for its Moscatels, only 107 hectares are currently planted with Moscatel vines. Other white grapes cover 100 hectares, but red grapes grow on a vast expanse of 11,800 hectares.

Chief amongst the red grapes is the Periquita, even more common here than in the remainder of southern Portugal, where it is the most widely planted grape (sometimes alias Castelão Frances or João de Santarém). The grape was christened Periquita after the small farm of that name where the founder of José Maria da Fonseca Successores started the business in 1834, and spread from there around the area.

José Maria da Fonseca's delightful 19th and early 20th century *adega* in Azeitão, between Palmela and Arrábida, is famous for its fortified Moscatel, but it in fact makes less of this wine than of its chief red brand, Peri-

quita, made from both Palmela- and Arrábida-grown grapes. Their two other principal red brands come from more specific vineyards or areas near Azeitão. Grapes for Pasmados are grown about three miles away at the base of the Arrábida mountains in a well-watered but sunny clay-soiled valley. Quinta de Camarate lies in the other direction on windy clay-lime slopes facing north towards Lisbon.

Maturation in old oak or chestnut casks has always been a characteristic feature of this company's wines, but they have made a cautious move into new oak for a proportion

Below: *The laboratory at João Pires, backup for a modern and innovative range of wines, made from both Portuguese and imported grape varieties.*

Above: *The impressive winery of da Fonseca Successores dominates the main street of the little town of Azeitão.*

of their latest vintages: about ten per cent of their red wines have recently been aged in new Portuguese oak, and even the whites have spent a very brief period in new wood.

A more international approach at the nearby João Pires *adega* shows how local and imported varieties grown on the Setúbal Peninsula can be turned into super-fruity, modern-style wines, yet still with a recognisably Portuguese character (partly from the rather piney-flavoured Portuguese new oak used to mature some of the young wines

made in the impressive stainless steel winery). Most of their huge output is bulk wine for the massive J. M. da Fonseca Internacional winery in Azeitão (now a separate enterprise from the family firm of Fonseca above). But a tiny proportion of their production is prestige wines in bottle: fresh, crisp dry whites, oaked and unoaked, and excellent reds, young Beaujolais-style Quinta de Santa Amaro from the foothills of the Serra da Arrábida, and rich, oaky Quinta da Bacalhôa, made from Cabernet and Merlot grapes grown near Azeitão, as well as a recently-introduced Champagne method sparkler. Their Australian wine guru Peter Bright is experimenting with a great variety of grape mixes and vinification methods.

Pick of the Setúbal Peninsula's Dry Wines

José Maria da Fonseca Successores High quality *adega* with California-trained winemaker making excellent (though inexpensive) wines in the best of Portuguese tradition. Reds: Periquita, made from Periquita grapes with Espaldeiro and Movedro, tannic, pruney-minty wine to be drunk by six years old at most; Quinta de Camarate, half Periquita, the rest half-and-half Espaldeiro and Cabernet Sauvignon, is rich in tobacco and blackcurrant flavours, and keeps its fruit well for six or more years; and Pasmados, excellent, rich, complex wine from local grapes Touriga Nacional, Periquita, Moreto and Alforcheiro, which will mature well for eight years or more. Camarate Garrafeira, sold simply as "TE", and Periquita Garrafeira, "CO" are especially rich and concentrated versions of these blends. Pasmados White and Quinta de Camarate Dry White are fresh, pleasant wines with the piney character of light, old-style white Riojas.

João Pires Super-modern *adega* with dynamic Australian winemaker. Top class modern wines from both local and international grape varieties, with a special emphasis on single *quinta* wines. Quinta da Bacalhôa is an excellent, meaty Cabernet (with a little Merlot) overlaid with vanilla oak, ageing well over six or so years to a tarry, figgy Portuguese character. Quinta de Santa Amaro (Periquita with 40 per cent Merlot) is young, honeyed, soft, cherry-fruity wine, half of it made by semi-carbonic maceration. White wines are amongst Portugal's very best: Catarina, very oaky, lemony-minty white made from Fernão Pires with five per cent Chardonnay, fermented in new oak; and João Pires White, light, crisp and grapy, made from early-harvest, skin-macerated, very cold-fermented Moscatel grapes, for drinking young.

Quinta de São Francisco Small estate near Azeitão with a good, traditional style, big, rich and piney red, Cepa da Serra.

The alleged laziness of the inhabitants of the vast, dry Alentejo region in the south may be the butt of frequent jokes in the rest of the country, but the wines are taken rather more seriously. They have been described as "Portugal's greatest undiscovered treasures". The process of discovery is now well under way, however. Many of the Alentejo wines are already on the road to international recognition, having been made in wineries that have adjusted to the 20th century much faster than many of their kind elsewhere in the country. For, despite their reputation of lying around in the sun all day, the natives of the Alentejo are revolutionaries at heart. (They were, indeed, among the most passionate supporters of the 1974 Revolution.)

In such a politically radical part of the country, it comes as no surprise to learn that the winemaking industry is dominated by co-operatives, and these, with a few exceptions, produce most of the wine. There are three main winemaking areas in the Alentejo: both reds and whites are made around Portalegre in the north; powerful, full-bodied reds (and a little white) east of Evora from Borba to Reguengos de Monsaraz; and strong whites around Vidigueira and Beja.

The vineyards and winemakers have to contend with tremendous heat and no more than 500mm average rainfall per year. Much of the Alentejo is a landscape of gently rolling hills, where the green of the spring quickly turns to brown in the blaze of midsummer. The soil is stony, and in the traditionally planted vineyards, with stumpy vines dotted haphazardly among twisted olive trees, the largest of these stones are piled around the bases of the tree trunks to clear the rest of the ground for cultivation.

Although the Alentejo has a reputation in Portugal for its white wines, it is the reds that are making the real progress. The Roupeiro grape struggles to contribute successfully to decent Alentejo white wines, like those from the Vidigueira co-operative and the new Esporão winery, giving them a touch of honeyed depth sadly lacking in most of the region's whites. Other white grapes used are the Rabo d'Ovelha, Manteudo, Perrum, Fernão Pires, Tamarez, Arinto and Diegalves. The red grapes Periquita, Moreto, Trincadeira and Aragonez cope with the Alentejo's harsh climate more consistently, particularly around Reguengos de Monsaraz. As well as having a large and efficient co-operative, this town is home to two of Portugal's most interestingly experimental wineries, those of Esporão and J. S. Rosado Fernandes.

What makes these particularly fascinating is the extraordinary contrast between them. The Rosado Fernandes estate and winery, bought in the spring of 1986 by José Maria da Fonseca Successores, is ultra traditional; Esporão is super-modern. Walking into the

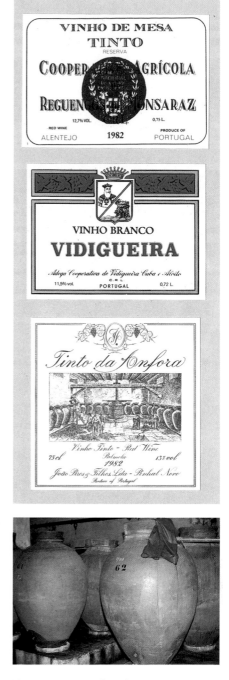

Above: *Green plastic string is the only concession to modernity among the clay pots of the Rosado Fernandes adega.*

Right: *Grapes for the João Pires Tinto da Anfora at Ferreira in the Baixo-Alentejo. The Alentejo's red grapes cope much better with the parched climate than the whites, particularly around Reguengos.*

Rosado Fernandes winery is like stepping back half a century in terms of winemaking technology. The wines are fermented in the tall clay pots traditional in the Alentejo, now

Pick of the Alentejo

Adega Cooperativa de Borba Co-op with traditional views on winemaking: no cool fermentation, ageing in cement more important than in wood. Reds are very good, both concentrated, cherry-like Tinto and rich, creamy, complex Reserva.

Adega Cooperativa de Reguengos de Monsaraz Large agricultural co-op, also dealing in olives and sheep. Adequate facilities, with intention of increasing refrigeration capacity, which will help the white wines. At present, reds are best, particularly the rich, cherry and plum-flavoured Reservas.

Adega Cooperativa da Vidigueira Attractive, young white (Colheita do Ano), with aromatic, lemon, apple and mint perfume.

Herdade do Esporão Enormous, ultra-modern estate, with plantations of over 50 grape varieties in 420 hectares of vineyard. Wines from the 1987-built winery have yet to be released, but previews are excellent.

J. S. Rosado Fernandes Most famous individual estate in the Alentejo, now owned by José Maria da Fonseca Successores, still making strong (13-14°) red Tinto Velho, which needs at least five years' maturation.

João Pires This modern winery on the Setúbal peninsula under the direction of Australian winemaker, Peter Bright, makes a lovely cedary, meaty red, Tinto da Anfora, from grapes grown in the north-west Alentejo, aged in chestnut and new oak casks, best drunk between four and six years old.

Adega Cooperativa de Redondo Co-operative making fresh, young reds and concentrated red Garrafeira, a bit woody, but with rich, cherry fruit.

quite rare, and the most recent development has been to become even *more* traditional by making a *garrafeira* in the best years, trodden in *lagares* before fermentation. Here, "cool fermentation" means hosing down the clay pots with cold water four or five times a day, and the only concession to modernity is the green plastic string that seems to be holding everything in the *adega* together.

Esporão is different. Owned by FINAGRA, a publicly quoted company, the estate has a brand-new winery (partly modelled on the Torres installations in Penedés), standing in 670 hectares of land, 420 of which are vineyards in production. Esporão has had a stormy history, confiscated during the 1974 Revolution, partly restored to its owners five years later, and eventually standing on its own feet after a row with the local co-operative and three new share issues in two years. Soon it may be one of the most widely-known wine estates in Portugal, if all goes well, and the winemaker repeats the success of the wines made from Esporão's grapes at the Reguengos co-operative in 1985-1986.

And the Alentejo as a region will not be far behind. When companies like Jóse Maria da Fonseca and João Pires (who have bought a 42 hectare estate in Moura) start buying land for vineyards, everyone sits up and takes notice. The forthcoming demarcation of the Alentejo will only set an official seal on an area already making some of Portugal's most exciting table wines.

Madeira the island is as unique as Madeira the wine. It rises sharply out of the Atlantic, soaring to heights of over 1,750 metres, 650km off the coast of Morocco, 480km north of the Canaries. Up towards its craggy summits, almost constantly shrouded in clouds, pines and heather thrive in the cool climate. A little further down towards the beachless coast, at between 330 and 750 metres above sea level, plums, apples and wheat grow along with the vines, while further down still, the vegetation becomes semi-tropical: sugar cane, lemons, avocados and bananas, more vines, vegetables and flowers.

The precipitous slopes are terraced up to a height of about 500 metres, divided into tiny plots belonging to thousands of smallholders. Madeira's naturally fertile volcanic soil is made more productive still by an intricate irrigation system – a network of canals, called *levadas*, that carry water all over the island.

Today, banana plantations cover far more of the terraces than vines. Grape yields are small, vines need regular and expensive spraying in this warm, moist climate if they are not to succumb to fungal diseases, and bananas earn twice as much per hectare as grapes. To allow plenty of aeration and to cope with the extreme vigour of vines grown in these conditions, they are usually trained on trellises of up to two metres in height, supported by wooden stakes. Nowadays, most of the quality grapes are planted around Camara de Lobos, eight kilometres west of Funchal.

Madeira's vineyards were utterly transformed a century ago when the phylloxera louse destroyed the vines. Most of the vineyards were replanted not with the traditional varieties but with poor quality American-European hybrid vines, which make insipid table wine drunk on the island (*vinho americano*), or brandy, or industrial alcohol. It has long been illegal to export hybrid wine.

Since the early seventies, however, the Madeira authorities, driven by impending membership of the EEC, have instituted a programme designed to restore the traditional varieties. There are cash grants for

Below: The island is terraced up to a height of about 500 metres, and divided into thousands of tiny smallholdings.

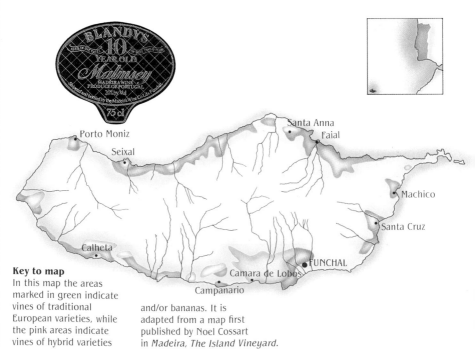

Key to map
In this map the areas marked in green indicate vines of traditional European varieties, while the pink areas indicate vines of hybrid varieties and/or bananas. It is adapted from a map first published by Noel Cossart in *Madeira, The Island Vineyard.*

Styles of Madeira

The following terms define the true Madeira styles, not the imitations made from the Tinta Negra Mole. Most Madeira has a characteristic tangy character owing to the heating process.

Sercial Pale, light, perfumed, dry or dryish. Undrinkably astringent in their first few years, but mellow and subtly, nuttily flavoured with eight or more years' ageing.

Verdelho Nutty, slightly richer than Sercial and discernably sweet to medium-dry, this has a golden colour, becoming drier and fuller with age.

Bual Dark, full, fragrant wine, sweet but not cloying because of its good balancing acidity.

Malmsey Dark, full bodied, fruity and muskily fragrant, and very sweet, though it can mellow and taste less sweet with age.

Reserve Five or more years old
Special Reserve Ten or more years old
Exceptional Reserve 15 or more years old
Vintage From a single year, aged for a minimum 20 years in cask, two in bottle.

Pick of Madeira

Blandy's Ten-year-old Malmsey is rich, pungent, exotically-flavoured wine with savoury concentration, sweet but with refreshing acidity.

Cossart Gordon The Reserves, "over five years", are excellent value, especially the Malmsey Reserve, very sweet, smokily pungent with a fresh, fruity, apricot-like flavour; and the off-dry Sercial Reserve is almondy, salty, fine and lean. Of the finer Special Reserves, the Verdelho has a salty, nutty, slightly cheesy tang and a little sweetness; and Cossart's Duo Centenary Celebration Sercial has a fine blend of salty and concentrated nutty flavours.

Leacocks Another brand name of the Madeira Wine Company. The Special Reserve Malmsey is rich, round, treacly and salty, beautifully balanced and complex.

Rutherford & Miles Reserve Bual is mellow and nutty, Special Reserve Malmsey concentrated, raisiny, treacly and spicy. Special reserve Verdelho is attractively toffee'd and salty; Special Reserve Sercial is soft, nutty, savoury and well balanced, though a touch sweetened.

uprooting the hybrids, compensation for temporary loss of income, subsidised hire of equipment, free technical advice and free, ready-grafted European vines, the original Bual, Verdelho, Sercial and Malvasia. Of the 90,000 hectolitres of wine made on Madeira in 1987, only half was hybrid wine. The hybrids are scheduled to have disappeared entirely by 1993.

The current figures look falsely optimistic, however, since about three-quarters of the European vines are the Tinta Negra Mole, a black grape without a lot of flavour. The four famous Madeira grapes represent about a quarter each of the remainder. Tinta Negra Mole is planted at all altitudes on the island at which grapes can be grown. But Bual and Malvasia (Malmsey to the English) tend to be planted in the hottest zone from sea level up to 400 metres, producing very sweet grapes; Verdelho is planted in the next zone, at between 400 and 600 metres, and Sercial (*Esgana Cão*, literally "dog strangler" in Portuguese), used for the driest wine, does best in the highest vineyards between 600 and 800 metres altitude.

Because of the shortage of the finer varieties, the Madeira producers have throughout this century used huge percentages of Tinta Negra Mole in wines labelled "Sercial", "Bual" and so on, attempting to make the wine in the style and at the level of sweetness historically sold under those names. You would be lucky to find five per cent of the named grape in the cheaper Madeiras, though the more expensive ones are mostly what they claim to be. All this is to change since Portugal's admission to the EEC, however. By 1993, any Madeira naming a variety on its label will have to be at least 85 per cent of that variety. The cheaper wines containing more than 15 per cent of Tinta Negra Mole will be sold as "Sercial-style" or "Verdelho-style" or under a brand name, simply labelled "dry", "medium dry", etc. Vintage dates on the label will also have to be respected under the new regime.

Madeira-making is the preserve of the large companies, many of them of British origin. The Madeira Wine company, a conglomerate of the British firms, makes about 40 per cent of bottled Madeira.

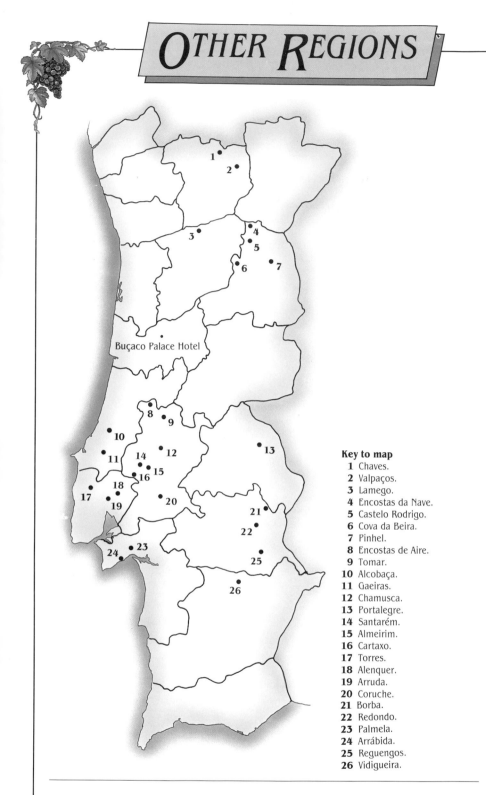

Buçaco Palace Hotel

Key to map
1 Chaves.
2 Valpaços.
3 Lamego.
4 Encostas da Nave.
5 Castelo Rodrigo.
6 Cova da Beira.
7 Pinhel.
8 Encostas de Aire.
9 Tomar.
10 Alcobaça.
11 Gaeiras.
12 Chamusca.
13 Portalegre.
14 Santarém.
15 Almeirim.
16 Cartaxo.
17 Torres.
18 Alenquer.
19 Arruda.
20 Coruche.
21 Borba.
22 Redondo.
23 Palmela.
24 Arrábida.
25 Reguengos.
26 Vidigueira.

The most important of the 26 regions hoping for demarcation by 1991 have already been described. The rest are covered briefly here, along with the Algarve and the wines from the Buçaco Palace Hotel.

Algarve

Most Portuguese dismiss the wines of the Algarve as unworthy of their demarcation in 1980. Almost all are red, made mainly from the Tinta Negra Mole (the main grape of Madeira), Trincadeira and Periquita, high in alcohol and low in acidity. Wines from the co-operatives at Lagoa and Tavira are marginally better than others in the region.

Beiras

If proof were needed that vines grow almost anywhere in Portugal, the provinces of Beiras bear it out. To the east of Dão and south of Trás-os-Montes, the Beira Alta and Beira Baixa fill in a space otherwise blank on Portugal's viticultural map, between north and south, Trás-os-Montes and Alentejo.

The more interesting wines are made in the northerly province. All the proposed demarcated regions are to be found here: Encostas da Nave, Castelo Rodrigo, Pinhel and Cova da Beira. Moimenta da Beira, south-east of Lamego, is said to make good Malvasia, suitable, with its high acidity, lowish alcohol and perfumed, musky scent, for the production of sparkling wines.

Close to the Douro region, several of the best-known port grapes are grown to make into red wine in some districts, including the Mourisco, Bastardo, Tinta Francisca and Touriga. These varieties give the wines good colour and alcohol, if not a great potential for ageing. The white wines (outnumbered four to one by reds) are made from the Arinto, Cercial, Malvasía, Rabo d'Ovelha, Alva and Folgazão grapes.

Buçaco

The red and white wines made by Senhor José Santos, general manager of the Buçaco Palace Hotel, a wonderfully extravagant, late 19th century edifice set in the glorious forest of Buçaco, are among the most delicious table wines of Portugal. They are made from grapes grown in and around Buçaco, which lies between the regions of Dão and Bairrada, and are sold only to guests staying at the Buçaco Palace Hotel and four other hotels (in Carcavelos, Coimbra, Curia and Lisbon).

Both red and white wines are trodden in traditional stone *lagares*, then the white is strained off and fermented for up to a month in barrel. The treading and fermentation of the reds continues for two or three days. Whites, made from the Bical, Maria Gomes, Moscatel and Rabo d'Ovelha varieties, spend 12 to 18 months in barrel before bottling. Reds have about three years in barrel, and are made from the Baga, Bastardo, Castellão Nacional and Tinta Mortágua.

Bottles are sealed with a mixture of beeswax and resin made at the hotel, which imparts a subtle, piney character to the naturally rich and elegant wine over the course of long bottle maturation. Guests at the hotel can enjoy vintages back to 1940, drawn from among 60,000 bottles kept in an immaculate cellar, with little piles of sawdust underneath the taps of the barrels in which the wine is aged to catch any rogue drips that might seek to offend against the prevailing order and cleanliness.

Trás-os-Montes

Trás-os-Montes, in the north-eastern corner of Portugal, has suffered more than any other part of the country from emigration, as the countryside is poor, and agriculture difficult. It is a region of mountains, thermal springs and river valleys, and local communities are working hard to woo tourists to the delights of fishing and "taking the cure".

Chaves and Valpaços, two areas within Trás-os-Montes, are both striving for full demarcated status, but are not the only wine-producing regions. Wines, mostly red, vary tremendously from one district to the next. At higher altitudes, as in Boticas and Carrazedo, the wines can be quite light and acidic (similar to *vinhos verdes*). Further up towards Portugal's north-eastern border with Spain, the districts of Mogadouro and Miranda do Douro used to produce much of Portugal's *rosé* before the large companies built new plants in the Douro and Bairrada.

Perhaps the best of the Trás-os-Montes wines come from Valpaços, rich red wines whose powerful, sour cherry fruit echoes the flavour of the cherry (*cereja de saco*) that is the speciality of the region.

Above: *The Buçaco Palace Hotel, set in forests between Dão and Bairrada, makes some of Portugal's finest wines.*

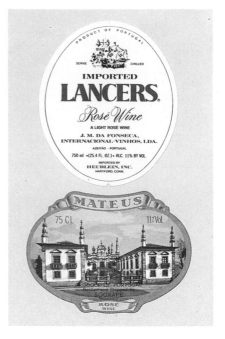

The palace of Mateus, near Vila Real, does not belong to the Guedes family, owners of Sogrape and inventors of Mateus Rosé. It is said that they offered the owners of the palace a choice of methods of payment for the privilege of using the illustration on the labels of bottles of the fledgling brand: a one-off payment, or a royalty on each bottle sold. The hapless owners played safe, and opted for the single payment.

Portugal's giant pink wine business, now responsible for two-thirds of all wine exports, was the 'fifties brainchild of the Guedes family. Their Mateus Rosé, a product designed to suit a particular market, has proved adaptable to varying market needs: the bottle of Mateus on the New York shelf may look the same as its counterpart in London, but the contents would shock devotees across the ocean. In America, Mateus (and, indeed, its main competitor Lancers) is a *still* wine, with none of the gentle fizz of the British version. In the 'fifties as today, even a lightly fizzy wine would have attracted a higher level of duty than still wine, so it made sense to dispense with the bubbles and keep the price down. And once the American market was used to its very own style of Mateus, that was how they liked it. Mateus' attempt to launch a fizzy American version in the 'sixties was a flop. Mateus and Lancers also vary in sweetness in different markets – consumers in the United States appear to like theirs sweeter.

These two superstars are by no means the only rosés of their kind on the market. Other Portuguese companies have their rosé brands in a similar sweetish-fruity and light (around 11°) style, and many companies, including the two brand leaders, make lookalikes under supermarkets' and liquor stores' own labels.

After years of growing success, however, Portuguese rosés began to fall in popularity a few years ago, to the extent that the big firms felt the need to diversify in order to survive a less 'rosy future. Mateus owners' Sogrape have been taking a much more active interest in finer Portuguese wines, Dão, Bairrada and *vinho verde* in particular. Meanwhile, J. M. da Fonseca Internacional, producers of Lancers, have turned their attention to other branded products, such as sparkling Lancers (see page 155) and Corado, a "blush" wine designed to fit the US fashion for very pale rosés. (Corado Blush has less than four hours' skin contact to obtain its pale pink colouring, compared with the 24 hours the more typical Lancers Rosé juice sits in contact with its skins at the beginning of its winemaking process.)

Below: *Mateus Rosé actually has nothing to do with the palace of Mateus, near Vila Real, pictured on its familiar label.*

Above: *Glistening white "Lollobrigida" storage tanks stay cool out in the sun at the da Fonseca Internacional winery.*

Both the Mateus and the Lancers production plants (and the João Pires winery that supplies all the base wine for Lancers) display the height of modern technology and hygiene. They need to, indeed, because the raw materials may arrive in far from perfect condition, from which only high technology winemaking can save them. In the 1986 vintage, for instance, when lorry-loads of grapes came in thick with grey mould after an appallingly rainy season, great batteries of centrifuges spun into motion to remove the rot before further damage could be done. And it takes many centrifuges to cope with the million or more kilos a day that pass through the larger of the two Mateus plants at the

height of the vintage. Mateus claim to have 20 kilometres of stainless steel piping connecting their serried ranks of winemaking equipment.

Both firms have had to work hard to convince their thousands of local grape suppliers of the need for cleanliness and speed of transit from vine to press. Mateus will accept no grapes until 11 o'clock in the morning in an attempt to ensure that the grapes are actually delivered on the day of picking. They are also trying to persuade growers to plant vine varieties separately in their vineyards, so that each variety can be picked at the appropriate moment. It has been a "seven or eight year war", according to J. M. da Fonseca Internacional, but they, too, seem at last to be winning. The land around both firms is peppered with the pointed-topped, glistening-white hemispherical insulated storage tanks, known irreverently as "Lollobrigidas" to the Portuguese, where the base wines are kept as cool as possible and protected from the air under a blanket of nitrogen until they are needed for blending.

While the rosé market was still ballooning at the end of the 'seventies, the Portuguese authorities decided to impose a few regulations. A ministerial order of August 1979 defines extensive areas in which a variety of specified grapes for such rosés may be grown. But in fact any red grapes of any Portuguese origin, in reasonable condition and processed in such advanced equipment, could turn out wines of a similar style. The Sogrape winery that currently makes the majority of Mateus, in the village of San Mateus near Anadia in the Bairrada region, may soon take over the whole of the production from the original Vila Real plant near the palace pictured on the label.

Below: *Packing Lancers at da Fonseca Internacional. Both Mateus and Lancers vary in sweetness for different markets.*

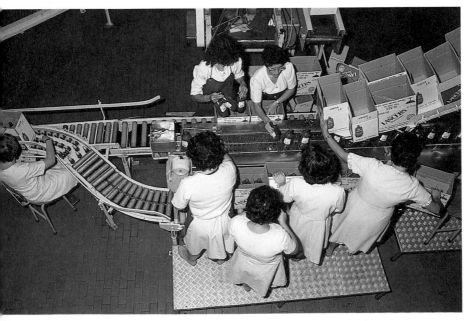

Portugal's sparkling wines have generally only been available to consumers within the country's borders, except for those that escaped to Brazil – this despite the fact that the best examples would compete favourably for quality with Spain's well-travelled *cavas*. However, sparkling Lancers and Raposeira have both recently made a determined appearance in export markets, both seeking favour through low prices. Neither of these two brands is typical of Portuguese sparkling wines. Lancers is made in Azeitão by the "Russian continuous" method, unique in Europe (see below), while Portugal's best-selling Raposeira brands contain varying amounts of "foreign" grapes including Chardonnay and Pinot Noir, and come from the beautiful hill town of Lamego some way south of the Douro town of Regua.

Bairrada is in fact the famed centre for sparkling wines in Portugal, and most of the Bairrada *adegas* make sparkling as well as still wines, in rapidly growing proportions. The usual base for the Bairrada sparkling wines is the pleasantly fruity but not very characterful Maria Gomes grape, along with the Arinto, Rabo d'Ovelha, Boal and Bical. Bairrada's most impressive winemaker, Luis Pato, believes the Arinto has greater potential, among the local grapes, especially for vintage fizz with greater bottle age. Its high acidity gives freshness and staying power, and though neutral-flavoured when young, it develops interesting flavours as it ages. The Cercial, he thinks, is even better, with good fruit and acidity, but it is susceptible to rot,

Above: *Periquita grapes arriving at the João Pires winery. Black Periquita grapes go into their delicious fizz, as well as the white Fernão Pires.*

How Sweet Are They?

Bruto Dry, less than 15gms/l of sugar
Seco Fairly dry, 17-35gms/l of sugar
Meio Seco Semi-sweet, 33-50gm/l of sugar
Doce Sweet, more than 50gms/l of sugar

Pick of the Portuguese Sparklers

Luis Pato Small family *adega* in Bairrada making delicious sparkling wines (as well as still Bairradas) from grapes from their own vineyards. The rosé is especially good, rich, creamy and rather reminiscent of Pinot Noir, though it is made from the local Baga grape. The white Brut is appley-lemony and seems sweet despite its dryness because of the character of the Maria Gomes grapes that make up half the blend, along with Bical and Cercialinho.

João Pires Super-modern *adega* in Pinhal Novo, south of Lisbon, making, among other things, Champagne method João Pires Bruto, a lovely, soft, appley-minty, honeyed but dry fizz. It is made from local white Fernão Pires and red Periquita grapes, fermented separately, then aged in small barrels until bottling for the second fermentation. It spends three years on its lees in bottle before disgorging for sale.

Raposeira Portugal's brand leader by far in sparkling wines has been producing them by the Champagne method since the end of last century, now in spotless, modern premises equipped with the latest in stainless steel, using grapes from their own and other vineyards around the town. Owned for many years by international liquor giants Seagram. Wines are inexpensive, and good value, without the earthiness of the typical Portuguese style. Full-bodied, simple, clean and fresh Raposeira Reserva made from Malvasia, Chardonnay, Cercial, Pinot Noir, Codega and Viosonho, aged for 12 months; and lighter, fresh, fruity Super Reserve, largely Chardonnay and Pinot Noir, with Malvasia and Cercial and two years' ageing.

Caves Aliança Large, forward-looking company, making all their own base wine for the sparkling side of their business. Particularly noteworthy is Bruto Espumoso, a Champagne method *red* with four to five years' bottle age, nice acidity and delicious raspberry-like fruit. The white Caves Aliança Espumante is pleasant, sweetish, lemony. A pleasant, drier version will soon be available.

Caves São João Bairrada's smallest sparkling wine producer, a medium-sized family company in the process of expansion and modernisation. Good, slightly yeasty-flavoured Champagne method sparkler.

and Pato is therefore trying out a cross between the Cercial and the Alvarinho, christened the Cercialinho.

Almost all Portugal's sparkling wines are made by the Champagne method, with just a little tank-produced and low-quality gas-injected wine (see pages 36 and 37 for details of these processes). But now a fourth method (the Russian continuous) has been introduced by American-owned J. M. da Fonseca Internacional, home of the long-successful, crock-bottled Lancers. This variation on the tank method is so highly automated and computerised that one man is able to run a plant that produces over 100,000 cases of sparkling wine a year.

The idea is to keep the wine moving slowly through a series of interlinked pressurised tanks tightly packed with washed-out wood shavings on which the dead yeasts are deposited, so that the yeasts are constantly rubbing up against the passing wine and transmitting their flavours to it. It takes eight and a half days for a given part of the continuous stream to make its way through the system. The result is very pleasant, clean, round and fruity, with nice acidity and good, fine, lasting bubbles – and it is very cheap.

Below: *The "Russian Continuous" plant at J. M. da Fonseca Internacional is a much improved version of the system used in the Eastern Bloc. Still wine goes in at one end and emerges just over a week later as slightly yeasty fizz.*

*I*NDEX

Names of wines, grape varieties, vineyards, and producers are indexed. The numerals in *italics* refer to illustrations.

A

APEVV, 166
Acorde Blanco Semi-Seco, 95
Adega Cooperativa da Vidigueira, 147
Adega Cooperativa de Almeirim, 137
Adega Cooperativa de Arruda dos Vinhos, 135
Adega Cooperativa de Borba, 147
Adega Cooperativa de Labrugeira, 135
Adega Cooperativa de Redondo, 147
Adega Cooperativa de Reguengos de Monsaraz, 147
Adega Cooperativa de Torres Vedras, 135
Adega Cooperativa de Ponte de Lima, 117
Adegas Regional de Colares, 138-9
adegas, 14, 30, 38
Agramont, 60
Agricola Castellana, 85
Agrupación de Cosecheiros Albariño do Salnes, 81
aguja, 39, 73
Airén grape, 44, 46, 83, 88-9, 90, 93, 94, 95, 104, 106-7
Alavesas, Bodegas, 54
Albariño Dom Bardo, 81
Albariño grape, 6, 44, 80, 81
Albariño Martin Codax, 81
Albero grape, 105
Albillo, 46, 83
Alcantara, 140
Alacanhões co-operative, 136
Alella, 64, 68, 69, 72-3
Alella Co-operative, 73
Alentejo, 41, 146-7
Alenquer, 135
Alfrocheiro Preto grape, 113, 132, 145
Algarve, 111, 150
Alicante, 93, 94
Alicante Bouschet grape, 136, 137
Alicante grape, 46, 81, 91
almacenista, 39, 102-3
Almansa, 91
Almeirim co-operative, 136, 137
almude, 124
Alta Alella, 72
Alta Mar, 75
Alva grape, 151
Alvarez y Diez, 84, 85
Alvarinho grape, 112, 116, 117
Alvear, *16*, *104*, 105, *105*
amforas, *16*
amontillado, 27, 39, 100, 101, 104
Amontillado Coliseo, 103
Amontillado del Duque, 103
amoroso, 100
Ampurdán-Costa Brava, 64, 69, *72*, 73, *73*
Angel Rodriguez, Bodegas, 84
ano, 38
año, 39
Antonio Bernardino Paulo da Silva, 139
Apostoles Oloroso Viejo, 103
Aragón, 43, 62-3, 82
Aragonés grape, 91, 113, 146
Arinto do Dão grape, 112, 132
Arinto grape, 112, 130, 134, 135, 140, 141, 142, 146, 151, 154
Arrábida, 144
arrope, 107
Arruda, 134, 135, *135*
Arruda co-operative, 134-5
Arruda dos Vinhos, 134
Artadi Blanco, 56
Artadi Tinto, 56
Assario Branco grape, 112, 132
Ascensio Carcelen, Bodegas, 95
Associacão dos Exportadores do Vinho do Porto, 119
Aureo, 76
autovinificators, 20, 30, *31*, 63, *118*, 128
Avesso grape, 112, 116, 117, 128
Ayuso Roig, Fermin, 89
Azal Branco grape, 112
Azal Tinto grape, 113
Azeitão, 142, 144, *145*
Azenhas do Mar, *139*

B

Baga grape, 113, 130, *130*, 131, 135, 136, 137, 151, 154
Bairrada, 11, 111, 130-1, 152
  sparkling wine, 154
  vintages, 41
Baixo Corgo, 128
Baladá, Ramon, 66, 67
Baladi, 104
Balearics, 43, 108-9
Barahonda, 95
Barba, Nuno, 140
Barbadillo, *29*, 103
Barca Velha, 6, 128, 129
Barcelo grape, 112, 132
barrels, 22-3, *22*, 25, 48, 49, *53*, 54, *55*, *58*-9, 59, *144*
Bastardo grape, 113, 128, 132, 151
Batalha, 1345

Beira, 150
Benavente, *19*
beneficio ratings, 122, 123
Bical do Bairrada grape, 130, 132
Bical grape, 112
Bierzo, Bodega Comarcal Co-operativa Vinos de, 83
Bierzo, El, 43, 82, 83
Binisalem, 43, 108, 109
black grapes, 6, 46-7, 112-13
Blanc Cru, 67
blanco, 39
Blandy's, 149
Bleda, Bodegas, 95
Boal grape, 112, 135, 136, 142, 154
Bobal grape, 46, 47, 62, 93
Bollulos co-operative, 96, 97
Bomfim, *118*, *120*, 126
Bordejé, Bodegas, 63
Borges & Irmão, 116
Borraçal grape, 113
Borrado das Moscas grape, 112, 132
Botaina Amontillado Viejo, 103
Boticas, 151
bottling, 8-9
Bradomin, 81
Brana Vieja, 60
Brencellão, 81
Bright, Peter, 145, 147
Bual grape, 34, 149
Buçaco, 151
Buçaco Palace Hotel, 7, 151, *151*
Bucelas, 111, 112, 140-1
Bucelas Velho, 140
Bullas, 43
Burdons Heavenly Cream Rich Old Oloroso, 103
butts *see* barrels

C

CALP Reserva Tinto, 95
CVC, 39
CVNE, *23*, *55*, 56, 57
COVISA, 63
Cabernet Franc grape, 82
Cabernet Sauvignon grape, 11, 44, 47, 53, 60, 63, 64, 66, 67, 72, 79, 86, 91, 108, 129, 136, 137, 145
Cacabelos co-operative, 82
Caino grape, 46, 81
Calatayud, 43, 63
Cálem, A.A., 133
Callet grape, 108
Camarate Garrafeira, 145
Camarate grape, 113, 134
Campo de Borja, 62, 63, 70
Campo Nuevo, 60
Campo Pleno, 60
Campo Viejo, 53, 56
canada, 124
Canaries, 43, 109-9
Canaveras, Bodegas, *91*
Cantanhede co-operative, 130
Carbonell, 104, 105
Carcavelos, 111, 141, *141*, 142
Cardallal, Bodegas, 81
Cariñena, 621, 63
  grape, *44*, 46, 65, 67, 73, 74, 75, 76, 77, 78
Carrazedo, 151
Carregado, 135
Cartaxo co-operative, *18*, 136, *136*
Cartoixa Scala Dei, 76, 77
Carvalho, Ribeiro & Ferreira, 133, 135, 137
Casa Agricola Herdeiros de Dom Luis de Margaride, 137
Casa Alta Vino Nuevo, 95
Casa de Cabanelas, 117
Casa de Calderon, 93
Casa de Compostela, 117
Casa do Douro, 119
Casa das Cunhas, 117
Casa la Teja, 89
Casal do Monteiro, 137
casks *see* barrels
Casa Lo Alto, 93
Castelão Frances grape, 113, 136, 144
Castelão Nacional, 151
Castell de Remei, 78, 79
Castelo Rodrigo, 150
Castilla la Vieja, Bodegas, 68, 70, 84, *84*, 85
Castilla-Léon, 43, 82-3
Castillo de Alhambra, 89
Castillo de Almansa, 91
Castillo Jumilla, 95
Castillo Ygay, 58
Catalonia, 43, 64-9, 70
  map, 70
Catarina, 145
cava, 39, 64, 68-71
  making, 36-7, *36*-7, 66, 70-1
Cava Reserva, 68
Cavas del Ampurdán, 73
Cavas del Castillo de Perelada, 73
Cavas Hill, 67, 68, 69
Cavas Murviedro, 93
Caves Aliança, 130, 131, 133, 154
Caves do Raposeira,

Caves Velhas, 136-7, 140, *140*, 141
Cayetana grape, 44, 46
Cebreros, 43, 83
Cebrian, Vincente, 58
Celler Hisenda Miret, 6, 67
Cellers de Scala Dei, *18*, *21*, 76, 77, *77*
Cellers, Robert, 67
Cenalsa, 60
Cencibel grape, 46, 47, 89, 90, 91, 93, 95
Cenicero co-operative, 52
Cepa da Serra, 145
Cercial grape, 112, 130, 132, 140, 151, 154
Cercialinho, 154, 155
Cerra Sol, Bodegas, 84
Champalimaud, Miguel, 122, 127, 128
Champalimaud family, 117
Chamusca co-operative, 136
Chardonnay grape, 44, 45, 60, 63, 65, 66, 70, 72, 79, 112, 129, 145, 154
Chaves, 151
Chenin Blanc grape, 53, 63, 65, 66, 72
Cherubino Valsangiacomo, 93
Chiva, 93
Chivite, Bodegas, 60, 61
Churchill Graham Lda, 126
Cigales, 43, 83
clarete, 21, 38, 39, 62, 81, 83, 90
Cockburn Smithes, 125, 126, 128
Codega grape, 154
Codorníu, 68, 69, *69*
Colares, 111, 138-9, *139-9*
Colheita do Ano, 147
Comarca Vinicola, 39, 43
Compañia Vinicola del Norte de España *see* CVNE
Con Sello, 95
Conca de Barberá, 43, 45, 64, 66-7, 68
Condado de Huelva, 44, 96-7
"Condado Palido", 96
Condado Viejo, 96
Conde de Santar, 133
Conde de Valdemar, 58
Consejo Regulador, 39, 49, 54, 81
Contino Reserva, 56
Convento da Serra, 137
Co-operativa de Cenicero, 56
Co-operativa del Campo Nuestro Padre Jesus del Perdón, 89
Co-operativa del Campo Nuestro Señora de Manjavacas, 89
Co-operativa del Campo San Juan Bautista, 63
Co-operativa La Purisima, 94, 95
Co-operativa Pazo Ribeiro, 81
Co-operativa San Isidro, 95
Co-operativa Somontana de Sobrarbe, 63
co-operatives, 6, 8-9, 13, 18, 42, 61
Corado, 152
cork trees, *97*
corks, 71
Correia family, 135
Cosecheros Alaveses, 56
Cossart Gordon, 149
Costanilla, 57
Costers, del Segre, 11, 12, 42, 43, 45, 47, 64, 69, 70, 78-9
Coto, El, 56
Coto de Imaz, 56
Côtto Grande Escolha, 129
Cova da Beira, 150
Croft Distinction, 126
Crucillon Rosado, 63
crusted port, 33
Cruzeiro, 126
Cune *see* CVNE

D

DO *see* Denominación de Origen
Dão, 111, 132-3, *133*, 152
  vintages, 41
dated port, 32
da Almeida, Fernando Nicolau, 128
De Muller, Bodegas, 74, 75, 76, 77
da Silva, A.B. Paulo, 139
De Soto, 103
Delaforce, 126
Delgado Zuleta, 103
Denominación de Origen (DO), 6-7, 39, 42
  regulations, 104
Denominación de Origen Provisional, 43
Denominación Especifica, 39, 43
Denominación Especifica Provisional, 43
Diagalves grape, 112, 146
Diego grape, 109
Diez Merito, 103
Dom Hermano, 137
Domecq, 12, 28, 53, *102*
Don Fadrique, 89
Don Gonzalo Old Dry Oloroso, 103
Don Mendo, 63
Don Tomás Amontillado, 103
Don Zoilo Fino, 103
Dona Antonia's Personal Reserve, 126
Douro, 33, 118-29
  climate, 122
  grapes, 121
  map, 128-9
  soil, 120-1
  vintages, 41

Bibliography

Bento de Carvalho & Lopes Correia, *The Wines of Portugal*, Junta Nacional do Vinho, Lisbon, 1985.

Noël Cossart, *Madeira, – The Island Vineyard*, Christie's Wine Publications, London, 1984.

Hubrecht Duijker, *The Wines of Rioja*, Mitchell Beazley, London, 1987.

A. Moreira da Fonseca, A. Galhano, E. Serpa Pimentel & J.R-P. Rosas, *Port Wine*, Instituto do Vinho do Porto, Porto, 1987.

Grupo Editorial Club de Gourmets, *Guia Práctica para Amantes y Profesionales de los Vinos de España*, Club G.S.A., 1987.

Julian Jeffs, *Sherry*, Faber & Faber, London, 1982.

Ben Howkins, *Rich, Rare & Red – a Guide to Port*, Christopher Helm, Bromley, 1987.

Jan Read, *The Mitchell Beazley Pocket Guide to Spanish Wines*, Mitchell Beazley, London, 1983.

Jan Read, *The Wines of Portugal*, Faber & Faber, London, 1987.

Jan Read, *The Wines of Spain*, Faber & Faber, London, 1982.

Jan Read, *Wines of the Rioja*, Sotheby Publications, London, 1984.

George Robertson, *Port*, Faber & Faber, London, 1982.

Jancis Robinson, *Vines, Grapes & Wines*, Mitchell Beazley, 1986.

Miguel Torres, *Los Vinos de España Cata*, Ediciones Castell, 1984.

Miguel Torres, *The Distinctive Wines of Catalonia*, Grupo Hymsa, Barcelona, 1986.

P. Truel, *Notes sur les Cépages du Portugal*, Progrès Agricole et Viticole, Montpellier, various issues between 1983 and 1985.

Picture Credits

The publishers would like to thank the many wine producers, importers, and photographers who have generously supplied pictures and labels for inclusion in this book. The photographs are here credited by page number.

Alvear S.A.: 105
J. Allan Cash Ltd: 109
Cephas Picture Library/Michael Rock: 2/3, 8, 10/11, 14, 15, 16, 17, 18 upper, 18 lower, 19, 21 upper, 22, 22/23, 23, 29, 32, 36, 37, 40, 44, 45, 47, 48/49, 50/51, 52/53, 53, 55, 61, 65, 67, 69 lower, 71, 72, 73, 74/75, 77, 82/83, 85 upper, 85 lower, 86, 87, 89, 90, 91, 96/97, 99 upper, 99 lower, 100 upper, 100 lower, 102, 104 upper, 104 lower, 106/107, 111, 115, 117, 118/119, 121, 132, 134/135, 137, 138/139, 141, 142/143, 144, 147, 151, 152, 153 upper, 153 lower, 154, 155
Codorníu S.A.: 37, 78/79, 79
Consejo Regulador de los Vinos Espumosos: 69 upper
Dows (Symington Port Shippers): 122/123
Ehrmanns: 145
José Maria da Fonseca Successores: 143
Garvey S.A.: 24/25, 25
Gonzalez Byass: 26, 26/27, 28
Graham & Co: 33, 124
Madeira Wine Co: 34/35, 35, 148
Charles Metcalfe/WINE Magazine: 20, 21 lower, 52, 57, 59, 63, 94/95, 130, 131, 136, 140, 146
Bodegas Osborne: 54
Quinta do Côtto: 129
Jon Wyand: 6/7, 13, 30, 31, 118, 120, 122

alabastro - Res - 2001 - Alentejano Region
Quinto de Terrugem
alabastro - 2661
Quinta De Baixo Res. 2000
Quinta de Baiso

Aliança Rosé med.dry

Trincadeira Joao Portugue Ramos
Alentejo 2002

Ribamar 1996 Particular Paulo De Siva
Casal D' Azenha Reserva 1995 Paulo
De Silva
Quinto Dos Quatro Vento Dauro 2000
Caves alianca

"T" da terrugem 1999/2000 Alentejo Caves
alianca